# 1000 SUBJECTS FOR
# SPEAKERS AND STUDENTS

# One Thousand Subjects

for

# Speakers and Students

COLLECTED BY
## HENRY PICKERING

Marshall Pickering

Pickering and Inglis
Marshall Pickering
3 Beggarwood Lane, Basingstoke, Hants RG23 7LP, UK

Copyright © 1925 by Pickering and Inglis Ltd.

First published in 1925 by Pickering and Inglis Ltd.
Part of the Marshall Pickering Holdings Group
A subsidiary of the Zondervan Corporation

Reprinted in 1927 1933, 1935, 1938, 1945, 1946, 1950, 1954,
1958, 1961, 1964, 1968
Re-issued in this format in 1986 by
Pickering and Inglis Ltd

**British Library Cataloguing in Publication Data**

Pickering, Henry
    One thousand subjects for speakers and
    students.
    1. Bible—Homiletical use      2. Preaching
    I. Title
    251      BV4211.2

    ISBN 0-7208-0697-6

Printed in Great Britain by
The Guernsey Press Co. Ltd., Guernsey, Channel Islands.

# PREFACE

THE unstinted welcome afforded to a previous volume of original outlines, gathered from active workers in all parts of the world, was sufficient to show that it had met a need in giving a hint, a thought, and an idea to those busy workers who could fill in from devout study, ample experience, or varied reading, but who were perplexed about the starting point of their subject.

Thus encouraged, the collection of the large amount of material for another volume has been undertaken, and there the compiler, in addition to many of his own outlines, has been favoured with contributions from able and active workers throughout the world.

Any speaker or student setting about his duties in a prayerful spirit, and seeking the help and guidance of the Holy Spirit, will find herein abundant material for ground thoughts for addresses, interesting themes for private and public Bible study, and numerous linkings and unfoldings of the wonderful Word, which will prove enlightenment to his mind and a joy to his heart.

The old, the hackneyed, the extract from another volume of studies, has been studiously avoided. If found herein, it comes from the memory, or through the penmanship of a worker of to-day to whom it must have appealed as freshly-gathered treasure. Indices of Titles, Subjects, and Texts are provided at the end of the volume for quick and easy reference.

In sending it forth we wish that the blessing of the Lord which maketh rich may rest in abundance upon every one who may derive help therefrom.      HYP

# CONTRIBUTORS

L. W. G. ALEXANDER
J. ANDREW
J. W. ASHBY

TOM BAIRD
V. A. BARTON
JAS. E. BEVAN
C. H. BRIGHT
HUBERT BROOKE
J. H. BROOKES
R. LUNDIN BROWN
JOHN BRUNTON
G. W. BUNCE
S. E. BURROW

J. R. CALDWELL
T. W. CANNING
J. B. CARTER
J. NORMAN CASE
JOHN CLIMIE
W. F. COLES
W. F. COX
HENRY CRAIK
DAN CRAWFORD
T. CROSKERY
T. R. CUPPLES

T. R. DALE
W. DALGETTY
M. DANIELS
J. C. M. DAWSON
H. K. DOWNIE
WM. DUDGEON
W. D. DUNN
S. E. DUTTON

JOHN H. ELLIOTT

ROBERT FARIE
W. W. FEREDAY
FRANKLIN FERGUSON
JAMES FORBES
HERBERT R. FRANCIS
H. R. FRANKLIN
DAVID FREW

A. GARDINER

W. J. GERRIE
WM. GILMORE
GEORGE GOODMAN
RICHARD GRAHAM
JOHN GRAY
HENRY GROVES

JAS. M. HAMILTON
WILL HARRISON
G. H. HATTON
JOHN HAWTHORN
HENRY HEATH
MATTHEW HENRY
T. SHULDHAM HENRY
G. HEPBURN
E. A. HEWITT
C. F. HOGG
THOS. HOLT
WM. HOSTE
WM. H. HOYTE
GEO. HUCKLESBY
S. HUGGETT
C. RUSSELL HURDITCH
GEO. J. HYDE

JOHN G. JOHNSTON
A. E. JONES
JOSEPH W. JORDAN

J. MUIR KELLY
HUGH KERR

J. P. LEWIS
ROBERT LOGAN
R. M. LORIMER
WM. LUFF

ARCHD. M'FADYEN
R. M'KILLIAM
ANGUS M'KINNON
FRANK M'LAINE
E. C. MACLAY
P. T. M'ROSTIE
ALFRED MACE
F. E. MARSH
H. H. MARTIN
GEO. MASCULL

ROBT. MATHESON
J. MEEK
W. J. MILLER
F. C. MOGRIDGE
J. MONYPENNY
G. H. MOWAT
T. D. W. MUIR

JAMES ORR
J. E. OWLES

RAY PALMER
ARCHIE PAYNE
HENRY PAYNE
I. W. PHIPPS
HY. PICKERING
A. T. PIERSON
A. J. POLLOCK
F. P. PRINDLE

W. T. RAE
WM. ROBERTSON

J. J. SIMS
JAMES SMITH
W. H. STANCOMBE
JAMES STEPHEN
M. STOTT
S. J. STREET

F. A. TATFORD
G. M. TAYLOR
W. H. GRIFFITH THOMAS
J. R. THOMPSON
WM. A. THOMSON
HENRY THORNE
R. A. TORREY
SAMUEL TURNER

H. J. VINE
W. E. VINE
R. J. G. VOISIN

HORATIO WALLIS
DAVID WARD
W. B. WESTCOTT
WALTER WILSON
FRED. P. WOOD

As the surnames of several contributors are unknown,
this list is therefore incomplete.

*"Because the preacher was wise, he gave good heed, sought out, and set in order"—Eccles. 12. 9.*

## The Soul.

1. Its Existence, - Gen. 2. 7; 35. 18; 1 Kings 17. 21
2. Its condition, - Ezekiel 18. 4; Ephesians 2. 1
3. Its Redemption, Psalm 49. 8
4. Its Salvation, - Isa. 55. 3; Heb. 10. 39; Matt. 16. 26

F.C.M.

## Seven Marks of a Christian.

1. A Christian is a man who is BORN AGAIN: "Born again, not of corruptible seed, but of incorruptible, by the Word of God, which liveth and abideth for ever" (1 Peter 1. 23).

2. A Christian is a man who doesn't seek for SALVATION THROUGH WORKS: "Not of works, lest any man should boast" (Eph. 2. 9); "God imputeth righteousness without works" (Rom. 4. 6).

3. A Christian is a man who shows by his works that he has got SALVATION THROUGH CHRIST: "Who gave Himself for us, that He might redeem us from all iniquity, and purify unto Himself a peculiar people, zealous of good works" (Titus 2. 14).

4. A Christian is a man who BUILDS ON A SURE FOUNDATION: "Other foundation can no man lay than that is laid, which is Jesus Christ" (1 Cor. 3. 11).

5. A Christian is a man who CONFESSES CHRIST among his fellows: "With the mouth confession is made unto salvation" (Rom. 10. 10).

6. A Christian is a man who SERVES THE LORD JESUS and WAITS FOR HIS COMING: He has "turned to God from idols to serve the living God, and to wait for His Son from Heaven" (1 Thess. 1. 9, 10).

7. A Christian is a man who CARRIES THE MESSAGE OF SALVATION to others and beseeches men, saying: "We pray you in Christ's stead be ye reconciled to God" (2 Cor. 5. 20).

J.C.

9

# SUBJECTS FOR SPEAKERS AND STUDENTS.

## Guidance for Servants.

1. A servant must be obedient, - - Titus 2. 9
2. A servant can be rewarded, - - Matt. 25. 21
3. A servant can be discharged, - - Matt. 20. 8-16
4. A servant cannot serve two masters, - Matt. 6. 24
5. A servant must not strive, - - - 2 Tim. 2. 24
6. Who is Master of the servant? - - Eph. 6. 5, 6, 7
7. The future place of service, - John 12. 26    F-T.

## A King Requited.

HOW ADONI-BEZEK WAS

Found, - Judges 1. v. 5
Fought, - ,,    ,, 5
Fled, - - ,,    ,, 6
Fared—"requited." ,, 7

HYP.

## Love in Four Aspects.

LOVE'S

1. Reproach, - Mal. 1. 2
2. Response, John 21. 15-17
3. Reciprocity, 1 John 4. 19
4. Rhapsody, - Rev. 1. 5

J.E.B.

## God-Given Portraiture.

1. Adam illustrates human nature; and what we are we have inherited from him (1 Cor. 15. 47, 48; Rom. 5. 12-19).
2. Cain illustrates the carnal mind, at enmity with God and with a religion of its own (Gen. 4. 1-16; 1 John 3. 12; Jude 11).
3. Abel illustrates the spiritual mind and discerns the value of the Blood (Gen. 4. 4; Heb. 11. 4).
4. Enoch illustrates communion with God that leads to separation from the world and to a testimony of Christ, and is a type of the Church caught up before the great tribulation (Gen. 5. 21-24; Heb. 11. 5-6; Jude 14, 15).
5. Noah illustrates regeneration—saved by the ark—and is a type of the Jewish remnant delivered safely through the tribulation (Heb. 11. 7).
6. Abraham illustrates faith, leading to strangership in this world (Gen. 12. 1, etc.; Heb. 11. 8-16; Gal. 3. 6-9).
7. Isaac illustrates sonship and heirship (Gal. 4. 1-7; 21-31).
8. Jacob illustrates service; he served fourteen years for both his wives, and six years for his cattle (Gen. 31. 38-42; Matt. 25. 21).
9. Joseph illustrates suffering and glory (Gen. 39. 20; 41. 41-45; 2 Tim. 2. 12).    F.F.

## A Complete Salvation.

1. Saviour from Sin's Penalty,    -    -    2 Cor. 9. 15
2. Deliverer from Sin's Power,    -    -    Rom. 6. 17
3. Leader in Service,    -    -    -    -    2 Cor. 2. 15
4. Hope in Resurrection,    -    -    -    1 Cor. 15. 54

J. G.

### Four I's (of Matthew 11. 28).

Inviting,    -    -    "Come." | Immediate,    -    "Give."
Individual, "Me," "You." | Invaluable,    -    "Rest."

HYP.

## The Righteous.

NONE RIGHTEOUS (Rom. 3. 10): "No, not one" of the human race.

ONE RIGHTEOUS (Luke 23. 47): The centurion's confession.

SOME RIGHTEOUS (Rom. 5. 19; 1 Cor. 1. 30): Made righteous by the obedience of the One.

ALL RIGHTEOUS (Isa. 60. 21; Rev. 21. 27): Of a future day it is written, "Thy people also shall be all righteous."    W. LUFF.

## Our Need of the Holy Spirit.

1. We need the Holy Spirit for Conviction,    John 16. 8
2. We need the Holy Spirit for Regeneration, John 3. 2
3. We need the Holy Spirit for Communion,    John 4. 14
4. We need the Holy Spirit for Consolation,   John 14. 16
5. We need the Holy Spirit for Revelation, - 1 Cor. 2. 9
6. We need the Holy Spirit for Demonstration, 1 Cor. 2. 4
7. We need the Holy Spirit for Sanctification, Rom. 8. 13
8. We need the Holy Spirit for Glorification, Rom. 8. 11

JS. FS.

## Cursing and Blessing.
### Jeremiah 17. 5-8.
#### WHAT IS CURSING? WHAT IS BLESSING?

1. THE CURSE.—(a) Its Evidence: useless, fruitless; (b) The Reason: robbing God, defeating His purposes.
2. THE BLESSING.—(a) Its Evidence: useful, fruitful, free from care (cf. 1 Peter 5. 7); (b) The Reason: gives opportunity for display of grace, provides trophies for Him, fills His purpose, satisfies His heart.

QUESTION: Can one be transferred? *Answer*: Galatians 3. 13, 14.   He was made a curse for us.    J.W.A.

## Divine Necessities.

### Six Groups—*three* in each Group.

1. We *must* needs die, - Condemnation, - 2 Sam. 14. 14
2. He that cometh to God *must believe that He is,* - Homologation, - Heb. 11. 6
3. Ye *must* be born again, - Regeneration, - John 3. 7

4. The Son of Man *must* be lifted up, - - - Propitiation, - John 3. 14
5. He *must* rise again, - Justification, - John 20. 9
6. What is written *must* be accomplished, - - Corroboration, - Luke 22. 37

7. The Gospel *must* first be published among all nations, - - - Evangelisation, - Mark 13. 10
8. There is no other Name whereby we *must* be saved, Salvation, - - Acts 4. 12
9. When the heaven *must* receive, - - - Approbation, - Acts 3. 21

10. He must increase, - - Appreciation, - John 3. 30
   (of Christ)
11. But I must decrease, - Depreciation, - John 3. 30
   (of self)
12. God is a Spirit, and they that worship Him *must* worship Him in spirit and in truth, - - Adoration, - - John 4. 24

13. I *must* work the works of Him that sent Me, - Consummation, - John 9. 4
14. Them also I *must* bring, - Unification, - John 10 16
15. For He *must* reign until, - Domination, - 1 Cor. 15. 25

16. We *must* through much tribulation enter into the kingdom of God, - Tribulation, - Acts 14. 24
17. We *must* all appear before the Judgment-seat of Christ, - - - Manifestation, - 2 Cor. 5. 10
18. This corruptible *must* put on incorruptibility, - Glorification, 1 Cor. 15. 53 T.R.D.

# SUBJECTS FOR SPEAKERS AND STUDENTS.

## Three Stages of Knowledge.

The knowledge of *God's Grace*, - - - Col. 1. 6
The knowledge of *God's Will*, - - - Col. 1. 9
The knowledge of *God Himself*, - - - Col. 1. 10

D-W—c.

| Five Open Doors. | Five Shut Doors. |
|---|---|
| 1. Restored Communion, 2 Chr. 29. 3 | 1. Safety, - - Gen. 7. 16 |
| 2. Deliverance - Acts 5. 19 | 2. Communion, Matt. 6. 6 |
| 3. Surrender, - Rev. 3. 20 | 3. Faith, 1 Kings 4. 5, 21, 33 |
| 4. Service, - - 1 Cor. 16. 9 | 4. Self - Sufficiency, Rev. 3. 20 |
| 5. Opportunity, Rev. 3. 8 | 5. Separation, - Matt. 25. 10 |
| I.W.P. | I.W.P. |

## "To Call to Remembrance."

How excellent is Thy Name, - - - Psalm 8. 1
How great is Thy Goodness, - - - Psalm 31. 19
How precious is Thy Lovingkindness, - Psalm 36. 7
How dear are Thy Tabernacles, - - - Psalm 84. 1
How sweet are Thy Words, - - - Psa. 119 103
How precious are Thy Thoughts, - - Psa. 139. 17

W. DUDGEON.

## "Sevens" in Scripture.

IT has been said that "the constant occurrence in Scripture of the number seven is the result of nothing short of Divine intention." This number has been traced in one form or another in nearly every book in the Old Testament and the New. It is wonderfully associated with the history of the life and teaching of our Lord. Note—

1. The seven stages of His history in Philippians 2. 6-9.
2. The seven characteristics of His wisdom in Proverbs 3. 15-18.
3. The seven parables in Matthew 13.
4. The seven miracles in John, chapters 2, 4, 5, 6, 9, 11.
5. The seven prayers in Luke, chapters 3, 5, 6, 9, 11, 22.
6. The seven petitions in the Lord's Prayer, Luke 11. 2-4.
7. The seven sayings on the Cross, Luke 23. 34; John 19. 26-28; Luke 23. 43; Matthew 27. 46; John 19. 30; Luke 23. 46.
8. The seven blessings from the throne, Revelation 1, 14, 16, 19, 20, 22.    HENRY THORNE.

# SUBJECTS FOR SPEAKERS AND STUDENTS.

## Three Great Facts.

1. Jesus Did It, - - John 19. 30; Heb. 1. 3; 10. 12
2. God Says It, - - Exod. 12. 13; Acts 13. 38-39
3. I Believe It, - - John 9. 38; Rom. 10. 8-11

*The finished work of Christ makes ME safe.*
*The written Word of God makes ME sure.* L-W.

## Sure Things in Isaiah.

1. A sure *place*—Christ our Support, .. .. ch. 22. 23
2. A sure *foundation*—Christ our Rock, .. ch. 28. 16
3. A sure *covering*—Christ our Defence, .. ch. 22. 17
4. A sure *supply*—Christ our Life, .. .. ch. 33. 16
5. A sure *resource*—Christ our Confidence, .. ch. 55. 3

M.

## "According to Thy Word" (Psalm 119).

1. Cleansing, - - - v. 9
2. Quickening, vv. 25, 107, 24
3. Strengthening - v. 28
4. Saving, - - - v. 41
5. Mercy, - - - v. 58
6. Blessing, - - - v. 65
7. Comforting, - - v. 76
8. Understanding, -v. 169
9. Delivering, - -v. 170

D.F.

## "Things to Come."

1. The Regeneration of all things, Matt. 19. 28
2. The Redemption of all things, - Eph. 1. 14
3. The Restitution of all things, - Acts 3. 21
4. The Reconciliation of all things, Col. 1. 28
5. The Restoration of all things, - Eph. 1. 10

H.K.D.

## Repentance.

1. Goodness of God leads to it, .. .. Rom. 2. 5
2. Authority of God commands it, .. .. Acts 17. 30
3. Compassion of God waits for it, .. .. 2 Peter 3. 9
4. Grace of God grants it, .. .. .. Acts 11. 18
5. Love of God rejoices over it, .. .. Luke 15. 7

W.W.F.

## "Together's."

1. Quickened Together, Eph. 2. 5
2. Raised Together, ,, 2. 6
3 Seated Together, ,, 2. 6
4. Framed Together, ,, 2. 21
5. Builded Together, ,, 2. 22
6. Joined Together, ,, 4. 16
7. Gathered Together, ,, 1. 10

Js.Fs.

## Four Banquets in Esther

1. The Banquet of *Deposition*, - ch. 1. 3
2. The Banquet of *Coronation*, - ch. 2. 18
3. The Banquet of *Petition*, - - ch. 5. 4-8
4. The Banquet of *Commemoration*, ch. 9. 17

M.

# SUBJECTS FOR SPEAKERS AND STUDENTS.

## Three Whosoevers.
1. A startling fact, - Rev. 20. 15
2. Solemn statement, „ 22.15
3. Sweeping invitation, „ 22.17
   H.K.D.

## The Ability of Christ.
1. Able to save, - Heb. 7. 25
2. Able to keep, - 2 Tim. 1.12
3. Able to subdue, Phil. 3.21
   W.N.Y.

## God's Side——and——Your Side.

"God so *loved* the world that He *gave* His only begotten Son."

The *loving* and *giving* are God's side.

(John 3. 16).

"That whosoever *believeth* in Him should not perish, but *have* everlasting life."

The *believing* and *having* are your side.

## Seven Crowns.
1. Crown of thorns, Matt. 27.29
2.   „  of life, Jas. 1.12; Rev. 2. 10    [2 Tim. 4. 8
3.   „  of righteousness,
4.   „  of rejoicing, 1 Thes. 2.19
5.   „  incorruptible, 1 Cor. 9.25
6.   „  of glory, - 1 Peter 5. 4
7.   „  of gold, Rev. 4. 4 J.H.B.

## Seven Mysteries.
1. Incarnation, - 1 Tim. 3. 16
2. Divine indwelling, Col. 1.27
3. The Church, - Ephes. 5.23
4. Iniquity, 2 Thess. 2.7,8
5. Translation, - 1 Cor. 15.51
6. Israel (condition of),
   Rom. 11.25
7. Restoration, Ep. 1.9,10 HYP.

## What God is——and——What God Gives.
### A Study of Psalm 84. 11, 12.
1. God is a sun, - Inward, - - Light, life, and love.
2. God is a shield, - Outward, - Protection, power, prosperity.
3. God gives grace, Time, Salvation, separation, sanctification.
4. God gives glory, Eternity, Rom. 8.17,18; 8.28-30; Col. 3.4. D.W.

## The Heart in Ephesians.
1. The blind heart, - - 4. 18
2. The filled heart, - - 3. 17
3. The melodious heart, 5. 19
4. The comforted heart, 6. 22
5. The single heart, - 6. 5 T.B.

## Threefold Writing.
1. Writing of justice, Ex. 31.18
2. Writing of grace, John 8. 6
3. Writing of judgment, - - - Dan. 5.25
   JS.FS.

## Ten Representative Lepers.
### A Study of Luke 17. 11.
1. They all had the same disease, - - Leprosy = sin.
2. They were all in the same place, - Afar off = distance.
3. They all cried to the same Person, - - Jesus = God.
4. They all cried for the same thing, - Mercy = helpless.
5. They all got the same prescription, - Go = obedience.
6. They all got the same blessing, Cleansing = regeneration.

15

# SUBJECTS FOR SPEAKERS AND STUDENTS.

## Four "Callings" in First Peter.

1. Called—"Out of darkness into His marvellous light, - - - Ch. 2. 9
2. Called unto—Suffering for well-doing, Ch. 2. 20, 21
3. Called unto—Rendering blessing for evil, - - - - - Ch. 3. 9
4. "Called...unto His eternal glory," Ch. 5. 10

"He which hath *called* you is holy" Ch. 1. 15. D.F.

| Life. | Nathaniel's Conversion. |
|---|---|
| 1. Manifested, John 1. 4 | 1. His Arrest, John 1. 45 |
| 2. Obtained, - John 3. 16 | 2. His Doubt, ,, 1. 46 |
| 3. Possessed, - John 4. 14 | 3. His Character, ,, 1. 47 |
| 4. Sustained, John 6. 35 | 4. His Question, ,, 1. 48 |
| 5. Ministered, John 7. 38 | 5. His Confession ,, 1. 49 |
| 6. Abounding, John 10. 10 | 6. His Faith, ,, 1. 50 |
| 7. Resurrection, ,, 11. 24 25 | 7. His Prospect, ,, 1. 51 |
| D.D.T | JS. FS. |

## Thou Art Mine.

1. POSSESSED—I in them, - - John 17. 23
2. ENCIRCLED—As by a wall of fire, - - Zech. 2. 5
3. UPHELD—By the everlasting arms, - Deut. 33. 27
4. CARRIED—Between His shoulders, - Deut. 33. 12
5. COVERED—In the shadow of His hand, - Isaiah 51. 16
6. COMPASSED—With favour, - - - Psalm 5. 12

F.F.

| "Choosing." | The Son of God |
|---|---|
| 1. A bad choice, Num. 10. 30 | THE MIGHTY ONE WHO |
| 2. A good choice, Gen. 24. 58 | Quickeneth, - John 5. 21 |
| 3. A better choice, Josh. 24. 15 | Judgeth, - John 5. 22 |
| 4. The best choice, Luke 10. 42 | Raiseth, - John 5. 25 |
| H.K.D. | W.S.M. |

## Seven "I Ams" of Christ
### (MEETING MAN'S NEED).

1. "I am" the Bread (for the unsatisfied one), John 6. 35
2. "I am" the Light (for the blind one), - John 9. 5
3. "I am" the Door (for the unsafe one), - John 10. 9
4. "I am" the Shepherd (for the lost one), - John 10. 11
5. "I am" the Way (for the ignorant one), John 14. 6
6. "I am" the Life (for the dead one), - John 11. 25
7. "I am" the Vine (for the fruitless one), - John 15. 1

A.G.A.

16

# SUBJECTS FOR SPEAKERS AND STUDENTS.

## Human Responsibility
### SEEN IN

1. Eden with the Tree, - - - Gen. 2. 17 —Eat not
2. Noah with the Ark, - - - Gen. 7. 1 —Come in
3. Egypt with the Blood, - - Exod. 12. 7—Strike
4. Rehab with the Cord, - - Josh. 2. 18—Bind
5. The Desert with the Serpent, - Num. 21. 8—Look
6. Sodom with Lot, - - - Gen. 19. 17—Escape
7. The World to-day with the Gospel, John 3. 16—Believe

JS.FS.

## God's Purpose
WITH HIS PEOPLE OF OLD
(Deut. 8. 2-16).

1. To humble thee.
2. To prove thee.
3. To do thee good.
   (Rom. 8. 28.) T-W.

## Word Links
EASILY JOINED TOGETHER.

Naught, - - Isa. 53. 3
Sought, - - Psa. 34. 4
Bought, - - 1 Cor. 6. 20
Caught, - - 2 Cor. 12. 16
Taught, 1 Thess. 4. 9 HYP.

## Seven Aspects of Salvation.
### WE ARE

1. Saved from the "penalty" of sin, - 1 Peter 3. 18
2. Saved from the "power" of sin, - Rom. 6. 7
3. Saved from the "power" of Satan, - Acts 26. 18
4. Saved from the "power" of the world, Gal. 1. 4
5. Saved from the "power" of the law, - Rom. 10. 4
6. Saved from the "power" of wrath, - 1 Thess. 1. 9, 10
7. We shall be saved from the "presence"
   of sin, - - - - - Heb. 9. 28

A.G.A.

## Why the Blood is Precious.
The following are a few of the precious things which His Blood has purchased for and brought to us:

Redemption - 1 Pet. 1. 19
Forgiveness - Eph. 1. 7
Deliverance
(see R.V.) - Rev. 1. 5
Justification - Rom. 5. 9
Atonement* - Lev. 17. 11
Propitiation*- Rom. 3. 25
Assurance - Exod. 12. 13
Nearness - Eph. 2. 13

Satisfaction - John 6. 55
Peace - - Col. 1. 20
Access - - Heb. 10. 19
Cleansing
(present) - 1 John 1. 7
Fellowship - 1 Cor. 10. 16
Sanctification- Heb. 13. 12
Victory - Rev. 12. 11
Testimony - 1 John 5. 8

* "Atonement" and "Propitiation" mean to cover, not only the sinner's sins forgiven, but the sinner covered (see Psalm 32. 1). T.

17

# SUBJECTS FOR SPEAKERS AND STUDENTS.

## "The Things of God" (1 Cor. 2. 11).

| | |
|---|---|
| The Purpose of God, | Exod. **3**. 7 |
| The Power of God, | Exod. **9**. 16 |
| The Provision of God, | Exod. **12**. 3 |
| The Punishment of God, | Exod. **12**. 30 |

## Two Remarkable Days. Js. Fs.

1. The *darkest* Day in Israel's history.
"There was no king in Israel: every man did that which was right in his own eyes," - Last verse of Judges.
2. The *brightest* Day in the Church's history.
"Neither said any of them that ought he possessed was his own; but they had all things common," - Acts 4. 30-35.

## Three Miracles Together.

1. A great Persecutor saved at midday, - - Acts 9. 6
2. A great Invalid cured after eight years, - „ 9. 34
3. A great Worker raised from the dead, - - „ 9. 40

HyP.

## The Lord Our Helper.

Vain is the help of man,
Psa. 60. 11
Fear not, I will help,
Isa. 41. 13
My Helper, I will not fear,
Heb. 13. 6
Very present help,
Psa. 46. 1
Help of His countenance,
Psa. 42. 5
Helped unto this day,
Acts 26. 22
Thy judgments help me,
Psa. 119. 175. F.F.

## Two Things in Matt. 7.

Gates—strait and wide,
v. 13
Ways—narrow and broad,
vv. 13, 14
Trees—good and corrupt,
v. 17
Fruits—good and evil,
v. 18
Men—wise and foolish,
vv. 24, 26
Foundations—rock and
sand, vv. 24, 26
Houses—fell and fell not,
vv. 25, 27. F.F.

## THE TEACHER'S MESSAGE
### IS A MESSAGE OF

| | |
|---|---|
| **M** atchless Grace, | Titus 2. 11 |
| **E** ngaging Interest, | Luke 19. 48 |
| **S** aving Power, | Rom. 1. 16 |
| **S** olemn Import, | Heb. 2. 3 |
| **A** ggressive Character, | 2 Tim. 2. 9 |
| **G** lad Tidings, | Luke 1. 19 |
| **E** verlasting Life, | John 3. 16 |

R. M. L.

# SUBJECTS FOR SPEAKERS AND STUDENTS.

## A Threefold " Arise."

1. I will arise and go *to* my Father—SALVATION, Luke 15.18
2. I will arise and go *for* my Father—SERVICE, Matt. 21.28,29
3. I shall arise and go *to* my Father—SATISFACTION,
John 14. 2, 3   G.H.

## Four Pointed Questions.

1. Where art thou ?   Condition and position,   -   Gen. 3. 9
2. What hast thou done ?   Responsibility to God, Gen. 4.10
3. To whom belongest thou? Ownership, service,1 Sam.30.13
4. Wilt thou be made whole?   Blessing and salvation,
John 5. 6   T.D.W.M.

## Trinities of Evil.

1. The lust of flesh,...eyes, and pride of life,   -1 John 2. 16
2 The dragon, beast, and false prophet,   -   - Rev. 16.13
3. Leaven of Pharisees, Sadducees, and Herod,
Mark 8. 15; Matt. 1 . 6
4. Three languages—Hebrew, Greek, and Latin, John 19.20
5. Cain, Balaam, and Core,   -   -   - Jude 11   W.W.F.

## The Full-orbed Gospel of Jesus Christ.

1. " Without Christ," the unsaved sinner's sad
condition, -   -   -   -   -   -   - Eph. 2.12
2. " Through Christ," the divine way of salvation
for contrite sinners,   -   -   -   - Eph. 2.7
3. " In Christ," the position of the believing sinner,Eph. 2.10
4. " With Christ," the prospect of the saved sinner,Eph. 2.5
G.H.

## Thoughts of Himself.

" My meditation of Him shall be sweet " (Psa. 104. 34).
1. His love,   -   -   -   - Gal. 2. 20; Eph. 3. 18, 19
2. His condescension, -   -   - Heb. 2. 14; Phil. 2. 7, 8
3. His exaltation,   -   -   - Phil. 2. 9; Heb. 1. 3, 8
4. His glory,   -   -   -   - John 17. 5; 17. 24
5. His present service for us,   -   - Heb. 9. 24; 7. 25
6. His return,   -   -   -   - John 14. 3   E.A.H.

## Love Giving.

1. The WORLD He Loved, -   -   -   - the *world*
2. The SON He Gave,   -   - His *only begotten* Son
3. The LIFE He Bestows, -   -   - *Everlasting* Life
4. The CONDITION He Imposes, -   whosoever *believeth*
5. The STATE from which He Saves,   should not *perish*

T. W. CANNING

# SUBJECTS FOR SPEAKERS AND STUDENTS.

## Kept by the Power of God.
### 1 Peter 1. 5.

The Lord will go *before* you, - - - Isa. 52. 12
The glory of the Lord shall be thy *reward*, - Isa. 58. 8
The Lord is *round about* His people, - - Psa. 125. 2
*Underneath* are the everlasting arms, - - Deut. 23. 7
His banner *over* me was love, - - S. of S. 2. 4. G-S.

## Spirituality.

1. Spiritual Blessings,
   Eph. 1. 3
2. Spiritual Meat,
   1 Cor. 10. 3
3. Spiritual Drink,
   1 Cor. 10. 4
4. Spiritual Gifts,
   1 Cor. 14. 1
5. Spiritual Songs,
   Eph. 5. 19
6. Spiritual Body,
   1 Cor. 15. 44
7. Spiritual Man,
   1 Cor. 14. 37 JS. FS.

## Fruitlessness.

1. Fruitless profession,
   Matt. 3. 8
2. Fruitless hearer,
   Mark 4. 7
3. Fruitless associate,
   Jude 12
4. Fruitless branch,
   John 15. 6
5. Fruitless vineyard,
   Matt. 21. 34
6. Fruitless account,
   Phil. 4. 17
7. Fruitless life, Rom. 6. 21
   JS. FS.

## Four Wonderful Books.

The Book of God's Counsels—"The
   Volume,"- - - - - - Heb. 10. 7
The Book of the Law—"Written in the
   law," - - - - - - Gal. 3. 10
The Book of Remembrance—"was written,"- Mal. 3. 16
The Book of Judgment—"Shall not come
   into," - - - - - John 5. 24. S-S.

## The Fruit of the Spirit.
### Galatians 5 22, 23.

1. Love is the - - - Source of Obedience.
2. Joy is the - - - Flower of Holiness.
3. Peace is the - - - Outcome of Trustfulness.
4. Longsuffering is the - Partner of Patience.
5. Gentleness is the - - Daughter of Love.
6. Goodness is the - - Activity of Grace.
7. Faith is the - - - Faithfulness of Courage.
8. Meekness is the - - Trait of Christ.
9. Temperance is the - - Mastery of Faith. C-C.

## Lot's Declension.

### Genesis 13 to 19. HIS MISTAKES.

1. Eyes not higher than Jordan, the way of the world, - - - - - - - Gen. 13. 10
2. Pitched his tent toward Sodom, - - Gen. 13. 12
   The mistake of seeing how far we can go towards the world, instead of how far we can keep from it.
3. Dwelt in Sodom, - - - - - Gen. 14. 12
   Brought him into trouble and loss.
4. Sat in the gate, - - - - - - Gen. 19. 1
   Identified entirely with the world.

Lot lost his (1) property, (2) communion, (3) testimony—
Gen. 19. 14—(4) faith—Gen. 19. 19.  G.J.H.

### Fourfold Fragrance.

1. The fragrance of God's knowledge, - 2 Cor.2.14
2. The servant, a fragrance of Christ, - - 2 Cor.2.15
3. The fragrance of death unto death, - 2 Cor.2.16
4. The fragrance of life unto life, - - 2 Cor.2.16

T.B.

### Seven Aspects of Love.

1. Manifested, -1 John 4. 9
2. Commended, Rom. 5. 8
3. Bestowed, -1 John 3. 1
4. Enjoyed, -Rom. 5. 5
5. Perceived, -1 John 3. 16
6. Perfected, -1 John 2. 5
7. Triumphant, Rom. 8. 39

JS. FS.

### The Righteousness of the Lord Jesus.

Heaven, earth, and hell bear witness to His righteousness.

1. Judas, - - - Matt. 27. 4
2. Pilate's wife, - „ 27. 19
3. Pilate, - - - „ 27. 24
4. Herod, - - - Luke 23. 15
5. The thief, - - Luke 23.41
6. The centurion, „ 23.47
7. Demons, - Mark 1.24; 3.11
8. The Father, Luke 3.22; 9.35

In type the testimony of the Spirit, Ex. 12. 5; Lev. 1. 3-10;
3. 1-6; 5. 18; 6. 6; 22. 21, &c.; Num. 19. 2

Holy, harmless, undefiled, separate from sinners, - Heb. 7.26

J.R.C.

### Four Aspects of Faith.

1. The security of faith, 1 Pet.1.5
2. The trials of faith, „ 1.7
3. The joy of faith, - „ 1.8
4. The end of faith, - „ 1.9

W.E.V.

### The Friend of Outcasts.

1. A seeking Saviour, John 9.35
2. A sincere Enquirer, „ 9.36
3. A surprising revelation, - - - - „ 9.37
4. A simple faith, - - „ 9.38

W.R.

# SUBJECTS FOR SPEAKERS AND STUDENTS

## God and His People.

### GOD'S PEOPLE HAVE

1. A place in His Heart, - - - - Deut. 33. 3
2. A place at His Feet, - - - - ,, 3
3. A place in His Hand, - - - - ,, 3
4. A place near His Side, - - - ,, 12
5. A place between His Shoulders, - - ,, 12
6. A place in His Arms, - - - - ,, 24 G.H.

## Christ is All.

### AS SEEN IN PHILIPPIANS.

Cross of Christ, - Phil. 3. 18
Work of Christ, - ,, 2. 30
Gospel of Christ, ,, 1. 27
Faith of Christ, - ,, 3. 9
Day of Christ, - ,, 1. 10
W. J. M.

## Five "I Wills"

### (Gen. 26. 3, 4).

1. "I will be with thee. "
2. "I will bless thee. "
3. "I will give. "
4. "I will perform the oath. "
5. "I will make thy seed to multiply. " F.F.

## Mephibosheth.—A Study.

1. David's desire, - 2 Sam. 9. 1 - Grace.
2. Dear departed, - ,, 1 - For Jonathan's sake.
3. Desert dwelling, - ,, 4 - Lo-debar.
4. Delightful deputation, ,, 5 - King's message.
5. Doubts dispelled, - ,, 7 - King's reception.
6. "Dead dog," - ,, 8 - Self-abasement.
7. Dainty dining, - ,, 10 - King's table.
8. Desirable dwelling, ,, 13 - In Jerusalem.
9. Daily dependence,- ,, 13 - King's provision.
10. Discomforting defect, ,, 13 - Lame on both feet.

## Acrostic Lesson on "PEACE." W.R.

**PLATFORM.**—"Justified by faith" (Rom. 5. 1). Explain righteous basis. Christ condemned, I am justified by faith.

**ENJOYMENT.**—"We have *peace* with God" (Rom. 5. 1). Not hope, but H.A.V.E. Possession means practical enjoyment.

**ACCEPTANCE.**—"By faith." Believing in Christ. I believe a letter, a newspaper, so I believe God's Word.

**CHANNEL.**—"Through Jesus Christ our Lord." Not good works, tears, prayers, etc. Salvation only through Christ.

**ENDURANCE.**—"Saved by His life" (Rom. 5. 10). As long as He lives all His own shall endure. HYP.

# SUBJECTS FOR SPEAKERS AND STUDENTS.

## A Solemn Threefold Cord.
1. The Saviour's gracious invitation, - - - Matt. 11. 28
2. The Saviour's plaintive lamentation, - - - John 5. 40
3. The Saviour's solemn declaration, - - John 8. 24 G.H.

## Threefold Privilege.
1. Abide *with* Me, 1 Sam. 22.23
2. Abide *in* Me, - John 15.4
3. Abide *for* Me, - Hos. 3.3
G.H.

## What the Thorns Teach.
1. Ruin, - - - - Gen. 3.18
2. Redemption, - Matt. 27.29
3. Regeneration, - Isa. 55.12
H.K.D.

## Five Points of Time.
1. The fulness of the time, - - Gal. 4.4, - The birth of Christ
2. The consummation of ages, - Heb. 9.26, The cross of Christ
3. The end of the age, - - Matt. 13.39, Close of Christianity
4. The fulness of the times, - Eph. 1.10, The millennium
5. The end of time, - - - - 1 Cor. 15. 24        W.W.F.

## Things Eternal
for the People of God.
1. The Son ... who became the Author of *eternal* salvation unto all them that obey Him, - - - Heb. 5.8,9
2. Hath obtained *eternal* redemption for us, - - - Heb. 9.12
3. That they might receive the promise of *eternal* inheritance, Heb. 9.15
E.A.H.

## Soul Prosperity.
1. Delighting in Lord, Psa. 34.2
2. Thirsting for God, ,, 42.2
3. Trusting in God, ,, 57.1
4. Waiting upon God, ,, 62.1
5. Satisfied and following closely, - - ,, 63.5-8
6. Praising the Lord, ,, 103.1
7. Keeping low, adhering to the Word, and loving it exceedingly, - - Psa. 119.25,167
8. Waiting for the Lord, Psa. 130.5,6 W.J.M.

## Lessons from Lazarus.
1. He was loved by Jesus, John 11.5
2. He was lifeless, John 11.14
3. He got life through Jesus, - - - - John 11.44
4. He got light, - - John 11.44
5. He got liberty, - John 11.44
6. He had life sustained, John 12.2
7. He manifested life, John 12.11
W.J.M.

## The Mounts of the Bible.
1. Sinai, the law, - Deut. 33.2
2. Ebal, the curse of the law, Deut. 27.13
3. Calvary, the curse removed, Luke 23.33
4. Gerizim, present blessing, Deut. 27.12
5. Pisgah, future inheritance, Deut. 34.1
6. Olives, coming, - Zech. 14.4
7. Zion, the final kingdom, Isa. 24. 23 J.H.B.

# SUBJECTS FOR SPEAKERS AND STUDENTS.

## Seven Things about Justification.

1. THE SOURCE.—"It is God that justifieth," Rom. 8. 33
2. THE SPRING.—"Being justified freely by His grace," - - - - Rom. 3. 4
3. THE GROUND.—"Being now justified by His Blood," - - - - - Rom. 5. 7
4. THE PROOF.—"He was raised again for (because of) our justification," - Rom. 4. 25
5. THE MEANS.—"Being justified by faith," Rom. 5. 1
6. THE EVIDENCE.—"By thy words thou shalt be justified," - - - - Matt. 12. 31
7. THE FRUIT.—"By works a man is justified," - - - - - - James 2. 24

G. GOODMAN.

## Scripture Enclosures.

1. In Adam, - - Humanity, - - - 1 Cor. 15. 22
2. In Isaac, - - Nationality, - - - Heb. 11. 18
3. In the Flesh, - Carnality, - - - Rom. 8. 8
4. In Sin, - - Depravity, - - - Rom. 6. 1
5. In the Spirit, - Spirituality, - - - Rom. 8. 9
6. In Christ, - - Christianity, - - - Eph. 1. 6
7. In God, - - Divinity, - - - 1 Thess. 1. 1

JS. FS.

## The Prayers of Christ in Luke.

1. At His baptism (3. 21).
2. After curing the leper (v. 16) He withdrew into the wilderness, in waiting upon His Father for more power.
3. All night before sending out His disciples (6. 12), praying for them and their work.
4. Alone praying (9. 18, 22). Notice what He says about His death.
5. In the transfiguration (9. 28). Still about His death.
6. In a certain place with His disciples (11. 1). The prayer given to us.
7.. Praying for Peter (22. 32). His divine interest in him.
8. For Himself (22. 41, 44), "Father, if Thou be willing, remove this cup from Me."
9. His dying prayer (23. 34), "Father, forgive them; for they know not what they do."
10. "Father, into Thy hands I commend My spirit" (23. 46).

W.H.

# SUBJECTS FOR SPEAKERS AND STUDENTS.

## "A Little Sanctuary"
### In Ezekiel 11.

1. WHO FOR?    Remnant, Small Company,
            Outcast, -     -     - verses 13, 15
2. WHERE? -   Among the heathen, scattered,   verse 16
3. WHAT?   -   "Yet"—a little word with a
            great God behind it, -    -  ,, 16
4. HOW?   -   A Person—"I will be a little
            Sanctuary,"   -   - verse 16    HYP.

## What Pleased God.

1. THE LIFE THAT PLEASED GOD.
   I do always the things that please
   Him, -   -   -   -   -   John 8. 29
   This is My beloved Son, in whom I
   am well pleased, -   -   -   Matt. 3. 17
2. THE DEATH THAT PLEASED GOD.
   It pleased the Lord to bruise Him,   -   Isa. 53. 10
   His death was a sweet smelling savour,   Eph. 5. 2
3. THE RESULTS THAT PLEASE GOD.
   The pleasure of the Lord shall prosper
   in His hand, -   -   -   -   Isa. 53. 10
   It pleased God by the foolishness of
   preaching to save them that believe,   1 Cor. 1. 21
                                             A.G.

## Sinners Paul Dealt With.

1. The careless sinner—Gallio, -   -   -   Acts 18. 17
   Callous indifference is a deadly
   enemy of the Gospel, and is a marked
   characteristic of our day in Britain
   (Jonah 1. 6; Amos 6. 1).
2. The convicted sinner—Felix,   -   -   ,, 24. 25
   Conviction is not conversion (Prov.
   27. 1).
3. The almost persuaded sinner—Agrippa,   ,, 26. 28
   Saddest of all, Agrippa; so near and
   yet so far. The closing words of
   Bunyan's vision may be fitly used:
   "Even from the Gates of Heaven there
   was a way to Hell."

*Note*.—All three perished, as far as the Scriptures
enlighten us.                              W.A.T.

# SUBJECTS FOR SPEAKERS AND STUDENTS.

## "Against Christ."

| | | |
|---|---|---|
| The Heart, | - | Matt. 12. 30 |
| The Mouth, | - | Luke 12. 10 |
| The Hand, | - | Luke 22. 21 |
| The Heel, | - | John 13. 8 |
| The Family, | - | Luke 12. 52 |
| The World, | - | Acts 4. 27 |
| The Devil, | - | Rev. 12. 4,5 |

## God Spared Not

1. Angels, - 2 Pet. 2. 4
2. Old World, 2 Pet. 2. 5
3. Egyptians, Psalm 78. 50
4. Idolater, - Deut. 29. 20
5. Israel, - - Rom. 11. 21
6. His Own Son, Rom. 8. 32
"Take heed, Rom. 11. 20

## The Names of the Patriarchs.
### 1 Chronicles 1. 1-4.

1. ADAM,    -   - Man
2. SHETH,    -   - Being set, or constituted, or having become a
3. ENOSH,    -   - Wretched
4. KENAN,    -   - Mourner,
5. MAHALALEEL,   - The Light of God, or the Blessed God,
6. JARED,    -   - Came down,
7. HENOCH,    -   - Consecrated
8. METHU-    -   - (by) His death
    SELAH,    -   - to send
9. LAMECH,    -   - to the poor, or oppressed,
10. NOAH,    -   - Comfort.     H. CRAIK.

Such are the meanings of the Hebrew words here used, and they show that when God named the Patriarchs, He had reference to redemption through the precious blood of His own dear Son; for read as follows they express that blessed truth:—Man having become (a) wretched mourner, the blessed God came down, consecrated (by) His death, to send to the oppressed comfort.

## Prayer is to be—

1. In Faith, - Mark 11. 24
2. In the Spirit, Jude 20.
3. To the Father, John 15. 16
4. In the Son's Name, John 14. 13, 14
5. Illimitable, Matt. 21. 22
6. According to God's Will, 1 John 5. 14
7. In Communion, John 15. 7. 14 T.R.D.

## A Hive of "B's" Worth Keeping.

1. Be ye separate, 2 Cor. 6. 17
2. Be ye kind one to another, - Eph. 4. 32
3. Be careful for nothing, - - Phil. 4. 6
4. Be ye thankful, Col. 3. 15
5. Be ye holy, 1 Peter 1. 16
6. Be ye also patient, Jas. 5. 8
7. And be content, Heb. 13. 5
         H. W.

## Three Sights of Christ.

1. Crucified, - - Luke 23. 48, - Humiliates.
2. Crowned, - - Hebrews 2. 9, - Encourages.
3. Glorified, - - 1 John 3. 2, - Transforms. H. K. D.

## God's Wonders in the Wilderness.

During "these forty years in the wilderness" (Deut. 8. 2)
God provided superbly for His people—

1. FOOD. Alike suitable for youth and age, Exod. 16. 35
   angels and men, - - - - - Psa. 78. 25
2. WATER. Clear and sparkling out of "the
   rock of flint," "that followeth them" Deut. 8. 15
   all the journey through, - - - 1 Cor. 10. 4
3. CLOTHING. Homespuns that "waxed not
   old," nor got threadbare, all these forty
   years, - - - - - - - Deut. 8. 4
4. FOOTWEAR. A very great essential in a
   desert march, which never was "waxen Deut. 29. 5
   old," and feet to match, for they did
   not become too big for the boots, - Deut. 8. 4

Well might God say, "Thou has lacked nothing." HYP.

## A Great Revival.

| PERSONAL CONDITIONS. | | NATIONAL CONDITIONS. | |
|---|---|---|---|
| 1. Hezekiah did *right* in the sight of the Lord, - - 2 Kings 18. 3 | | 1. Temple doors were *opened* and *repaired*, 2 Chron. 29. 3 | |
| 2. He *removed* the images, - - - ,, 4 | | 2. A covenant was *made* with the Lord, - ,, 10 | |
| 3. He *trusted* in the Lord, - - - ,, 5 | | 3. The priests and Levites were *sanctified*, - - - ,, 15 | |
| 4. He *clave* to the Lord, ,, 6 | | 4. The Temple was *sanctified*, - - - ,, 15 | |
| 5. He *followed* the Lord, ,, 6 | | 5. The Temple was *cleansed*, - - - ,, 16 | |
| 6. He *kept* His commandments, - - ,, 6 | | 6. The sacrifice was *offered*, - - - - ,, 22 | |
| RESULT. | | RESULT. | |
| 1. The Lord was *with* him, 7 | | 1. Hezekiah *rejoiced*, - ,, 36 | |
| 2. The Lord *prospered* him, 7 | | 2. There was *great joy* in Jerusalem, 2 Chr. 30. 26 | |

J. G.

# SUBJECTS FOR SPEAKERS AND STUDENTS.

## The Gospel in Names.

1. GALLIO.—"Cared for none of these things," Acts 18. 17
2. ONESIMUS.—"Put that to my account," - Philemon 18
3. SIMON.—"Neither part nor lot in matter," Acts 8. 21
4. PAUL.—"I was not disobedient to heavenly
        vision," - - - - - - Acts 26. 19
5. ELYMAS.—"The sorcerer withstood them," Acts 13. 8
6. LYDIA.—"Whose heart the Lord opened," Acts 16.14

E.V.G.

## Our God
### IS THE

God of Truth,
        Deut 32. 4; Jer. 10. 10
God of all Grace, 1 Peter 5.10
God of Peace, - - Phil. 4.9
God of Love, - 2 Cor. 13. 11
God of all Comfort,
                2 Cor. 1. 3
God of Patience, Rom. 15. 5
God of Hope, - Rom. 15. 13
God of Glory, - - Acts 7. 2
God of Judgment, Isa. 30. 18
God of Mercies, - 2 Cor. 1. 3

J. H. B.

## Spiritual Maladies
### AND THEIR DIVINE REMEDIES.

Bad temper, - Psa. 34. 1
Evil speaking, ,, 35. 28
Melancholy, - ,, 70. 4
Scandal, - ,, 71. 8
Self-righteousness, ,, 71. 15
Fear, - - - ,, 71. 24
Songs, - - - ,, 52. 9
Boasting, - - ,, 44. 8
Envy, - - -Prov. 23. 17
Evil Thoughts, Psa. 119. 9

R.L.B.

## Things to Know.

1. Be it Known—The Knowledge of Resurrection, - - - - - Acts 4. 10
2. Be it Known—The Knowledge of Justification, - - - - - Acts 13. 38
3. Be it Known—The Knowledge of Salvation, - - - - - - Acts 28. 28

JS. FS.

## Seven Precious Possessions of the Lord
### Psalm 100. 3, 4, 5.

1. His people, - His creation—"He made us."
2. His pastures, - ,, ,,
3. His gates, - His command—"Enter with
4. His courts, - praise."
5. His name, - His Characteristics—"For the
6. His mercy, - Lord is good."
7. His Truth, - ,, ,, D.F.

# SUBJECTS FOR SPEAKERS AND STUDENTS.

## Four Women in Revelation.

1. Jezebel, - - Popery, - - - Rev. 2. 20
2. Sun-clothed woman, Israel, - - - Rev. 12. 1
3. Babylon, - - Re-united Christendom, Rev. 17. 5
4. The Bride, - - The true Church, Rev. 19.7 w.w.f.

## In the Morning

1. Ponder the Word, Ezek.12.8
2. Plant the seed, Eccles.11.6
3. Praise the Lord Psa. 59. 16
   "Day by Day," w.t.r.

## The Heart in 1 John.

1. Subject heart, - 1 John 3.20
2. Condemning heart, ,, 3.20
3. Uncondemning heart, ,, 3.21
4. Assured heart, - ,,3.19 t.b.

## Seven Aspects of Sanctification.

1. In Christ - Positional, - - - 1 Cor. 1. 2
2. By blood, - Sacrificial, - - - Heb. 13. 12
3. By the Spirit, Spiritual, - - 2 Thess. 2. 13
4. By faith, - Experimental, - - Acts 26. 18
5. Through the truth, Scriptural, - - John 17. 17
6. By association, Social, - - - 1 Cor. 7. 14
7. In heart, - Internal, - - 1 Pet. 3. 15 js.fs.

## Four Questions.

1. A question of place, Gen.3.9
2. A question of property,
   1 Sam. 30. 13
3. A question of profit,
   Matt. 16. 26
4. A question of purpose,
   Matt. 27. 22 h.k.d.

## Christians should be

1. Full of Faith, - Acts 6. 5
2. Abound in Faith, 2 Cor.8. 7
3. Continue inFaith,Acts 14.22
4. Be strong in Faith,
   Rom. 4. 20
5. Stand fast in Faith,
   1 Cor. 16. 13

## Remission of Sins.

1. The source of remission, Grace, - - Eph. 1. 7
2. The ground of remission, The blood, - Heb. 9. 22
3. The object of remission, His name's sake, 1 John 2. 12
4. The possessors of remission, Those in Christ, Col. 1. 14
5. The evidence of remission, Compassion, Matt. 18. 33
6. The enjoyment of remission,Confession, 1 John 1. 9
7. The heralds of remission, Disciples, Acts 13. 38 js.fs.

## Nine Kinds of Tongues.

1. A backbiting, - Prov.25.23
2. A deceitful, - Psa.120.2
3. A lying - Psa.109.2
4. A froward, - Prov.10.31
5. A naughty, - Prov.17.4
6. A perverse, - Prov.17.20
7. A stammering, Isa.33.19
8. A soft, - - Prov.25.15

9. A wholesome tongue, - Prov. 15. 4

"Whoso keepeth his mouth and his tongue, keepeth his soul from troubles" (Prov. 21. 23). j.s.

# SUBJECTS FOR SPEAKERS AND STUDENTS.

## A Happy Band
### as seen in Acts 1. 14.

1. PERSEVERANCE,
   "These all continued"
2. UNITY, "with one accord"
3. PETITION, -"in prayer"
4. INTENSITY,
   "and supplication." HyP.

## "The Glorious Gospel"
### (1 Tim. 1. 11) and the

1. Deliverance it works, 1 Tim. 1. 12
2. Honour it confers, „ 1. 14
3. Riches it bestows, „ 1. 15
4. Hope it gives, - „ 1. 16
5. Song it inspires, - „ 1. 17

## Peter's Fishing Expedition
### in John 21. A picture for "fishers of men."

1. FAILURE—"That night they caught nothing," verse 3
   It is *hard* to fish and catch nothing.

2. FRIEND—"Jesus stood on the shore," - „ 4
   A Friend ever ready in "the morning."

3. FAITH—"Cast the net on the right side of
   the ship, and ye shall find," - - - „ 6
   The *right* side is the side He commands.

4. FIND—"They were not able to draw for the
   multitude of fishes," - - - - „ 6
   He knows where to *find* the fish.

5. FELLOWSHIP—"Come and dine," - - „ 12
   Master and disciples had "*fish* likewise."

*The Response*—"LORD, . . . Thou knowest that
I love Thee," - - - - - - „ 17
   HyP.

## John 3. 16.

1. LOVE AT ITS LOFTIEST SOURCE, For *God* so loved
2. LOVE AT ITS WIDEST RANGE, - - - the *world*,
3. LOVE IN ITS DEEPEST MANIFESTATION,
   that *He gave* His only begotten Son,
4. LOVE IN ITS HIGHEST PURPOSE,
   that whosoever believeth in Him should *not perish*, but
   *have everlasting life.* Mr. WOOD (of Fritz and Arthur Wood)

## Outlines of John 3. 16.

1. God - - - - - - THE AUTHOR
2. so loved - - He gave His Son, THE MEASURE
3. the world, - - - - - - THE OBJECT
4. Whosoever believeth should not perish, THE PURPOSE
5. Have eternal life, - - - - THE END. J.H.

30

# SUBJECTS FOR SPEAKERS AND STUDENTS.

## Fourfold Assurance.
### "BE OF GOOD CHEER."

1. Assurance of Forgiveness, - - - Matt. 9. 2
2. Assurance of Companionship, - - Mark 6. 50
3. Assurance of Victory, - - - - John 16. 33
4. Assurance of Eternal Safety, - - Acts 23. 11

I.W.P.

## Four Precious Words of Christ.

"*Come* to Me"—Rest, - - - - Matt. 11. 28
"*Follow* Me"—Fishers, - - - - Mark 1. 17
"*Remember* Me"—Lord gets something, - Luke 22. 19
"*Abide* in Me"—Fruit (cf. ver. 8), - John 15. 4

W.F.C.

## Seven "Looks of Jesus" in Mark.

1. In chapter 3. 5 we read: "He *looked round* about on them with anger, being grieved at the hardness of their hearts."
2. Ch. 3. 34 there is a great contrast: "*He looked around* them that sat about Him, and said, Behold my mother and my brethren!"
3. Ch. 5. 32, 34: "*He looked round* about to see the woman who had touched Him, and said, Daughter, thy faith hath made thee whole; go in peace."
4. Ch. 8. 33: "He *looked* on His disciples, and rebuked Peter, saying, Get thee behind Me, Satan; for thou savourest not the things that be of God, but the things that be of men."
5. Ch. 10. 21. The young man who came to Him: "Then Jesus, *beholding* him, loved him, and said, One thing thou lackest: go thy way, sell whatsoever thou hast, and give to the poor, and thou shalt have treasure in Heaven; and come, take up the Cross, and follow Me."
6. Ch. 10. 23-27. In reply to His disciples: "Who then can be saved? And Jesus, *looking upon them*, saith, With men it is impossible, but not with God; for with God all things are possible."
7. Ch. 11. 11: "And Jesus entered into Jerusalem, and into the temple; and when He had *looked round about* upon all things, He went out unto Bethany with the twelve;" and Luke adds, "He beheld the city, and wept over it." W.H.

# SUBJECTS FOR SPEAKERS AND STUDENTS.

## Bible Reckonings.

| | |
|---|---|
| The Reckoning of God, - - - | - Rom. 4. 9 |
| The Reckoning of the King, - - | - Matt. 18. 24 |
| The Reckoning of the Owner, - - | - Matt. 25. 19 |
| The Reckoning of the Saint, - - | - Rom. 6. 11 |
| The Reckoning of the Sufferer, - - | - Rom. 8. 18 |
| The Reckoning of the Unbeliever, - | - Luke 22. 37 |
| The Reckoning of the Apostle, - | Heb. 10. 29. JS. FS. |

## The Corinthians were

1. Begotten, - 1 Cor. 4. 15
2. Brethren, - 1 Cor. 2. 1
3. Builded, - 1 Cor. 3. 9
4. Bought, - 1 Cor. 6. 20
5. Baptised, - 1 Cor. 12. 13
6. Body of Christ 1 Cor. 12. 28
7. Beloved, - 1 Cor. 15. 57

JS. FS.

## The Heart by Grace.

1. Broken, - Psalm 51. 17
2. Clean, - - Prov. 51. 10
3. Having love of God,

Rom. 5. 5
4. Having peace Phil. 4. 7
5. Singing - Col. 3. 16
6. Crieth for God,

Psalm 84. 2. F.F.

## Under the Blood.

| | |
|---|---|
| 1. We have redemption, - - - | - Eph. 1. 17 |
| 2. We are saved from wrath, - - | - Rom. 5. 9 |
| 3. We are reconciled to God, - - | - Col. 1. 20 |
| 4. Our sins are forgiven, - - | - 1 John 1. 7 |
| 5. We are justified, - - - | Rom. 3. 24, 25 |
| 6. Brought nigh to God, - - | Eph. 2. 13-18 |
| 7. We have eternal life, - - | John 6. 53-57. F.F. |

## The Servant of the Lord.

1. HIS CALL.—"The Holy Ghost said, Separate Me
   Barnabas and Saul for the work whereunto *I have
   called* them," - - - - Acts 13. 2
2. HIS DIRECTOR.—"Being sent forth by
   the Holy Ghost," - - - - Acts 13. 4
3. HIS SPHERE.—"Wherever directed of the
   Lord," - - - - - - Acts 8. 26
4. HIS GUARANTOR.—"My God shall supply
   all your need," - - - - Phil. 4. 19
5. HIS AMBITION.—"To preach the Gospel
   in the regions beyond," - - - 2 Cor. 10. 16
6. HIS RESPONSIBILITY.—"To study to show
   himself approved of God," - - 2 Tim. 2. 15
7. HIS JOY.—"To spend and be spent on
   behalf of others," - - 2 Cor. 12. 15 F.E.G.

## Three Vitals.

1. The brevity of life, Jas.4.14
2. The certainty of death,
Isa.38.1
3. The eternity of destiny,
Matt.25.46
H.K.D.

## He that Trusteth

1. In his riches shall fall,
Prov.11.28
2. In his own heart is a fool,
Prov.28.26
3. In the Lord, happy is he,
Prov.16.20    H.P.,Jr

## Thoughts concerning Communion.

1. Communion established through the revelation of life, - - - - - 1 John 1.3
2. Communion maintained through the light by the blood, - - - - - 1 John 1.7
3. Communion manifested through the unity of the saints, - - - - Acts 2.42 J.H.

## Christ the Centre.

STUDY OF "ME" IN JOHN'S
GOSPEL.

1. Unto Me, - Attraction, 12.32
2. Against Me, Treason,  13.18
3. By Me,  - Access,  14.6
4. Without Me, Failure, 15.5
5. In Me,  - Peace,  16.33
6. With Me, - Glory,  17.24
W.T.R.

## Attitudes of the Believer.

1. Sitting, Lu.8.35; Deut.33.3
2. Standing, Eph.6.13; Phil.4.1
3. Walking, Eph.2.10; Gal.5.25
4. Running,
1 Cor.9.24; Heb.12.1
5. Mounting up,
Isa.40.31; 1 Thess.4.17
6. Leaning, - - - John13.23
7. Lying down, - Psa.23.2 N.B.

## The False and the True—A Solemn Contrast.

BABYLON.

1. A habitation of demons,
Rev.18.3
2. A table of demons,
1 Cor.10.21
3. A cup of demons, 1 Cor.10.21
4. Doctrines of demons,
1 Tim.4.1
5. Sacrifices to demons,
1 Cor.10.20

All planned and carried out in the energy of that wisdom which is "earthly, sensual, *devilish*" (Jas. 3. 15).

I would not that ye should have fellowship with demons (1 Cor. 10. 20).

THE CHURCH.

1. A habitation of God,
Eph.2.22
2. The table of the Lord,
1 Cor.10.21
3. The cup of the Lord,  ,,
4. The doctrine according to godliness,  1 Tim.6.3
5. Spiritual sacrifices,
1 Peter 2.5

All planned and carried out by that wisdom which is pure, peaceable, gentle, ... without hypocrisy (Jas. 3. 17).

Truly our fellowship is with the Father, and with His Son, Jesus Christ (1 John 1.3). T.B.

# SUBJECTS FOR SPEAKERS AND STUDENTS.

| The Trumpet of | Hope. |
|---|---|
| Gloom, - - - Josh 6. 4,5 | Exhortation, - - Psa. 42. 5 |
| Grace, - - - Lev. 25. 9 | Consolation, - - Joel 3. 16 |
| Glory, - 1 Cor. 15. 52 w.t.r. | Anticipation, - Tit. 3. 7 w.t.r. |

## Most Wonderful.

The omnipotence of Christ, - - - - John 1. 3
The omniscience of Christ, - - - - John 2. 24
The omnipresence of Christ, - - John 3. 13 Js. Fs.

| The Postures of our Lord. | Sheep and Shepherd. |
|---|---|
| Jesus sitting, - Luke 7. 36 | Saved *through* Him, John 10.9 |
| Jesus sinking, - Psa. 69. 2 | Sustained *by* Him, ,, 10.9 |
| Jesus singing, - Heb. 2. 12 | Submissive *to* Him, ,, 10.4 |
| W. T. R. | W. T. R. |

| A Mighty Man. | A Brave Young Man. |
|---|---|
| Moses and his | Daniel as a man of |
| 1. Choice, - - - Heb. 11. 24 | 1. Purpose, - - Dan. 1. 8 |
| 2. Prospects, - Heb. 11. 24 | 2. Prayer, - - Dan. 6. 10 |
| 3. Meekness, - - Num. 12. 3 | 3. Faith, - - - Heb. 11.33 |
| 4. Faithfulness, - Num. 12. 7 | 4. Excellent spirit, Dan. 6. 3 |
| 5. Fellowship, - Num. 12. 8 | 5. Testimony, - Dan. 6. 4, 5 |
| 6. Work, Exod. 3. 10 s.j.s. | s. j. s. |

## The Spirit.

1. The possession of the Spirit, - - - Rom. 8. 11
2. The leading ,, - - - ,, 8. 14
3. The witness ,, - - - ,, 8. 16
4. The firstfruits ,, - - - ,, 8. 23
5. The help ,, - - - ,, 8. 26
6. The intercession ,, - - - ,, 8. 26
7. The mind ,, - Rom. 8. 27 h. k. d.

| The Redeemer's Return. | The Prodigal Son. |
|---|---|
| A Sevenfold Result. | A New Setting. |
| 1. Revelation, - 1 Pet. 1. 13 | 1. Desire, - - - Luke 15. 12 |
| 2. Resurrection, | 2. Departure, - ,, 15. 13 |
| 1 Thess. 4. 16; 1 Cor. 15.52 | 3. Destitution, - ,, 15. 14 |
| 3. Redemption, - Eph. 4. 30 | 4. Degradation, - ,, 15. 15 |
| 4. Refreshing, - Acts 3. 19 | 5. Despair, - - ,, 15. 17 |
| 5. Rapture, 1 Thess. 4. 13-18 | 6. Decision, - - ,, 15. 18 |
| 6. Reception, - - John 14. 3 | 7. Delight, - - ,, 15. 24 |
| 7. Recompense, - Rev. 22. 12 | W. J. M. |
| J. M. | |

## Continually

| 1. Praying, - - Acts 6. 4 | 4. Resorting, - Psa. 71. 3 |
|---|---|
| 2. Praising, - - Psa. 34. 1 | 5. Hoping, - - Psa. 71. 14 |
| 3. Serving, - - Dan. 6. 16 | 6. Watching, Isa. 21.8 w. j. m. |

# SUBJECTS FOR SPEAKERS AND STUDENTS.

## A Precious Threefold Link.

1. Peter's precept, - That ye may grow, - 1 Pet. 2. 2
2. God's purpose, - That ye should show, - 1 Pet. 2. 9
3. Paul's prayer, - That ye may know, Eph. 1. 18 W.T.R.

| Threefold Counsel. | Threefold Comfort. |
|---|---|
| 1.Stand still and see, Ex.14.13 | 1.God for us, - - Rom.8.31 |
| 2.Stand still and hear,Num.9.8 | 2.God with us- - Matt.1.23 |
| 3.Stand still and reason, | 3.God in us, - - 1 John 4.16 |
| 1 Sam.12.7 JS.FS. | Who against us? E.C.M. |

## The Call of the Master.

"The Master is come, and calleth for thee" (John 11. 28).

1. He calls "for *thee*," personal, - - - John 11. 28
2. He calls to *save*, - - - - - Isa. 45. 22
3. To give *rest*, - - - - - - Matt. 11.28
4. To *sympathise*, Jesus wept, - - - John 11. 35
5. To *raise the dead*, "Lazarus, come forth,"- John 11. 43
6. To *explain difficulties*, "I am the resurrection and the life," - - - - John 11. 25
7. To renew fellowship, "They made Him a supper," - - - - - John 12. 2 A.P.W.

## The Lamb in Revelation.

| "WORTHY IS THE LAMB." | 4.Song of the Lamb, - 15.3 |
|---|---|
| 1.Wrath of the Lamb, - 6.16 | 5.Marriage of the Lamb, 19.7 |
| 2 Blood of the Lamb, - 7.14 | 6.Supper of the Lamb, - 19.9 |
| 3.Book of life of the Lamb, 13.8 | 7.Throne of the Lamb,22.1 J.B. |

## Seven Exceeding Things.

1. Sinfulness of sin, - - - - Rom. 7.13
2. Sorrow of the Saviour, - - - - Matt. 26.38
3. Greatness of God's power, - - - - Eph. 1.19
4. Abundance of God's grace, - - - 1 Tim. 1. 14
5. Great and precious promises, - - - 2 Peter 1. 4
6. Growth of faith, - - - - - 2 Thess. 1.3
7. Joy to come, - - - - - Jude 24 G.H.

| Moses' Seven Objections. | Inexhaustible Riches. |
|---|---|
| 1.Who am I? - - Ex. 3.11 | THE RICHES OF GOD'S |
| 2.What shall I say? Ex. 3. 13 | 1.Goodness, - - Rom. 2.4 |
| 3.Will not believe me, Ex.4.1 | 2.Forbearance and |
| 4.I am not eloquent, Ex. 4. 10 | longsuffering, Rom. 2. 4 |
| 5 Send Aaron, - - Ex. 4. 13 | 3.Wisdom and know- |
| 6.Israel have not | ledge, - - Rom. 11.33 |
| hearkened, - - Ex. 6. 12 | 4.Mercy, - - - Eph. 2. 4 |
| 7.I am of uncircum- | 5.Grace,- - - - Eph. 1. 7 |
| cised lips, Ex.6.30 JS.FS. | 6.Glory,- - Eph. 1. 18 G.H. |

# SUBJECTS FOR SPEAKERS AND STUDENTS.

### Brotherly Love.

The Weak Brother,
　　　　　　Rom. 14. 1.
The Offended Brother,
　　　　　　Matt. 5. 13
The Trespassing Brother,
　　　　　　Matt. 18. 15
The Overtaken Brother,
　　　Gal. 6. 1. w.w.f.

### Great Questions.

Are there few that be saved?
(Luke 13.23)—The Heedless.
Who then can be saved?
(Luke 18. 26)—The Hopeless.
What must I do to be
saved? (Acts. 16. 30)—The
Helpless.　　　　　　d.f.

### The Love that Never Fails.

| | |
|---|---|
| For the love that never fails, | 1 Cor. 13 |
| And the Blood that sure avails, | Heb. 10. 19 |
| The Source we'll praise. | Rom. 16. 27 |
| To the Priest who must prevail, | Heb. 7. 25 |
| Though the foe our ranks assail, | 2 Cor. 2. 11 |
| Our song we'll raise. | Acts 4. 24. j.s. |

### Some of the Little Foxes

Which spoil the tender fruit of the Spirit, as detailed in
Gal. 5. 22, 23.

1. Selfishness　　..　　.. that spoils Love.
2. Disappointment,　　..　,,　,,　Joy.
3. Anxiety　　..　　..　,,　,,　Peace.
4. Impatience　..　　..　,,　,,　Long Suffering.
5. Bitterness　　..　　..　,,　,,　Gentleness.
6. Indolence　　..　　..　,,　,,　Goodness.
7. Doubt　　..　　..　,,　,,　Faith.
8. Pride　..　　..　　..　,,　,,　Meekness.
9. Indulgence　　..　　..　,,　,,　Temperance. hyp.

### Faithful Servants of God.

1. ABRAHAM—*Faithful* Abraham,　　-　　- Gal. 3. 9
2. MOSES—My servant, who is *faithful* in
　　all My house,　　-　　- Num. 12. 7; Heb. 3. 5
3. PAUL—Christ Jesus counted me *faithful*, - 1 Tim. 1. 12
4. TYCHICUS—A *faithful* minister and fellow-servant;
　　a *faithful* minister in the Lord, Col. 4. 7; Eph. 6. 21
5. ONESIMUS—A *faithful* and beloved brother, Col. 4. 9.
6. EPAPHRAS—A *faithful* minister of Christ, Col. 1.7; 6.12
7. TIMOTHY—*Faithful* in the Lord, -　　- 1 Cor. 4. 17
8. SILVANUS—A *faithful* brother,　　-　　- 1 Peter 5. 12
9. DANIEL—He was *faithful*, -　　-　　- Dan. 6. 4
10. ANTIPAS—Was My *faithful* martyr, Rev. 2. 13　s.t.

# SUBJECTS FOR SPEAKERS AND STUDENTS.

## The Love of God.

"Behold what manner of love the Father hath bestowed on us."

1. Its origination, - - God's own heart, - John 3. 16
2. Its manifestation, - Christ dying, - - 1 John 4. 9, 10
3. Its communication, By the Spirit, - - Rom. 5. 5
4. Its demonstration, - On our side, - - 1 Cor. 13
5. Its compensation, - Them that love Him, 1 Cor. 2. 9 A.M'K.

## With Christ at Sea.

1. A reasonable suggestion, - Let us go over, - - Mark 4. 35
2. A wise action, - - They took Him, - Mark 4. 36
3. A dangerous position, - The ship was now full, Mark 4. 37
4. A peaceful condition, - He was asleep, - - Mark 4. 38
5. An unkind question, - Carest Thou not ? - Mark 4. 38
6. A complete subjection, - Was a great calm, - Mark 4. 39
7. A deserved admonition, - Why are ye so fearful? Mark 4. 40
8. A happy conclusion, - Feared exceedingly, Mark 4. 41

H.K.D.

## The "Widows" in Luke's Gospel.

1. A widow who served and worshipped, - Luke 2. 37
2. A widow who was honoured and provided for, Luke 4. 26
3. A widow who sorrowed, but was comforted, Luke 7. 12
4. A widow who prayed and was answered, - Luke 18. 3
5. A widow who was commended and extolled, Luke 21. 3

W.J.M.

## A Complete Sermon.

1. Lord hath spoken, - Isa. 1. 2
2. Addresses sinners, - ,, 4
3. Reveals their disease, ,, 5, 6
4. Rejects offerings, - 11, 15
5. Commands repentance,
   Matt. 3. 2, 8; Isa. 1. 16, 17
6. Announces pardon, Isa. 1. 18
7. Warns of judgment, Isa. 1. 20

H. P., Jr.

## An Ideal Address.

1. A consecrated life, Acts 10. 38
2. A criminal's death, ,, 39
3. A confirmed resur-
   rection, - - - 40, 41
4. A coming judgment, ,, 42
5. A complete salvation, ,, 43
6. A converted company, ,, 44
7. A command obeyed, ,, 48

H.K.D.

## Seven Aspects of Justification in Romans.

1. Justified by God, - - The authority, - Rom. 8. 33
2. Justified by grace, - - The source, - Rom. 3. 24
3. Justified by blood, - - The means, - Rom. 5. 9
4. Justified by faith, - - The enjoyment, - Rom. 5. 1
5. Justified by Christ risen, - The proof, - - Rom. 4. 25
6. Justified from sin, - - The dead, - - Rom. 6. 7
7. Justified by the law, - The doers, Rom. 2. 13 JS.FS.

37

# SUBJECTS FOR SPEAKERS AND STUDENTS.

| **Full Assurance.** | **A Threefold Invitation.** |
|---|---|
| 1.Faith, - Heb. 10. 22 | To the Guilty, Isaiah 1. 18 |
| 2.Understanding, Col. 2. 2 | To the Weary, Matt. 11. 20 |
| 3.Hope, - - Heb. 6. 11 | To the Thirsty, John 7. 37 |
| H.K.B. | JS.FS. |

## Forgiveness of Sins.

1. The need of Forgiveness—Guilt, - - Rom. 3. 23
2. The Ground of Forgiveness—Christ's
   Blood, - - - - - - Heb. 9. 22
3. The Authority of Forgiveness—God, - Mark 2. 7
4. The Knowledge of Forgiveness—Through
   preaching, - - - - - Acts 13. 38
5. The Condition of Forgiveness—Repentance, - - - - - - Luke 24. 47
6. The Assurance of Forgiveness—The Word
   of God, - - - - - 1 John 2. 12
7. Evidence of Forgiveness—The Walk, 1 Thess. 1. 4 JS.FS.

| **The Sin Offering.** <br> Hebrews 13. 12. | **"Meet" for the Kingdom.** <br> HE HATH MADE US MEET. |
|---|---|
| 1.The Person—Jesus. | 1.As to Title, Col. 1. 12 |
| 2.The Purpose—Sanctify. | 2.As to Service, |
| 3.The Price—His Blood. | Luke 9. 62 |
| 4.The Place—Outside the gates. H.K.D. | 3.As to Fruitfulness, Mark 4. 29. A.M.P. |

## Divine Necessities.

1. EXCEPT ye repent, ye shall all likewise
   perish, - - - - - - Luke 13. 3

2. EXCEPT a man be born again, he cannot
   see the Kingdom of God, - - John 3. 3

3. EXCEPT ye be converted, and become as
   little children, ye shall not enter
   into the Kingdom of Heaven, Matt. 18. 3 A.J.P.

## The Mission of the Master
(John 9. 4).

1. Great necessity, - I must work.
2. A great commission, The works of Him that sent Me.
3. A great opportunity, While it is day.
4. A great incentive, - The night cometh when no man
   can work. R.M.

# SUBJECTS FOR SPEAKERS AND STUDENTS.

## The Sight of Sights.

1. Past: Mine eyes have seen the King,    -    Isa. 6. 5
2. Present: We see Jesus,   -   -   -   -   Heb. 2. 9
3. Future: We shall see Him as He is,    1 John 3. 2 W.T.R.

## Contrasted Experiences.

| | | |
|---|---|---|
| 1. He is good, -   - Ps. 107. 1 | 1. They wandered, - Ps. 107. 4 | |
| 2. He hath redeemed,   ,,   2 | 2. Hungry and thirsty,   ,,   5 | |
| 3. And gathered them out, ,,   3 | 3. They cried unto Lord, ,,   6 | |

H. P., Jr.

## Various Aspects of Justification.

1. By blood we have salvation from wrath,   -    Rom. 5. 9
2. By faith we have peace with God,   -   -    Rom. 5. 1
3. By grace, heirs of heaven,   -   -   -    Titus 3. 7
4. By works, the evidence, "offered up Isaac,"    Jas. 2. 20

"As the body without the spirit is dead, so faith without works is dead also."    N.B.

## Some New Things.

1. The new Jerusalem, -   A new centre,   -   Rev. 21. 2
2. The new commandment, New rule,   -   -   John 13. 34
3. The new way, -   -   New access to God,   Heb. 10. 20
4. The new bottle,   -   Regeneration,   -   Luke 5. 38
5. The new garment,   -   Righteousness of God, Luke 5. 36
6. The new wine, -   -   Joy of the Holy Spirit, Gal. 5. 22
7. The new name,   -   New character,   Rev. 2. 17 Js. Fs.

## Seven Eternal Realities

### In the Hebrews.

| | Jehovah. |
|---|---|
| 1. Salvation, -   - Heb. 5. 9 | 1. Thy presence to search us, Ps. 17. 2 |
| 2. Judgment, -   - Heb. 6. 2 | 2. Thy lips to speak to us,   ,,   4 |
| 3. Redemption,   - Heb. 9. 12 | 3. Thy paths to separate us,   5 |
| 4. Spirit, -   -   Heb. 9. 14 | 4. Right hand to save us,   ,,   7 |
| 5. Inheritance,   - Heb. 9. 15 | 5. Wings to shelter us,   ,,   8 |
| 6. Covenant, -   Heb. 13. 20 | 6. Face to shine on us,   ,, 15 |
| 7. Perfection, -   - Heb. 7. 28 | 7. Likeness to satisfy us,   ,, 15 |
| J.H.E. | W.J.M. |

## The Believer's Confidence.

1. His past,   - Justified by faith,   -   -   Rom. 5. 1
2. His present, - This grace wherein we stand,   Rom. 5. 2
3. His prospect, - The glory of God,   -   -   Rom. 5. 2
4. His experience, Tribulations also,   -   -   Rom. 5. 3
5. The outcome, - Hope, the love of God shed abroad in our hearts by the Holy Ghost,   - Rom. 5. 5 J.H.

# SUBJECTS FOR SPEAKERS AND STUDENTS.

## The Saviour and the Sinner.
### (Mark 2).

Pattern Preacher,  -v. 2    —Sinner gets Pardon,  - v.  5
Powerful Physician, v. 10  —Saint gets Power,     - v. 11
Pilgrims' Guide,  - v. 14   —Saviour gets Praise, - v. 12

W.J.M.

| Wages, for the | Peter's Declension. |
|---|---|
| 1. Lover,  - Gen. 29. 16; 30. 28; 31. 7-41 | 1. He Boasts,  Matt. 26. 33 |
| 2. Nurser (Moses' Mother), Exod. 2. 9 | 2. He Sleeps,  Matt. 26. 40 |
| | 3. He Fights,  Matt. 26. 51 |
| 3. Soldier,  - Luke 3. 14 | 4. He Follows Afar off, Matt. 26. 58 |
| 4. Reaper,  - John 4. 36 | |
| 5. Sinner,  - Rom. 6. 23 | 5. He Denies Christ, Matt. 26. 70 |
| 6. Preacher,  2 Cor. 11. 8 | 6. He Swears,  Matt. 26. 72 |
| 7. Seer  -  - 2 Pet. 2. 15 | 7. He Curses,  Matt. 26. 74 |
| (see 1 Sam. 9. 9).  D.F. | J.F. |

## Paul's Sufferings.
### THEIR FRUIT FOR OTHERS.

Eph. 3. 13.—*Instruction*.  We owe the written unfoldings concerning Christ and the Church to his imprisonment.

2. Cor. 1. 3-7.—*Comfort*.  He had it to communicate to others.

Phil. 1. 12-14.—*Courage*.  Brethren gained confidence in God, beholding His wonderful way of working.  W.W.F.

## Various Aspects of Salvation.

1. SAVED BY GRACE—The Source of Salvation,  -  -  -  -  -  - Eph. 2. 5
2. SAVED BY FAITH—The Reception of Salvation,  -  -  -  - Acts 16. 31
3. SAVED BY BAPTISM—The Confession of Salvation,  -  -  - 1 Peter 3. 21
4. SAVED BY WORKS—The Manifestation of Salvation,  -  -  - James 2. 14
5. SAVED BY HIS LIFE—The Support of Salvation,  -  -  -  - Rom. 5. 10
6. SAVED BY FIRE—The Proof of Salvation,  -  -  -  -  - 1 Cor. 3. 15
7 SAVED BY HOPE—The Prospect of Salvation,  -  -  - Rom. 8. 24.  JS.FS.

# SUBJECTS FOR SPEAKERS AND STUDENTS.

## Christian Progress.

1. Prayer: That which I see not, teach Thou me, Job 34. 32.
2. Precept: Grow in...knowledge...Jesus Christ, 2 Pet. 3. 18
3. Promise: The meek will He teach, - Psa. 25.9 W.T.R.

### Christ Greater than

1. The temple, Matt. 12. 6
2. Jonah, - Matt. 12.41
3. Solomon, - Matt. 12.42

W.W.F.

### A Three-fold MeetingPlace

1. The mercy-seat, Ex. 25. 22
2. The brazen altar, Ex.29.42
3. The golden altar, Ex. 30. 6

JS. FS.

## Great Contrasts.

1. The Lord's hand is not shortened—your
   iniquities have separated, - - - Isa. 59. 1, 2
2. Neither His ear heavy—your sins have hid
   His face, - - - - - Isa. 59. 1, 2 H.P.,Jr.

### A Three-fold Trial.

1. A trial of walk, Ex. 16. 4
2. A trial of worship, Deu.13.2
3. A trial of warfare, Jud. 3. 1

JS. FS.

### Men who Settle Down.

1. The worldling, Luke 12. 19
2. The false professor, ,, 12. 45
3. The saint by-and-by,
   Luke 12. 37 W.W.F.

## Immeasurable Comparisons in Psalm 103.

1. As the heaven is high above the earth, so great is His
   mercy.
2. As far as the east is from the west, so far hath He removed
   our transgressions. H.P., Jr.

## A Contrast oft repeated To-day.

### RECEIVING GOD'S GIFTS.

1. They took, - Neh.9 .25
2. Possessed - ,, 9. 25
3. Did eat, - ,, 9. 25
4. Were filled, - ,, 9. 25
5. Became fat, - ,, 9. 25
6. Delighted themselves, 9. 25

### REJECTING GOD THE GIVER.

1. They were disobeient,
   Neh. 9.26
2. Rebelled, - - ,, 9.26
3. Cast Thy law, ,, 9.26
4. Slew Thy prophets, ,, 9.26
5. Wrought provocations,9.26

H.P., Jr.

## Tears Shed by Different Persons.

1. The Saviour's Tears, - Luke 19. 41; John 11. 35
2. The penitent sinner's tears, - Luke 7. 38-44
3. The saint's tears, - - John 20. 11; Acts 20. 37
4. The servant's tears, - Acts 20. 19-31; Phil. 3. 18
5. The backslider's tears, - - Luke 22. 62
6. The lost sinner's tears, - Matt. 8. 12; 22.13 W.J.M.

41

# SUBJECTS FOR SPEAKERS AND STUDENTS.

## "No Respect of Persons"
IN THREE WAYS.
1. In Death, - 2 Sam. 14. 14
2. In Salvation, Acts 10. 34
3. In Judgment, 1 Pet. 1. 17

H.K.D.

## The Gospel in Genesis 3.
Deceived by Satan,    v. 13
Death by Sin, - -    v. 19
Debarred by Sword,    v. 24
Delivered by Sacrifice, v. 21

D. WARD.

## The Secure Hiding-Place.

"A man shall be as an hiding-place from the wind, and a covert from the tempest; as rivers of water in a dry place, as the shadow of a great rock in a weary land" (Isa. 32. 2).

1. Secured *from the wind*, which is symbolical of Satan's power. "Life is hid with Christ in God" (Col. 3. 2).

2. Sheltered *from the tempest*. The coming storm of judgment (1 Thess. 1. 10). "We shall be saved from wrath through Him" (Rom. 5. 9).

3. Satisfied *with rivers of water*. The world is a dry and thirsty land where no true satisfaction is found (John 4); "rivers of living water" (John 7).

4. Succoured *under the shadow of a great rock*. The world is a place of tribulation where the heat—symbolical of the trying influences of the day—tests the spirit and tends to make the pilgrim faint. "He is able to succour them that are tempted" (Heb. 2. 18).

## Heroes of Faith
As seen in Heb. 11.
1. Abel, - - The Sacrifice of Faith.
2. Noah - The Simplicity of Faith.
3. Abraham, The Sojourn of Faith.
4. Isaac, - The Sanguinity of Faith.
5. Moses, - The Suffering of Faith.
6. Rahab, - The Salvation of Faith.
7. The Rest, The Supremacy (v. 32, etc.) of Faith.

H.K.D.

## The Great Invitation
of Matt. 11. 28.
1. Come unto Me,
     The Person
2. Ye that labour,
     The People.
3. I will give, The Promise.
4. Take my yoke,
     The Precept.
5. I am meek and lowly,
     The Pattern.
6. Ye shall find rest,
     The Product.
7. My yoke is easy—burden light,
     The Proof.
Blessed Invitation. D.F.

# SUBJECTS FOR SPEAKERS AND STUDENTS.

## In His Heart.

"As he thinketh in his heart, so is he" (Prov. 23. 7)

1. Abraham,  -  Weakness of faith,    - Gen. 17. 17
2. Esau,  - -  Revenge,  - - -  - Gen. 27. 41
3. David,  - -  Unbelief,  - - -  - 1 Sam. 27.1
4. Jeroboam,  -  Subtlety,  - - - 1 Kings 12. 26
5. Evil servant,   Worldliness,  - Luke 12. 45 w.w.f.

## His Presence.

1. A searching place, Ps. 139.7
2. A humiliating place,
   1 Cor.1.29
3. A hiding place,  Ps. 31.20
4. A dwelling place, Ps. 140.13
5. A joyful place,  - Ps.16.11
6. An interceding place,
   Heb.9.24
7. A perfect place,  - Jude 24
   w.j.m.

## A Four-fold Command.

1. Pray ye: A quickened
   interest,    - Luke 10. 2
2. Bring ye: The com-
   missariat established,
   Mal. 3.10
3. Tarry ye: Preparation
   for the conflict,Luke24.49
4. Go ye: Forward march,
   Matt.28.19   w.r.

## The Church.

1. The Saviour's Promise: On this Rock I will
   build My Church,  - - - -  - Matt.16.18
2. The Father's purpose; Christ, Head over
   all things,  - -  - Eph. 1. 18-23; 2. 20; 3. 10
3. The Lord's purchase: He loved, and gave
   Himself,  - - - -  - Eph. 5. 25
4. His present performance: Sanctify and
   cleanse, present it faultless,  - -  - Eph. 5. 26
5. Its earthly place: Pillar and ground of the
   truth,  - - - - 1 Tim. 3. 15 j.h.

## Afterward.

1. The fruit of sin, Prov.20.17
2. The result of grace, Joel 2.28
3. The path of disciple-
   ship,  -  - John 13.36
4. The result of dis-
   cipline, -  - Heb. 12.11
5. The resurrection of
   the saints,  - 1 Cor. 15.23
6. The glory that is to
   follow,    - Psa. 73. 24
7. The eternal remorse
   of the lost, Heb.12.17 g.h.

## Seven Marks of Disciple-ship.

1. To be very happy,Rom.4.7,8
2. To have peace with God,
   Rom.5.1
3. To joy in God, - Rom. 5. 11
4. To be ashamed of the past,
   Rom.6.21
5. To delight in God's Word,
   Rom.7.22
6. To have an inward conflict,
   Rom.8.13
7. To pray in the spirit,
   Rom.8.15   js. fs.

43

# SUBJECTS FOR SPEAKERS AND STUDENTS.

## Progressiveness, as Seen in the Christian.

The "go on" to perfection, - - - Heb. 6. 1
The "press toward" for the prize, - - Phil. 3
The "more and more" of love, - - 1 Thess. 4. 9, 10
The "abound" of hope, - - - Rom. 15. 15
The "increase" of knowledge, - - Col. 1. 10
The "growth" of faith - - - - 2 Thess. 1. 3
The "continue" in the Word, - - John 8. 31 L-F.

| Things Worth Knowing | Things " of God." |
|---|---|
| 1. Mystery of His will, - - Eph. 1. 9 | 1. The Gospel of God, - -Rom. 1. 1 |
| 2. Hope of His calling, - ,, 1. 18 | 2. The Son, - - ,, 1. 4 |
| 3. Riches of His glory, - ,, 1. 18 | 3. The Beloved, - ,, 1. 7 |
| 4. Greatness of His power, - ,, 1. 19 | 4. The will, - - ,, 1. 10 |
| | 5. The power, - ,, 1. 16 |
| 5. Wisdom of God, - - ,, 3. 10 | 6. The righteous- ness, - - ,, 1. 17 |
| 6. Love of God, ,, 3. 19 | 7. The wrath, - ,, 1. 18 |
| 7. Son of God, ,, 4. 13 | 8. The glory, - ,, 1. 23 |
| | 9. The truth, - ,, 1. 25 |
| | 10. The judgment ,, 1. 32 |
| H.K.D. | H.K.D. |

## Seven Requirements in Keeping the Passover.

### (As seen in Exodus 12).

1. Roasted Lamb (v. 8),
    Corresponding to Christ slain - - 1 Cor. 5. 7
2. Bitter Herbs (v. 8),
    Corresponding to repentance, - - Luke 15. 10
3. Unleavened Bread (v. 8),
    Corresponding to holiness, - - 1 Cor. 5. 8
4. Girded Loins (v. 11),
    Corresponding to habits controlled, - 1 Peter 1. 13
5. Feet Shod (v. 11),
    Corresponding to Gospel testimony, - Eph. 6. 15
6. Staff in Hand (v. 11),
    Corresponding to pilgrim characters, 1 Peter 2. 11
7. Eaten in Haste (v. 11),
    Corresponding to the Coming One, - Rev. 22. 20

JS. FS.

# SUBJECTS FOR SPEAKERS AND STUDENTS.
## Past—Present—Future
1. CONVERSION, - Turned to God from idols, 1 Thes. 1. 9
The sphere of faith.
2. CONSECRATION, Serve the living and true God, 1 Thes.1.9
The domain of love.
3. CONTEMPLATION,Wait for His Son from heaven,1Thes.1.10
The place of hope. W.R.

| **A Three-fold Loss.** | **Three Rejoicing Men.** |
|---|---|
| **S**aviour's **L**oss, Phil. 3. 7 | **R**ejoicing **P**risoner,Phil.1.18 |
| **S**aint's **L**oss, 1 Cor. 3.15 | **R**ejoicing **P**urser, Acts 8.39 |
| **S**inner's **L**oss, Matt.16.26 | **R**ejoicing **P**atriarch, Jn.8.56 |

Js.Fs.

## Backsliding—Four Steps Away.
1. Gone far from Me, and become vain, - Jer. 2. 5
2. Two evils; forsaken Me, and hewed out
broken cisterns, - - - - - Jer. 2. 13
3. My fear not in thee, - - - - - Jer. 2. 19
4. Said no hope (verse 25), and turned their back, Jer. 2. 27

A.M.P.

## The Aggressive Christian's Position.
1. A pupil sitting at the feet of Jesus, - - John 11. 32
2. A soldier putting on his spiritual armour, Eph. 6. 14
3. A runner laying aside every weight, - - Heb. 12. 1
4. A sower sowing beside all waters, - - Isa. 32. 20
5. An ambassador beseeching men to be reconciled,2 Cor.5.20
6. A priest offering spiritual sacrifice, - - Rom. 12. 1
7. A fisher casting the net on the right side, John 21. 6 R.L.

## Utilisation of Pressure the Secret of Power.
1. Pressed out of measure, - - - - 2 Cor. 1. 8
2. Pressure of sins, - - - - - Psa. 32. 4
3. Pressure of temptation, - - - - Acts 20. 24
4. Pressure of Satan, - - - - Eph. 6. 12
5. Pressure of circumstances, - - - 2 Cor. 11. 23-28
6. Pressure of the spirit and prayer,
Luke 22. 44; 1 Thes. 3. 10
7. That the power of Christ may rest, - 2 Cor. 12. 9
8. Confession and forgiveness, - - - Psa. 32. 5
9. God-given escape, - - - - - 1 Cor. 10.13
10. The destroyer of the would-be destroyer, 1 John 3. 8
11. Pleasurable weakness, - - - - 2 Cor. 12.10
12. Was heard, - - - - - - Heb. 5. 7
13. Was Spirit helped, - - - Rom. 8. 26 B.C.M.

# SUBJECTS FOR SPEAKERS AND STUDENTS.

## What it is to be " In Christ."

In Christ—The place of relationship,   - 2 Cor. 5. 17
In Christ—The place of nearness to God. - Eph. 2. 13
In Christ—The place of security,   -   - Rom. 8. 1
In Christ—The place of joy,   -   -   - Phil. 3. 3
In Christ—The place of fruitfulness, -   - John 15. 4;
   1 John 2. 28

A person is either in Christ and bound for *Heaven*.
or in their sins and bound for *Hell*.   W.J.M.

## Marks of the Unsaved.

1. He is without life,
   Eph. 2. 1
2. He is without strength,
   Rom. 5. 6
3. He is without righteousness, -   - Rom. 3. 10
4. He is without hope,
   Eph. 2. 21
5. He is without the Holy
Spirit,   - Jude 19
6. He is without Christ,
   Eph. 2. 12
7. He is without God
   Eph. 2. 12
   JS. FS.

## Hidden Things

OF THE BIBLE.

1. Hidden Ones
   Psa. 83. 3
2. Hidden Treasures,
   Prov. 2. 4
3. Hidden Riches,
   Isa. 45. 3
4. Hidden Things,
   Isa. 48. 6
5. Hidden Wisdom,
   1 Cor. 2. 7
6. Hidden Life,
   Col. 3. 3
7. Hidden Manna,
   Rev. 2. 17   R.L.B.

## Comforting Words about "Home."

1. For the *Stranded*—"In my Father's
house are many mansions,"   -   - John 14. 2
2. For the *Tired*—"There remaineth a rest," Heb. 4. 9
3. For the *Anxious*—"My servants shall
sing for joy of heart,"   -   -   - Isa. 65. 14
4. For the *Tempted*—"There the wicked
cease from troubling,"   -   -   - Job 3. 17
5. For the *Busy*—"Mine elect shall long
enjoy the work of their hands,"   - Isa. 65. 22
6. For the *Lonely*—"So shall we ever be
with the Lord,"   -   -   -   - 1 Thess. 4. 17
7. For the *Trustful*—"Thine eyes shall see
the King in His beauty,"   -   - Isa. 33. 17

H. H. MARTIN.

# SUBJECTS FOR SPEAKERS AND STUDENTS.

## A Three-fold Formula.
1. For immersion, Matt. 28.19
2. For supplication, Eph. 5.20
3. For benediction, 2 Cor.13,14

## Sovereignty of the Spirit.
1. In regeneration, John 3.8
2. In ministration, 1 Cor.12.11
3. In inspiration, 2 Tim. 3.16
Js. Fs.

## The Touch.
1. The touch of restoration, - - - - Dan. 8. 18
2. The touch of instruction, - - - - Dan. 9. 21
3. The touch of comfort, - - - - - Dan. 10.10
4. The touch of renewed intercourse, - - Dan. 10.16
5. The touch of imparted strength, - Dan. 10 18 w.e.v.

## The Lord's Coming.
1. A word of comfort,
1 Thess. 4. 18
2. A word of warning, Matt.25
3. A word of encouragement,
Rev. 3. 11
A. M'K.

## Tychicus,
which means Fortunate (Col. 4. 7).
1. Beloved brother,
Relationship
2. Faithful minister, Service
3. Fellow-servant, - Unity

## Triple Testimony of John the Baptist.
1. Repent ye . . . He that cometh after me, - Matt. 3. 1-12
2. Behold the Lamb of God, which taketh, &c., John 1.29-34
3. He that believeth on the Son . . . He that
believeth not . . . - - - - John 3.26-36
All things that John spake of this Man were true (John 10.41)
H. P., Jr.

## What God Knows.
1. Our bodies, - - - Psa. 103. 14; 1 Kings 19. 1
2. The secrets of our hearts, - Psa. 44. 20, 21; Luke 1. 4
3. Those things which we need, Matt. 6. 5-8; Phil. 4. 19
4. Those who are His, - - 2 Tim. 2. 19
5. Those who trust in Him, - Nah. 1. 7; 2 Peter 2. 4-8
6. All things, - - - 1 John 3. 20, 21 A.P.

## Things Said of the Believer's Sins.
1. They have been laid on Christ, - Isa. 53. 6; 1 Pet. 2.24;
2 Cor. 5. 21
2. They have been blotted out, - - Isa. 44. 22; Col. 2. 14
3. They have been removed, - Psa. 103. 12; Lev. 16.21,22
4. They have been forgiven, Rom.4. 7; Eph. 1. 7; Luke7.48;
Col. 2. 13
5. They have been cast behind God's back, - Isa. 38. 17
6. They are cast into the depths of the sea, - Micah 7. 19
7. They are forgotten, Jer. 31.34; Heb. 8. 12; 10. 17 J.H.B.

# SUBJECTS FOR SPEAKERS AND STUDENTS.

## "So Great"

1. So great a people,
   1 Kings 3. 9
2. So great a God,
   Psa. 77. 13
3. So great mercy,
   Psa. 103. 11
4. So great faith, Matt. 8. 10
5. So great a death,
   2 Cor. 1. 10
6. So great salvation,
   Heb. 2. 3
7. So great a cloud of witnesses, - Heb. 12. 1

H.K.D.

## Seven Aspects of Peace.

1. Peace Sought,
   1 Peter 3. 11
2. Peace Absent,
   Isa. 57. 21
3. Peace Made,
   Col. 1. 20
4. Peace Preached,
   Rom. 10. 15
5. Peace Enjoyed,
   Rom. 5. 1
6. Peace Bequeathed,
   John 14. 27
7. Peace Ruling,
   Col. 3. 15

JS. FS.

## Living Pictures of Faith.

| | | |
|---|---|---|
| Abel, - - | The faith that justifies, - - Heb. 11. 4 |
| Enoch, - - | The faith that sanctifies, - - ,, 11. 5 |
| Noah, - - | The faith that testifies, - - ,, 11. 7 |
| Abraham, - | The faith that determined, - ,, 11. 8 |
| Sarah, - - | The faith that multiplies,- - ,, 11. 11 |
| Isaac, - - | The faith that looked forward, ,, 11. 20 |
| Jacob, - - | The faith that looked upward, ,, 11. 21 |
| Joseph, - | The faith that looked homeward, ,, 11. 22 |
| Moses, - - | The faith that looked Godward, ,, 11. 27 |

W.R.

## "Life's Greatest —."
(Rom. 6. 23.)

1. Life's greatest reality—
   "Sin."
2. Life's greatest certainty—
   "The wages of sin is death."
3. Life's greatest offer—
   "The gift of God."
4. Life's greatest issues—
   "Death"—"Life."
5. Life's greatest choice—
   "Wages"—"Gift."
6. Life's greatest medium—
   "Through Jesus Christ." s.o.

## Seven Aspects of Hope.

1. Hope given, 2 Thess. 2. 16
2. Hope abounding,
   Rom. 15. 13
3. Hope in exercise,
   Rom. 8. 25
4. Hope as an anchor,
   Heb. 6. 19
5. Hope as an helmet,
   1 Thess. 5. 8
6. Hope as an effect,
   1 John 3. 3
7. Hope abiding,
   1 Cor. 13. 13

JS. FS.

48

# SUBJECTS FOR SPEAKERS AND STUDENTS.

## Unchangeable Things.
"They shall perish . . . Thou remainest" (Heb. 1. 12).

1. Unchangeable God (Mal. 3. 6). As Creator — Redeemer—Judge. Not to Abram, the faithful, Isaac, the obedient, but to Jacob, the crooked, the worm.
2. Unchangeable Saviour (Heb. 13. 8). Yesterday He bore our sins on the Cross; to-day He bares our cares on the throne; to-morrow ourselves into Glory.
3. Unchangeable Spirit (John 14. 16). Another Comforter, paraclete, agent. May grieve, quench, but never banish.
4. Unchangeable Word, (1 Pet. 1. 25). Grass, ordinary man, withereth; flower of grass, wise and mighty men, falleth away.
5. Unchangeable Inheritance (1 Pet. 1. 4). No moth to damage from without, no rust to corrode from within, no thief to venture within or without. HYP.

## "The Lord my Banner."

1. Banner of Salvation. "Put it on a *pole*." Num. 21. 8 Same word as banner. Christ on Cross.
2. Banner of Victory (Exod. 17. 15). "He that keepeth thee will not slumber, - - - Psa. 121. 3
3. Banner of testimony. "That it may be displayed," Psa. 60. 4
4. Banner of glory. "A root of Jesse shall stand for an *ensign* of the people." *Ensign* same word as banner, - - - Isa. 11. 10, 12. R.M.

## "Without Blemish."

1. A lamb without blemish and without spot, 1 Pet. 1. 19
2. Your lamb shall be without blemish, - Exod. 12. 5
3. Burnt sacrifice . . without blemish, - - Lev. 1. 3
4. Red heifer . . . without spot, - - Num. 19. 2
5. Christ offered Himself without spot, - Heb. 9. 14
6. We should be holy and without blame, - Eph. 1. 4
7. A glorious Church, not having spot, or wrinkle, or any such thing, but holy and without blemish,
Eph. 5. 27 J.R.

## "Precious Thoughts"
Concerning our Lord in Hebrews 10.

1. Incarnation, "a body prepared," - - - - v. 5
2. His work, "Lo, I come to do Thy will," - - v. 9
3. On the throne, "Sat down on the right hand," v. 12
4. Ascension. "Holy Ghost also is a witness, v. 15
5. Living for us. "Having an High Priest over the House of God," - v. 21
6. Coming for the Church. "Yet a little while," v. 37
7. Final Triumph. "His enemies made His footstool," - v. 13 L.W.G.A.

# SUBJECTS FOR SPEAKERS AND STUDENTS.

## Incorruptible.

1. The Son of God, Acts 13.37
2. The Saviour's Blood,
   1 Pet. 1. 18.19
3. The Scriptures of Truth,
   1 Pet. 1. 23
4. The Saint's Inheritance,
   1 Pet. 1. 4
5. The Sister's Ornament, 3.4
6. The Saint's Resurrection Body, 1 Cor. 15.52
7. Servant's Crown,
   1 Cor. 9. 25. w.j.m.

## A Sevenfold Coming to Christ.

"To whom coming" (1 Peter 2. 4).

1. For rest, -   Matt. 11. 28
2. For satisfaction,
   John 7. 37
3. For communion,
   John 1. 39
4. For help, -   Heb. 4. 16
5. For service,   Mark 1. 17
6. For victory, Matt. 14. 26
7. For home,      Rev. 4. 1
"Let us COME."      G.H.

## Christ the Hope of—

1. The *Individual*—"All changed,"      - 1 Cor. 15. 51
2. The *Family*—"Them also which sleep
   in Jesus will God bring with Him," 1 Thess. 4. 14
3. The *Church*—"They all may be one," - John 17. 11
   Divided now, united at His Coming again.
4. The *World*—Unrest on every hand. The
   exhortation is, "Be patient, the
   Coming of the Lord draweth nigh," James 5. 7, 8
   All wrongs righted then, but not till then.
5. The *Glory*—"He shall see of the travail
   of His soul, and shall be satisfied," Isa. 53. 11
   Satiated, filled like a sponge.      HYP.

## The Fruit of Love.

1. Continue in love,
   John 15. 9; Heb. 13. 1
2. Increase in love,
   1 Thess. 3. 12
3. Abound in love,
   1 Thess. 4. 10
4. Walk in love, as Christ
   hath loved us, Eph. 5. 2
5. Be fervent in love,
   1 Peter 1. 22; 4. 8
6. Be unfeigned in love,
   2 Cor. 6. 6; Rom. 12. 9
7. Be perfected in love,
   1 John 4. 18 G.M.T.

## "The Joy of Salvation."

CONSISTS IN

1. The knowledge of
   forgiveness, Psalm 51. 2
2. The enjoyment of God's
   presence,      Psa. 51. 11
3. The realisation of Spirit's
   power,      Psa. 51. 11.
4. The pleasure of winning
   souls,      Psa. 51. 11.
5. The ascent of praise,
   Psa. 51. 11.
6. The surrender of all to
   God,      Psa. 51. 16, 17.
   H.K.D.

## Peter's Mother-in-Law. (Mark 1.30, 31).

| 1. Sin: | 2. Sympathy : | 3. Sufficiency: | 4. Service : |
|---------|---------------|-----------------|--------------|
| Fever. | They tell Him. | He came...lifted up. | She ministered. |

W.R.

## Which Way to Look.

1. If you wish to be distracted—look around, - Psa. 73. 1-15
2. If you wish to be miserable—look within, - Psa. 77. 1-9
3. If you wish to be happy—look up, - Psa. 73. 16-28 B.E.

## Knowing the Lord Leads One to Know Oneself.

1. Mine eye seeth Thee. Wherefore I abhor
   myself, - - - - - - - Job 42. 5
2. Mine eyes have seen the King. Then said
   I, woe is me . . . the Lord of hosts, - - Isa. 6. 1, 5
3. When Simon Peter saw it. . . . I am a sinful
   man, O Lord (a fuller revelation of Christ), Luke 5. 8
   In 1 repentance is prominent (Job 42. 6)
   In 2 cleansing is prominent (Isa. 6. 7)
   In 3 service is prominent (Luke 5. 10) H. P., Jr.

| Christ's Seven Offices. | Satan's Seven Offices. |
|-------------------------|------------------------|
| 1. Saviour to deliver, Matt. 1.21 | 1. The tempter, - -Gen. 3. 1 |
| 2. Redeemer to restore, | 2. The deceiver, - John 8. 44 |
| 1 Peter 1. 18, 19 | 3. The persecutor, 1 Pet. 5. 8 |
| 3. Head to characterise, Col. 1.18 | 4. The hinderer, -1 Thes. 2. 18 |
| 4. Mediator to reveal, 1 Tim. 2. 5 | 5. The buffeter, - 2 Cor. 12. 7 |
| 5. Priest to maintain, Heb. 4. 14 | 6. The impersonator, |
| 6. King to rule, -Matt. 27. 11 | 2 Cor. 11. 14 |
| 7. Judge to award, Acts 17. 31 | 7. The accuser, - Rev. 12. 10 |
| Js. Fs. | Js. Fs. |

## The Subject of Isaiah 53.

"He began at the same Scripture, and preached unto him Jesus"
(Acts 8. 35.)

| 1. The Sensitive One, - | A tender plant, - | - verse 2 |
|---|---|---|
| 2. The Sorrowing One, - | A Man of Sorrows, | - ,, 3 |
| 3. The Smitten One, - | Smitten of God, - | - ,, 4 |
| 4. The Suffering One, - | He was wounded, | - ,, 5 |
| 5. The Sin-bearing One, | The Lord hath laid on Him, ,, 6 |
| 6. The Silent One, - | He opened not His mouth, ,, 7 |
| 7. The Stricken One, - | The stroke was upon Him, ,, 8 |
| 8. The Sincere One, - | No deceit in His mouth, ,, 9 |
| 9. The Submissive One, | It pleased the Lord, - ,, 10 |
| 10. The Satisfied One, - | He shall be satisfied, - ,, 11 |
| 11. The Successful One, - | He shall divide the spoil, ,, 12 |

H.K.D.

# SUBJECTS FOR SPEAKERS AND STUDENTS.

## A Picture of Grace,
### As seen in 2 Kings 25.

1. Emancipation (Out of Prison), - - - v. 27
2. Consolation (Spake kindly to him), - - v. 28
3. Exaltation (Set his throne, etc), - - v. 28
4. Transformation (Changed his prison garments), v.28
5. Acceptation (Did eat bread continually before Him), - - - - - - - v. 29
6. Preservation (A continual allowance...every day, all the days of his life), - v. 30. D.W.

## Private Study.

In connection with private Scripture study there are five important things:
1. Reading - 1 Tim. 4. 13
2. Searching - Acts 27. 11
3. Finding - Psa. 69. 162
4. Meditating- Jer. 15. 16
5. Practising James 1. 22-25
S.J. B.C.

## Together,
### or How Christians are united to Christ.

1. Quickened - Chron. 2. 5.
2. Raised - ,, 6.
3. Sealed - ,, 6.
4. Planted - Rom. 6. 5
5. Sufferers - ,, 8. 17
6. Heirs - ,, 8. 17
7. Glorified - ,, 8. 17
R.L.B.

## Things which are " Set."

1. A set Child, - Luke 2. 34
2. A set Light, - Acts 13. 47
3. A set Ruler, - Heb. 2. 7
4. A set Hope, - Heb. 6. 18
5. A set Priest, - Heb. 8. 1
6. A set Race, - Heb. 12. 1
7. A set Joy, - Heb. 12. 2

## Christ our Life.

Source of our life Eph. 2. 1
Sustenance - Gal. 2. 20
Solace - John 6. 51
Object - Heb. 13. 5
Pattern - Phil. 1. 21
Crown - Col. 3. 20
R.L.B.

## Seven Things Came by the Fall,
### and these have their full measure in Christ.

1. Pain, - - Gen. 3. 16, - - Isa. 53. 11
2. Subjection, - ver. 16, - - Gal. 4. 4
3. The Curse, - ver. 17, - - Gal. 3. 13
4. Sorrow, - - ver. 17, - - Isa. 53. 3
5. Thorns, - - ver. 18, - - Matt. 27-29
6. Sweat, - - ver. 19, - - Luke 22. 24
7. Death, - - ver. 19, - - Phil. 2. 8

Night has fallen upon the guilty pair, Adam and Eve; but in the night there is a star that leads on to a manger, a child, a Saviour (Matt. 2. 9). F.E.

# SUBJECTS FOR SPEAKERS AND STUDENTS.

## "Conditions of Blessing."

"Who shall abide" (Psalm 15).

1. A godly personal life, - - - - Psa. 24. 4
2. Walking with God, - - - - - 1 John 3. 18
3. Unity amongst brethren, - - - Psa. 133. 1   R.M.

## The New Covenant.

1. The covenant maker, God, - - Titus 1. 2
2. The covenant head, Christ, - - Eph. 1. 3
3. The covenant victim, Christ, - - 1 Peter 1. 20
4. The covenant seal, Jesus' blood, - Heb. 13. 20
5. The covenant blessing, eternal life, - Titus 1. 2
6. The covenant people, the saved, - 2 Tim. 1. 9
7. The covenant duration, everlasting, - Heb. 13. 20   W.W.F.

## Beyond Expression.

1. Mercies innumerable,
   Psa. 68. 19
2. Peace incomprehensible,
   Phil. 4. 7
3. Joy unspeakable,   1 Pet. 1. 8
   G.H.

## I am the Resurrection.

(John 11. 25.)

1. The dead hear His voice,
   Luke 7. 14, 15; 8. 54, 55;
   John 11. 43, 44
2. The dead shall hear,
   1 Thess. 4. 16, 17   E.A.H.

## Mistakes of God's Famous Men.

1. Moses smote the rock twice, - - Num. 20. 11, 12
2. Joshua believed the Gibeonites, - - - Joshua 9. 15
3. David believed Ziba, - - - - 2 Sam. 16. 4
4. Hezekiah received ambassadors, - 2 Chron. 32. 31
5. Peter separated from the Gentiles, - - Gal. 2. 12
6. Barnabas dissembled, - - - - Gal. 2. 13
7. John wanted fire from heaven, - - Luke 9. 54   JS. FS.

## A Model Church.

The Church of the Thessalonians was a Model, as shown in Chapter 1.

1. Election. "Your election of God," - - - verse 4
2. Conversion. "Turned to God from idols," not
   from God to idols, - - - - - verse 9
3. Assurance. "Our Gospel came unto you . . . in
   much assurance," - - - - - verse 5
4. Dwelling place. "In God the Father and in the
   Lord Jesus Christ," - - - - verse 1
5. Character. "Ye were ensamples unto all that
   believe," - - - - - - - verse 7
6. Testimony. "From you sounded out the Word
   of the Lord," - - - - - - verse 8
7. Hope. "Turned . . . to wait for His Son from
   heaven," - - - - - - - verse 10   T.B.

# SUBJECTS FOR SPEAKERS AND STUDENTS.

## God's Appearances.

| | |
|---|---|
| To Abraham as a Traveller, - - - | Gen. 18. |
| To Jacob as a Wrestler, - - - - | Gen. 32. |
| To Joshua as a Captain, - - - - | Joshua 5. |
| To Zechariah as Redeemer, - - | Zech. 3. 1 HYP. |

## Seven Springs,
#### Affording streams of perfect and perennial joy.

| JOY. | | KNOWN BY |
|---|---|---|
| 1. In Sins forgiven, | - | Accepting Christ. |
| | | Acts 16. 34; Psa. 32. 1 |
| 2. In His Presence, | - | Communion with Christ. |
| | | Psalm 16. 11. |
| 3. In His Word, - | - | Feeding upon Christ. |
| | | Jeremiah 15. 16. |
| 4. In His will, - | - | Obeying Christ. |
| | | John 13. 17. |
| 5. In suffering, - | - | Loyalty to Christ. |
| | | 1 Peter 4. 13, 14; Acts 4. 51. |
| 6. In prospect of coming Glory, | | Looking for Christ. |
| | | Romans 5. 2. |
| 7. Service and reward, - | | Living for Christ. |

1 Thess. 2. 19-20; Phil. 2. 16; Matt. 25. 21.   D.W.

## Brother.
#### His qualifications by degree.

| | | | |
|---|---|---|---|
| 1. Quartus, - | - | "*A*" brother, | - Rom. 16. 23 |
| 2. Quartus, - | - | "*The*" brother, | - 2 Cor. 8. 18 |

"Whose praise is in the Gospel in all the churches."

| | | | |
|---|---|---|---|
| 3. Epaphroditus, | - | "*My*" brother, | - Phil. 2. 25 |
| 4. Timotheus, | - | "*Our*" brother, | - Philemon 1. 1 |
| 5. Tychicus, - | - | "*Beloved*" brother, | Col. 4. 7 |
| 6. Silvanus, - | - | "*Faithful*" brother, | 1 Peter 5. 12 |
| 7. Onesimus, | - | "*Faithful* and *Beloved*" | |
| | | brother, | Col. 4. 9 D.F. |

## It's Just Like Him.

| | |
|---|---|
| 1. He came near to Adam to *clothe* him, - | Gen. 3. 21 |
| 2. He came near to Enoch to *walk* with him, | Gen. 5. 24 |
| 3. He came near to Abraham to *befriend* him, | Gen. 18. 17 |
| 4. He came near to Jacob to *bless* him, - | Gen. 32. 30 |
| 5. He came near to John to *encourage* him, | Rev. 1. 17 |
| 6. He came near to Zaccheus to *save* him, - | Luke 19. 9, 10 |

H.H.M.

# SUBJECTS FOR SPEAKERS AND STUDENTS.

## The Pith and Essence of the Gospel in Two Words.

1. WHOSOEVER—for those without,    -    John 3. 16
2. WHATSOEVER—for those within,    -    John 14. 13 N.B.

### The Cross to the Glory.

1. Redeemed, - - 2 Cor. 5. 21
2. Reconciled, - - 2 Cor. 5. 18
3. Righteous, - - 2 Cor. 5. 21
4. Regenerated, - 2 Cor. 5. 17
5. Rewarded, - - 2 Cor. 5. 10

W.J.M.

### Three Essentials for Enjoyment.

1. Cleave unto the Lord,
   Acts 11. 23
2. Love one another, 1 John 4. 7
3. Always abounding in the
   work of Lord, 1 Cor. 15. 58

### A Three-fold Hindrance.

1. A hindrance to prayer,
   Dan. 6. 7
2. A hindrance to obedience,
   1 Kings 13. 18
3. A hindrance to victory,
   Judges 7. 2

### Transforming of a Priest.

1. An unclean man, - Isa. 6. 5
2. A convicted man, - „ 6. 5
3. A contrite man, - - „ 6. 5
4. A cleansed man, - „ 6. 7
5. A consecrated man, „ 6. 8
6. A commissioned man, 6. 9

W.J.M

## The Effect of Receiving the Spirit.

1. Godward,    -    PRAYER,    -   -   -   Rom. 8. 15
2. Soulward,    -    CONFLICT,    -   -   -   Gal. 5. 17
3. Churchward,    LOVE,    -   -   -   -   Acts 4. 31
4. Worldward, -    SEPARATION, -   -   Acts 5. 13   JS. FS.

### Preach the Word.

1. It is life, - - - Phil. 2. 16
2. It is light, - Psa. 119. 105
3. It is power, - - Rom. 1. 16
4. It is pure, - Psa. 119. 140
5. It is unchanging, Ps. 119. 89
6. It searches, - - Heb. 4. 12
7. It judges, - - John 12. 48

J.H.B.

### The God of all Comfort.

1. Yesterday: The Lord hath
   comforted His people,
   Isa. 49. 13
2. To-day: I am He that comforteth you, - Isa. 51. 12
3. To-morrow: They shall be
   comforted, - - Matt. 5. 4

W.T.R.

## Sacrifices Accepted by God.

1. Abel (transitoriness), -    Gen. 4. 4 (see Psa. 20. 3, marg.)
2. Moses (drawer out), -    -    -    -    -    Lev. 9. 24
3. Gideon (feller, hewer),    -    -    -    Judges 6. 19-21
4. David (beloved),    -    -    -    -    1 Chron. 21. 26
5. Solomon (peace),    -    -    -    -    - 2 Chron. 7. 1
6. Elijah (my God is Jehovah),    -    - 1 Kings 18. 36-38
7. Christ (anointed), the Lamb of God, -    - John 1. 29

God's answer of acceptance (Matt. 27. 50, 51; Acts 2. 1-4).

F.P.P.

# SUBJECTS FOR SPEAKERS AND STUDENTS.

## The Lord's Supper.
### Heads of an address on 1 Cor. 11. 23-26.

1. The Person we remember, - - "Me."
2. The Fact we announce, - - "His death."
3. The Event we wait for, "Until He come." J.J.S

## The Saint's Song of Degrees.
### As given in Psalm 126.

1. Dreaming, - verse 1
2. Laughing, - ,, 2
3. Singing, - ,, 2
4. Magnifying, - ,, 3
5. Weeping, - verse 5
6. Reaping, - ,, 5
7. Rejoicing, - ,, 6
"We are glad." HYP.

## The Purifying Process
### As revealed in Zechariah 3. 4, 5.

CONDEMNED, - "Take away the filthy garments."
CLEANSED, - "Caused thine iniquity to pass."
CLOTHED, - "Clothed with a change of raiment."
CROWNED, - "Set a fair mitre upon his head."
The Lord planned and provided all. HYP.

## Some Striking Contrasts.

The "Old Serpent" cast down, - - - Gen. 3. 14
The Son of Man lifted up, - - - John 3. 14
Eternal Death, - - - - - Gen. 3. 15
Eternal Life, - - - - - John 3. 15
Bad tidings of great sorrow, - - - Gen. 3. 16
Good tidings of great joy,- - - - John 3. 16
The ground cursed, - - - - - Gen. 3. 17
That the world...might be saved, John 3. 17 J.G.J.

## Beware Lest Ye Be
### (2 Peter 3. 17).

1. Savourless—
   Salt, - - Matt. 5. 13
2. Covered—
   Candles, - Luke 8. 16
3. Foundation-
   less—Builders, ,, 6. 49
4. Fruitless—
   Branches, - John 15. 6
5. Sleeping—
   Virgins, - Matt. 25. 5

## "These Three Men"
### Mentioned in a peculiar place, Ezek. 14. 14-20.

NOAH - - - Salvation.
DANIEL - - - Separation.
JOB - - Stability. HYP.

## Aspects of Rest.

Come unto Me=
    Rest obtained.
Learn of Me=
    Rest retained.
Yoked with Me=
    Rest maintained. D.F.

# SUBJECTS FOR SPEAKERS AND STUDENTS.

## Three Glorious Themes.

1. "God is my salvation," - - - - Psa. **62.** 7.
2. "God is my helper," - - - - - Psa. 54. 4
3. "God is my portion," - - - Psa. **73.** 26 G.H.

## A Striking Exhortation.

1. Passover and unleavened bread, - - Exod. 12
2. "Christ our Passover; ... keep the feast," - 1 Cor. 5. 7, 8
3. " The leaven of *malice and wickedness;* ...
unleavened bread of *sincerity and truth,*" 1 Cor.5.6-8 C.F.H.

## Moses—A Hidden Man.

1. Hidden in the house, - - - - Heb. 11. 23
2. Hidden in the Nile, - - - - - Exod. 2. 3
3. Hidden in the desert, - - - - Exod. 3. 1
4. Hidden in the mount, - - - - Exod. 32. 1
5. Hidden in the wilderness, - - - - Exod. 15. 22
6. Hidden in the rock, - - - - Exod. 33. 22
7. Hidden in the grave, - - - Deut. 34. 6 T.B. & T.B.

## An Impressive Manifestation.

1. Impressive time. The year the leper king
passed away, - - - - - Isa. 6. 1
2. Impressive way. He saw the Lord, heard
the seraphim, felt the posts of doors move, Isa. 6. 1-4
3. Impressive effect. He said, " Woe is me ! "
Six times " woes " on others ; seventh
for himself, - - - - - - Isa. 6. 5
4. Impressive application. Then flew one of
the seraphim ; touched, live coal, - - Isa. 6. 6
5. Impressive commission. Who will go ?
Send me. " Go and tell," - - - Isa.6.8 W.J G.

## The Friend of God.

1. Secrets are revealed to friends. " Shall I
hide from Abraham ?" - - - Gen. 18. 17
2. Friendship produced humility. Abram said,
"I am but dust and ashes [Heb., cinders]" Gen. 18. 27
He counted himself worthy of the same
deserts as Sodom, which was "turned
to ashes [cinders]," - - - - 2 Peter 2. 6
3. Divine friendship is lasting. "Abram thy
friend for ever," - - - - - 2 Chron. 20. 7
4. Obedience the proof of friendship. " Ye
are My friends if ye do whatsoever I
command you," - - - - John 15. 14 H.P.

# SUBJECTS FOR SPEAKERS AND STUDENTS.

## The Perfect Work of a Perfect Saviour.

1. Commencement—He hath begun a good
   work in you, - - - - - Phil. 1. 6
2. Continuation—It is God which worketh
   in you, - - - - - - Phil. 2. 13
3. Completion—Who shall change our vile
   body, etc., - - - Phil. 3. 21.    G.H.

## The Whole World.

1. Guilty, - Rom. 3. 19
2. Provided for, 1 John 2. 2
3. Informed, - Matt. 26. 13
4. Speaking, - Rom. 1. 8
5. In Wicked-
   ness, - - 1 John 5. 19
6. Deceived, - Rev. 12. 9
7. Gained, - Matt. 16. 26

JS. FS.

## Visions of Christ.

1. Humble One, Mark 1. 9
2. Tempted One, ,, 13
3. Gathering One, ,, 17
4. Healing One, ,, 34
5. Approved One, ,, 11
6. Preaching One, ,, 14
7. Holy One, - ,, 24
8. Praying One, - ,, 35

W.J.M.

## Three Salvation Requisites.

1. Conviction is illustrated
   in John 8. 9; Job 40. 4;
   Isaiah 6. 5; Luke 5. 8.
2. Conversion in Acts 3. 19;
   Psalm 51. 13; Matthew
   18. 3; Psalm 19. 7.
3. Confession in Romans 10.
   9, 10; Luke 12. 8; 1
   John 1. 9; Psalm 32. 5;
   Proverbs 28. 13; Luke
   15. 21.    T.R.D.

## Five Great Pillars.

1. Stone—*Witness*,
   Gen. 28. 18; 31. 52
2. Truth—*Wisdom*,
   Prov. 9. 1; 1 Tim. 3. 15
3. Cloud—*Guidance*,
   Exod. 13. 21, 22
4. Brass—*Stability*,
   1 Kings 7. 15
5. Salt—*Judgment*,
   Gen. 19. 26; Judges 16. 25-29
6. Reward—*Rest*, Rev. 3. 12

T.R.D.

## The Atonement.

1. NECESSITY, seen in the righteousness of God and the
   unrighteousness of man.
2. POSSIBILITY through the grace and mercy of God
   (Rom. 3. 24-26).
3. ACTUALITY, as accomplished by the death of the Lord
   Jesus Christ (Rom. 5. 7-11).
4. PRACTICABILITY, or how it works out in daily life.
   Paul could say, "God forbid that I should glory,
   save in the Cross of our Lord Jesus Christ" (Gal.
   6. 14).    J.G.

58

# SUBJECTS FOR SPEAKERS AND STUDENTS.

## Three Eternal Verities.

1. The Son ... who became the Author of *eternal* salvation unto all them that obey Him, - - - - - - - Heb. 5. 8, 9
2. Hath obtained *eternal* redemption for them, - Heb. 9. 12
3. That they might receive the promise of *eternal* inheritance, - - - Heb. 9. 15 E.A.H.

| Elijah's Character. | Elisha's Prescription. |
|---|---|
| | 2 Kings 5. 10. |
| 1. A prayerful man, James 5. 17 | |
| 2. A powerful man, 1 Kings 17.1 | 1. "Go," - - Responsibility |
| 3. A perusing man, Deut. 13.5 | 2. "Wash," - Applicability |
| 4. A provided-for man, | 3. "In Jordan," - Locality |
| 1 Kings 17.6 | 4. "Seven times," Extremity |
| 5. A protected man, „ 18.10 | 5. "And thou," Individuality |
| 6. A patient man, „ 17.7 | 6. "Shalt be,"- - Certainty |
| 7. A persecuted man, „ 19.2 | 7. "Clean," - - Recovery |
| Js. Fs. | Js. Fs. |

## Past Condition—Present Position—Future Prospect.
### A Study of Ephesians 2.

### I. PAST CONDITION.

1. "*In times past*" (Πυτὲ), "walking according to course of this world, according to prince of power of air," - - - - - - verse 2
2. "*In times past*" (Πυτὲ), "fulfilling desires of flesh and of mind; by nature children of wrath," - verse 3
3. "*In times past*" (Πυτὲ), "Gentiles in the flesh called Uncircumcision; without Christ; aliens from commonwealth of Israel; strangers from covenants of promise, without hope and without God," - - - - - - verse 11
4. "*In times past*" (Πυτὲ), "far off," - - - verse 13

### II. PRESENT POSITION.

1. "*Now* in Christ Jesus made nigh by blood," - verse 13
2. "*Now* by grace *are* ye saved," - - - verse 8
3. "*Now* we *are* His workmanship," - - verse 10
4. "*Now* we *have* access ... unto the Father," - verse 18
5. "*Now* ye *are* fellow-citizens with the saints," - verse 19
6. "*Now* ye *are* built upon the foundation," - - verse 20

### III. FUTURE PURPOSE AND PROSPECT.

1. "*In the ages to come* that He might show the exceeding riches of His grace in His kindness toward us through Christ Jesus," - - verse 7
2. "*In the ages to come* all the building ... a holy temple in the Lord," - - - - verse 21 W.H.

# SUBJECTS FOR SPEAKERS AND STUDENTS.

## True Things.

1. True Judgment,
   Ezek. 18. 8
2. True Riches,
   Luke 16. 17
3. True Light, John 1. 9
4. True Worshippers,
   John 4. 23
5. True Bread,
   John 6. 32
6. True Vine, John 15. 1
7. True Tabernacle,
   Heb. 8. 2    H.K.D.

## "Lovest Thou Me."
(John 21. 17).

1. A Pardonable Question.
   (Christ asks it.)
2. A Personal Question.
   (Addressed to the individuals.)
3. A Plain Question.
   (Language is simple.)
4. A Pointed Question.
   (Message is searching.)
5. A Practical Question.
   (Issues are important.)S.O.

## What is Right for a Believer to do?

1. To walk more firmly or earnestly,      - Eph. 5. 15
2. To work with more purpose of heart,  - Col. 3. 23
3. To suffer more patiently,  -    -    - 1 Peter 2. 18-24
4. To fight more faithfully,  -    -    - 1 Tim. 6. 12
5. To be more contented,  -    -    - Heb. 13. 5
6. To pray always,    -    -    - 1 Thess. 5. 17
7. To preach more faithfully,    -    - 2 Cor. 5. 20
8. To love more, -    -    -    2 Tim. 4. 8.    J.G.

## Our Heavenly Father's Treasures.

My Father's House
(earthly),  John 2. 16
My Father's Name,
   John 5. 43
My Father's Will,
   John 6. 39
My Father's Hand,
   John 10. 29
My Father's House
(heavenly),  John 14. 2
My Father's Word,
   John 4. 24
My Father's Command-
ments, -  - John 15. 10
   R.L.B.

## The Hope.

Holy Hope - 1 John 3. 3
Overcoming, Rom.8.24, 25
Patient,   - 1 Thess. 1. 3
Encouraging, Rom. 5. 5
   T.R.D.

## Peace.

P  A *Present* Peace
   Luke 7. 50
E  An *Enjoyed* Peace,
   Rom. 5. 1
A  It must be an *Accepted*
   Peace, - John 14. 27
C  It is a *Changeless* Peace,
   Eph. 2. 14
E  It is an *Eternal* Peace,
   Psa. 72. 7   G.H.

# SUBJECTS FOR SPEAKERS AND STUDENTS.

## The Christian's Comparative Degrees.

GOOD—Giving thanks always for *all things*, - Eph. 5. 20
BETTER—Honour the Lord with thy *substance*, Prov. 3. 9
BEST—Present your *bodies* a living sacrifice, Rom. 12. 1 W.T.R.

## What Jehovah Does.

1. Weigheth the actions, - - - - 1 Sam. 2. 3
2. Humbleth the sinner, - - - - 1 Sam. 2. 6
3. Giveth life, - - - - - - 1 Sam. 2. 6
4. Maketh rich, - - - - - - 1 Sam. 2. 7
5. Exalteth the poor, - - - - - 1 Sam. 2. 8
6. Keepeth His saints, - - - - - 1 Sam. 2. 9
7. Judgeth the wicked, - - - - 1 Sam. 2. 10 W.J.M.

## Christ's Ten Characters in Hebrews.

1. As the Great Sehpherd, Heb. 13. 20
2. As the Leader, Heb. 12. 2
3. As the Victim, Heb. 10. 12
4. As the Mediator, Heb. 9. 15
5. As the Minister of the Sanctuary, Heb. 8. 2
6. As the Surety, Heb. 7. 22
7. As the High-Priest, Heb. 5. 10
8. As the Apostle, - Heb. 3. 1
9. As the Captain, Heb. 2. 10
10. As the Son of God, Heb. 1. 2 JS. FS.

## " Beware ! "

On considering this word in the Scriptures with its immediate connections, I find that it occurs ten times, warning of ten evils, which are specified hereunder. We are told to beware :

1. Of forgetting God (Deut. 6. 12; 8. 11). Both these warnings are uttered after promise of an entrance into the promised land.

2. Of evil and uncharitable thoughts (Deut. 15. 9). Uttered after promise of great riches.

3. Of things forbidden (Judges 13. 4-13). Uttered in connection with Samson's consecration to the Lord.

4. Of dangers foretold (Job 36. 18). A warning to unsaved.

5. Of the wrath of God (Acts 13. 40). Uttered immediately after the glorious Gospel message.

6. Of false teachers and their leaven (Matt. 7. 15; 16. 6 11).

7. Of men (Matt. 10. 17). Alas! our great snare. Uttered after the Lord Jesus' statement, " Behold, I send you forth."

8. Of evil workers (Phil. 3. 2).

9. Of the error of the wicked (2 Peter 3. 17). Uttered in connection with the danger of the last days being evil.

10. Of covetousness (Luke 12. 15). A warning to those desirous of possessing riches and inheritances. W. M'C.

61

# SUBJECTS FOR SPEAKERS AND STUDENTS.

## Three Important Things.
1. The Will of God,
      Heb. 10. 7
2. The Witness Holy Ghost,
      Heb. 10. 15
3. The Way unto the Holiest
      Heb. 10. 19, 20   H.K.D.

## Abiding Things.
1. Comforter,  John 14. 16
2. Christians,  John 13. 4
3. Service,  - 1 Cor. 3. 14
4. Christ,  - John 12. 24
5. Scriptures,  1 Peter 1. 23
                        H.K.D.

## "My Father Worketh"
### (John 5. 17).
1. God chooses His people, -  -  -  - 1 Cor. 1. 27
2. God calls His people,  -  -  -  - Rom. 8. 28
3. God cleanses His people,  -  -  - 1 Cor. 6. 11
4. God chastens His people,  -  -  - Heb. 12. 6
5. God counsels His people,  -  -  - Rev. 3. 18
6. God comforts His people,  -  -  - 2 Cor. 1. 4
7. God crowns His people,  Psa. 103. 4   JS. FS.

## Divinely Guided
1. With His eye, Psa. 32. 8
2. With His counsel
      Psa. 73. 24
3. With His strength
      Exod. 15. 13
4. With His skilful hands
      Psa. 78. 72
5. In judgment,  Psa. 25. 9
6. Into all truth, John 16. 3
7. Continually,  Psa. 58. 11
                        H.K.D.

## The Great Redeemer
### (Luke 19. 10).
His position to man,
      "The Son of Man."
His picture of man, "Lost."
His poverty on behalf of
      man,  - "Is come"
      (From glory to earth).
His patience toward man,
      "Seeking."
His purpose with man,
      "Saving."   S.O.

## A Study of John the Baptist.
1. His fashion of dress (plain)—
      Camels' hair, -  -  -  -  - Matt. 3. 4
2. His food (plain)—
      Locusts and wild honey,  -  - ,, 3. 4
3. His fervour or fearlessness—
      Rebuked a king,  - Matt. 14. 4; Luke 3. 7-19
4. His followers—
      They now follow Christ,  -  - John 1. 35-7
5. His faith (flickering)—
      Art Thou HE?  -  -  -  - Matt. 11. 3
6. His fears—Do we look for another?  - ,, 11. 3
7. His fame—None greater,  -  -  - ,, 11. 11

62                        D.F.

## Three Precious Things in One Verse.

1. Propitiation—"Christ hath once suffered
   for sins," - - - - - - 1 Peter 3. 18
2. Substitution—"The Just for the unjust," - 1 Peter 3. 18
3. Reconciliation—"That He might bring us
   to God," - - - - - 1 Peter 3. 18 H.D.

### The Woman of Samaria.

1. Conversation commenced,
   John 4. 7
2. Confidence gained, John 4. 15
3. Conscience reached,
   John 4. 18, 19
4. Conversion effected,
   John 4. 26
5. Change manifested,
   John 4. 29
   W.J.M.

### "The Spirit of God"
as revealed in 1 Corinthians 12. Ver.

1. Confession of the Spirit, 3
2. Baptism of the Spirit, - 13
3. Drinking of the Spirit, - 13
4. Gifts of the Spirit, - - 8
5. Dividing of the Spirit, - 11
6. Working of the Spirit, - 11
7. Manifestation of Spirit, 7-10
   The aim—"to profit
   withal," verse 7. T.B.

### Revival of the Prayer Life.
"ASK—SEEK—KNOCK" (Matt. 7. 7).

1. Prayer must be directed to God, - - Matt. 6. 9
2. Prayer must be made in the name of the
   Lord Jesus Christ, - - - John 14. 13, 14
3. Prayer must be in faith, - - - Matt. 21. 22
4. Prayer must be joined with "abiding" in
   Christ, - - - - - - John 15. 7
5. Prayer must be linked with avoidance of all
   known sins, - - - - - Psa. 66. 18
6. Prayer must be made "without ceasing," - 1 Thess. 5. 17
   Acts 12. 5 A.M.

### The Use of the Commonplace.

1. Moses and his *rod*, - - - - - Exod. 4. 2
   Trace history of rod, Exod. 4. 2, 17, 20; 7. 15, 17;
   14. 16; 17. 5. Had to be "cast."
2. Gideon and his *pitchers*, - - - - Judges 7. 16
   Had to empty, and "broken."
3. Widow and her two *mites*, - - - Mark 12. 42
   Her all; had to be "given."
4. The Master and the *towel*, - - - John 13. 4
   Had to be "girded."
5. Dorcas and her *needle*, - - - Acts 9. 39
   Needs "use" to keep bright.
   Blessing not in the commonplace, but in the *use* of that
   which is wholeheartedly given to the Lord. HYP.

# SUBJECTS FOR SPEAKERS AND STUDENTS.

## Points About Prayer.
Given by the Lord in Matthew 6. 6.

1. PERIOD, - - - - "When thou prayest."
2. PLACE, - - - - "Enter thy closet."
3. PRIVACY, - - - - "In secret."
4. PERSON, - - - - "To thy Father."
5. PROMISE, - - - - "Shall reward." HYP.

## Joy.

The Source from whence it comes—God, - Rom. 5. 11
Hab. 3. 18
The Channel through which it comes—The
Lord Jesus Christ, - - - - Rom. 5. 11
The Means by which it is imparted—The
Holy Spirit, - - Gal. 5. 22; Acts 13. 52
The Principal upon which it is obtained—
Faith, - - - - Rom. 15. 13; 1 Peter 1. 8
D.W.

| Our Behaviour. | Wondrous Grace. |
|---|---|
| 1. Changed, 1 Sam. 21. 13 | What I was earthly, |
| 2. Wise, - Psa. 101. 2 | 1 Cor. 15. 48 |
| 3. Princely,- Hosea 12. 3 | What I am heavenly, |
| 4. Seemly, - 1 Cor. 13. 5 | 1 Cor. 15. 48 |
| 5. Orderly, - 2 Thess. 3. 7 | What I shall be, |
| 6. Reverent, 1 Tim. 3. 15 | 1 Cor. 15. 49 |
| 7. Holy, - Peter 3. 2 | What I ought to be, |
| H.K.D. | 1 Cor. 15. 58. R.L.B. |

## Some Mountains of Scripture.
These will well repay the climber.

1. Ararat—Sin and sorrow, saving grace, - Gen. 8. 4
2. Moriah—The typical sacrifice, Isaac foreshadowing Christ,- - - - Gen. 22.
3. Horeb—The call of Moses, - - - Exod. 3. 1-10
4. Sinai—God and man face to face, - Exod. 19. 17
5. Pisgah—Vision of Promised Land, - Deut. 3. 27
6. Transfiguration—A Millennial glimpse,
and fellowship with God, - - Matt. 17.
7. Calvary—Reconciliation, - - - Luke 23. 33
8. Olivet—The Lord's coming, - - Acts 1. 12 F.F.

## Fanning and Sifting.

Christ fans to get rid of the chaff, - - Matt. 3. 12
Satan sifts to get rid of the wheat, - Luke 22. 31. G-T.

# SUBJECTS FOR SPEAKERS AND STUDENTS.

| The Master's Messages of Salvation and Service. | The Spirit's Coming in Four Aspects. |
|---|---|
| 1. Come unto Me, Matt. 11.28 | 1. As wind to vivify, John 3.6 |
| 2. Abide in Me, - John 15.4 | 2. As water to satisfy, ,, 4.16 |
| 3. Follow Me, - - Luke 9.23 | 3. As oil to qualify, 1 John 2.27 |
| 4. Go for Me, - - Matt. 28.19 | 4. As fire to purify, 1 Thes.5.19 |
| O.F.H. | Js. Fs. |

## John the Baptist.

Promised of God, and great in His sight, - Luke 1.13-15
Filled with the Holy Ghost, and used of God, Luke 1.15, 16
A just and holy man, and sent from God, Mark 6.20; John 1.6
Preached the Word, and warned the people, - Luke 3.3-9
Exalted Christ, and reproved a king, John 1.29; Luke 3.19
Suffered imprisonment, and died a martyr,

Luke 3.20; Matt. 14.10 W.J M.

## Grace and its Results.
### Could be used as Blackboard or Object Lesson in School or Bible Class.

G R-A-C-E.

**G**od **R**evealed **A**nd **C**hrist **E**xtended (Mephibosheth),

I-N-V-I-T-E-S. John 3.16

**I**s **N**ot **V**alued **I**f **T**here **E**xists **S**uspicion (Hanun),

F-R-E-E-L-Y. John 3.19

**F**reely **R**eceived: **E**nsures **E**verlasting **L**ife **Y**ours, John 3.36

T-A-K-E.

**T**ake **A**nd **K**eep **E**ternally, - - John 10.28 R.M.L.

## God's Chosen Priest.

1. The person of the Priest, Jesus, Son of God, Heb. 5.5
2. The preparation through suffering, - - Heb. 5.8
3. The purpose of the Priest, to offer sacrifices, Heb. 5.1
4. The people of the Priest, the redeemed, - Heb. 6.20
5. The place of the Priest, Heaven, - - Heb. 9.24
6. The pattern of the Priest, Melchisedec, - Heb. 5.10
7. The power of the Priest, Almighty, - Heb. 7.25 JS. FS.

| The Scriptures are | The Scriptures should be |
|---|---|
| 1. Precious, - - Psa. 19.10 | 1. Pondered over, Psa. 1.2 |
| 2. Perfect, - - Psa. 19.7 | 2. Prayed about, - Psa.119.12 |
| 3. Powerful, - - Heb. 4.12 | 3. Prized highly, - Job 23.12 |
| 4. Profitable, - - 2 Tim. 3.16 | 4. Practised daily, James 1.22 |
| 5. Prophetic, - - 2 Pet. 1.19 | 5. Preached freely, Deut. 6.7 |
| 6. Pure, - - - Psa. 12.6 | 6. Producing faith, John 20.31 |
| 7. Purifying, - - Psa. 119.9 | 7. Promoting growth, 1 Pet. 2.2 |
| | W.T.B. |

# SUBJECTS FOR SPEAKERS AND STUDENTS.

## Trial and Trust.
### As seen in Psalm 3.

1. TRIAL,   - 2 verses, - "Lord" once, ends Selah.
2. TRUST,   - 2 verses, - "Lord" twice, ends Selah.
3. TRIUMPH, - 4 verses, - "Lord" thrice, ends Selah

HyP.

## The Perfections of God.

1. His *work* is Perfect,  -  -  - - Deut. 32. 4
2. His *way* is Perfect,  -  -  - - 2 Sam. 22. 31
3. His *knowledge* is Perfect,  -  - Job 36. 4
4. His *law* is Perfect,  -  -  - - Psalm 19. 7
5. His *will* is Perfect,  -  -  - - Rom. 12. 2
6. His *love* is Perfect,  -  -  - - 1 John 4. 18
7. He *Himself* is Perfect,  -  - Matt. 5. 48 T.B.

## Seven Weak Things
### in JUDGES.

1. Left hand,   Judges 3. 21
2. The ox goat,   ,,   3. 31
3. A woman,   ,,   4. 4
4. A nail, -   - ,,   4. 21
5. Piece of
   millstone,   ,,   9. 53
6. Pitcher and
   trumpet,   ,,   7. 20
7. Jaw bone of an ass
   Judges 15. 16   R.L.B

## The Centurian's Faith.
### Matthew 8.

1. Personally presented,
            Matt. 8. 5
2. Pleadingly exercised,
            Matt. 8. 5
3. Practically illustrated,
          Matt. 8. 8, 9
4. Publicly honoured,
          Matt. 8. 10
5. Plentifully rewarded,
     Matt. 8. 13.   H.K.D.

## Three Bible Contrasts.

1. God's first recorded utterance to man:
    "Thou shalt *surely* die,"   -   - Gen. 2. 17
   His last recorded utterance to man:
    "*Surely* I come quickly,"   -   - Rev. 22. 20
2. Man's first recorded utterance to God:
    "I was *afraid*, . . and I hid myself," - Gen. 3. 10
   Man's last recorded utterance to God:
    "Even so, *come*, Lord Jesus,"   - Rev. 22. 20
3. The first question in the Old Testament:
    "Where art *thou*?"—man a lost
      sinner,   -   -   -   - Gen. 3. 9
   First question in the New Testament:
    "Where is *He*?"—the Saviour,   - Matt. 2. 2 F.F.

# SUBJECTS FOR SPEAKERS AND STUDENTS.

## Satan.

Prince of the power of the air (Eph. 2. 2), head of spiritual
forces above.

Prince of this world (John 14. 30), head of temporal powers
below. W.W.F.

## Foundation Truths.

1. INCARNATION—A little lower than angels, - Heb. 2. 9
2. ATONEMENT—The suffering of death, - Heb. 2. 9
3. RESURRECTION—We see Jesus, - - Heb. 2. 9
4. EXALTATION—Crowned with glory, - Heb. 2. 9 J.M.H.

## Our Characters.

Our characters can be safely left in His keeping, for God
vindicates His servants. He speaks about :

1. Moses not fearing the wrath of the King, - Heb. 11. 27
2. The patience of Job, - - - - James 5. 11
3. The meekness of Moses, - - - - Num. 12. 3
4. The righteous vexings of Lot, - - 2 Peter 2. 7 HYP.

| World in Seven Aspects. | The Outstretched Hand. |
|---|---|
| 1. Loved world, - John 3. 16 | 1. To heal, - - - Matt. 8. 15 |
| 2. Guilty world, - Rom. 3 19 | 2. To cleanse, - - Luke 5 13 |
| 3. Crucified world, Gal. 6. 14 | 3. To give life, - Luke 7. 14 |
| 4. Deceived world, Rev. 12. 9 | 4. Make straight, - Luke 13. 13 |
| 5. Evil world, - - Gal. 1. 4 | 5. Deliver, - - Matt. 14. 31 |
| 6. Enslaved world, 1 John 5. 19 | 6. Bless, - - - Mark 10. 16 |
| 7. Endless world, Eph. 3. 21 | 7. Revive, - - - Rev. 1. 17 |
| Js. Fs. | H. P., Jr. |

## God's Trial Ground.

1. Moses in the wilderness, - - - - Exod. 3. 1
2. Elijah in the wilderness, - - - - 1 Kings 19. 4
3. David in the wilderness, - - - - 1 Sam. 26. 3
4. John the Baptist in the wilderness, - - Matt. 3. 1
5. Paul in Arabia, - - - - - - Gal. 1. 17
6. The apostle John in Patmos, - - - Rev. 1. 9
7. Jesus in the wilderness, - - - Luke 4. 1 Js. Fs.

## Three Abominations in Proverbs 15.

1. The *sacrifice* of the wicked (verse 8). Compare Gen. 4. 5
2. The *way* of the wicked (verse 9). Compare 1 Peter 1. 18
3. The *thoughts* of the wicked (ver. 26). Compare Matt. 15. 8

AND THE THREE CONTRASTS.

1. The prayer of the upright (a *sacrifice*, Psa. 141. 2) is His
delight.
2. Him that followeth after righteousness (a *way*) He loveth.
3. The words of the pure (the expression of *thoughts*) are
pleasant. H. P., Jr.

# SUBJECTS FOR SPEAKERS AND STUDENTS.

## "My Beloved."

"My Beloved is mine, and I am His" (Song of Solomon 2. 16).

| My Beloved | - | *Precious* Possession, | - 1 Peter 2. 7 |
| | | | Psa. 73. 25 |
| Is | - | *Present* Possession,- | - Psa. 16. 5 |
| | | | Heb. 13. 6 |
| Mine | - | *Personal* Possession, | - Luke 1. 47 |
| | | | John 20. 28 |
| I | - | *Prized* Possession, - | - Isa. 43. 4 |
| | | | Eph. 5. 25 |
| Am | - | *Permanent* Possession, | - John 6. 39 |
| | | | ,, 10. 28 |
| His | - | *Purchased* Possession, | - 1 Cor. 6. 20 |
| | | | Titus 2. 14   D.W. |

## Seven Great Things.

1. Great wickedness,
    Gen. 6. 5
2. Great death, 2 Cor. 1. 10
3. Great white throne,
    Rev. 20. 11
4. Great mercy, Psa. 103.11
5. Great salvation,
    Heb. 2. 3
6. Great reward, Psa. 19.11
7. Great gulf between,
    Luke 16.26.   F.F.

## Far Off—Made Nigh.

Study of Ephesians 2. 13.

But now,   - - The Present
In Christ Jesus, The Place
Ye,   - - - - The People
Who sometimes, The Past
Were made far
    off,   - - - The Position
Are made nigh, The Portion
By the Blood, - The Price
Of Christ,   - - The Person
Js. Fs.

## "Prepared."

The Keyword of Jonah and Solution of all Difficulties.

1. Prepared (sent out) a great *wind* to turn
    the backslider,   -   -   -   -   Jonah 1. 4
2. Prepared a great *fish* to swallow Jonah,   ,,   1. 17
    (Whatever it was, God made it for the
        purpose).
3. Prepared a *gourd* to cover the despondent
    penitent,   -   -   -   -   -   ,, 4. 6
4. Prepared a *worm* to wither all man's
    hopes of earth,   -   -   -   -   ,, 4. 7
5. Prepared a silent *east wind* to cast him
    only upon Jehovah,   -   •   -   ,, 4. 8
Great grace at last (v. 11).   HYP.

# SUBJECTS FOR SPEAKERS AND STUDENTS.

## Righteousness—Four Symbols.
1. Gold—Intrinsic divine righteousness,       - Exod. 25. 11
2. Brass—Divine righteousness in connection
      with sin, - - - - - Exod. 27. 2; 30. 18
3. Fine Linen—The righteousness of saints, -   Rev. 19. 8
4. Filthy Rags—Fleshly righteousness, -  Isa. 64. 6  w.w.f

### A Threefold Choice.
1. Moses' choice—
      To suffer, - - Heb. 11.25
2. Lot's choice—
      To possess, - Gen. 13. 11
3. Mary's choice—
      Jesus' feet, - Luke 10. 39
                              Js. Fs.

### A Threefold End.
1. The end of the law,
                        Rom. 10. 4
2. The end of the ages,
                        Heb. 9. 26
3. The end of the unbeliever,
                        1 Peter 4. 17
                              Js. Fs.

## Seven Marks of Discipleship
included in the one word, "OBEDIENCE" (John 8. 31).
1. Love, - - - - - - John 13. 34, 35
2. Lowliness, - - - Matt. 10. 24, 25; 11. 29, 30
3. Denial of self, - - - - - -⎫
4. Taking up the Cross—Act, Daily, Continuance,⎬ Luke 9.23
5. Following Christ, - - - - - -⎭   ,, 14.27
6. Loving service and hospitality, Matt. 10 42; 25.40; Heb. 6. 10
7. Fruit-bearing, - - - - - John 15. 8  L.J.T.

## David and Mephibosheth.
1. Mephibosheth had wrong thoughts of the
      Rightful King, - - - - - 2 Sam. 4. 4
   See Adam hiding behind the trees of the garden (Gen. 3).
      The unfaithful servant (Matt. 25. 44).
2. Mephibosheth was sought and saved by a
      Gracious King, - - - - - 2 Sam. 9. 1-5
   See God seeking Adam (Gen. 3).   The Shepherd seeking
      the lost sheep (Luke 15).
3. Mephibosheth dwelt with a Powerful King,  2 Sam. 9. 13
   Result: He had peace with the King; privileged to
      feast with the King, and was satisfied by the King.
4. Mephibosheth suffered with a Rejected King, 2 Sam. 16. 1-4
   Compare Phil. 1. 28; Matt. 5. 10-12; Rom. 8. 17
5. Mephibosheth was faithful to an Absent King, 2 Sam. 19. 24
   Compare Luke 19. 13; Rev. 2. 10; 2 Tim. 4. 7
6. Mephibosheth welcomed a Returning King, 2 Sam. 19. 24-30
   Compare Luke 12. 37; 1 John 2. 28
7. Mephibosheth secured by a Faithful King, - 2 Sam. 21. 7
   Compare John 10. 28; Jude 1-24; 1 John 4. 17; Heb. 13. 20

# SUBJECTS FOR SPEAKERS AND STUDENTS.

## At Jesus' Feet.

1. To hear His WORD  as a DISCIPLE,  - Luke 10. 39
2. To WEEP -  -  in  DISTRESS,  - John 11. 32
3. To WORSHIP  -  in  DEVOTION,  John 12. 3  G-T.

## A Successful Christian Life.

1. Begin right,  -  -  -  -  - John 1. 12
2. Confess Christ openly,  -  -  - Matt. 10. 32
3. Study the Word,  -  -  -  - 1 Peter 2. 2
4. Pray without ceasing,  -  -  - 1 Thess. 5. 17
5. Go to work for Christ,  -  -  - Matt. 25. 29
6. Give largely,  -  -  -  -  - 2 Cor. 9. 6-8
7. Keep pushing on,  -  -  Phil. 3. 13, 14  F.F.

## The Work of the Lord.

1. Directs, Acts 8. 29; 19. 20
2. Restrains, - Acts 13. 2-4
3. Warns,  -Acts 21. 4
4. Reveals,  1 Cor. 2. 10;
  Eph. 3. 5
5. Empowers,  Rom. 15. 19
  W.W.F.

## Jeremiah—A Study.

1. Supplication, Jer. 15.15
2. Suffered,  -  ,, 15
3. Strengthened,  ,, 16
4. Satisfied,  -  ,, 16
5. Separated,  -  ,, 17
6. Supported,  -  ,, 20
  W.J.M.

## The Saint and his Saviour

### Could both join in the 7 "I ams" of Psalm 69 and 71.

1. I am come into deep waters,  -  - Psa. 69. 2
2. I am weary of my crying, -  -  -  ,, 3
3. I am become a stranger unto my brethren, ,, 8
4. I am in trouble—hear me speedily,  -  ,, 17
5. I am full of heaviness—"none," -  -  ,, 20
6. I am poor and sorrowful,  -  -  ,, 29
7. I am as a wonder unto many,  Psa. 71. 7  HYP.

## Wilderness Experience.

### Psalm 63.

### THE PILGRIM AND HIS GUIDE.

1. Seeking for Thee,  -  -  -  - Verse 1
2. Thirsting for Thee,  -  -  -  -  ,, 1
3. Longing for Thee,  -  -  -  -  ,, 1
4. Praising Thee, -  -  -  -  - verses 3-5
5. Remembering Thee,  -  -  -  - verse 6
6. Meditating on Thee,  -  -  -  ,, 6
7. Rejoicing in Thee,  -  -  -  - verses 7-11
8. Following after Thee,  -  -  - verse 8 W.J.M.

70

## SUBJECTS FOR SPEAKERS AND STUDENTS.

### Ten Points of Salvation in one Precious Verse.

John 3. 16.

| | |
|---|---|
| 1. The SOURCE of Salvation, - - - | For *God* |
| 2. The SUPERLATIVENESS of Salvation, - | *so* loved |
| 3. The SUBJECTS of Salvation, - - - | the *world*, |
| 4. The SPONTANEITY of Salvation, - | that He *gave* |
| 5. The SECURER of Salvation, - | His only begotten *Son*, |
| 6. The SCOPE of Salvation, - - - | that *whosoever* |
| 7. The SIMPLICITY of Salvation, - | - *believeth* in Him |
| 8. The SOLACE of Salvation, - | - should *not* perish, |
| 9. The SURENESS of Salvation, - - | - but *have* |
| 10. The STABILITY of Salvation, - | - *Everlasting* Life |

### A Great Rallying Centre.

"Unto Him shall the gathering of the people be" (Gen. 49. 10).

1. For salvation, - Luke 15. 1
2. For prayer, - Matt. 18. 20
3. For home, - 2 Thess. 2. 1
4. For judgment, Matt. 25. 32
5. For communion, Psa. 50. 5
6. For service, - - Mark 3. 14
7. For millennial worship,
Zech. 14. 16

"Christ all in all." G.H.

### What We Are.

| | |
|---|---|
| Babes in the family, - - - - - | 1 Peter 2. 2 |
| Living stones in the building, - - - | 1 Peter 2. 5 |
| Strangers in the world, - - - - | 1 Peter 2. 11 |
| Servants in our sphere, - - - - | 1 Peter 2. 16 |
| Followers in the way, - - - - | 1 Peter 2. 21 |
| Sheep in the flock, - - - | 1 Peter 2. 25 W.J.M. |

### Our Past—our Present—our Future.

PAST EXPERIENCE—There failed not ought of any good thing which the Lord had spoken unto the house of Israel; all came to pass (Joshua 21. 45).

PRESENT PRIVILEGE—Casting all your care upon Him; for He careth for you (1 Peter 5. 7).

FUTURE RESOLVE—I will trust, and not be afraid (Isa. 12. 2) W. D. D.

### In Christ's Name.

"The Name above every Name" (Phil.

1. Preaching, - - Luke 24. 47
2. Baptising, - - Acts 8. 16
3. Gathering, - - Matt. 18. 20
4. Receiving, - - Matt. 18. 5
5. Praying, - - John 14. 14
6. Giving, - - - Mark 9. 41
7. Ruling, - 2 Thess. 3. 6 Js.Fs.

### Seven Phases of Quickness.

1. Quick to agree, Matt. 5. 25
2. Quick to obey, Matt. 28. 7
3. Quick to compel, Luke 14. 21
4. Quick to deceive, Luke 16. 6
5. Quick to betray, John 13. 27
6. Quick to judge, - Rev. 2. 16
7. Quick to come, - Rev. 22. 20
T. B.

# SUBJECTS FOR SPEAKERS AND STUDENTS.

## The New Birth.

1. The Sovereignty of New Birth - Jas. 1. 18
2. The Means of New Birth, - - 1 Pet. 1. 23
3. The Nature of New Birth, - 1 John 3. 9
4. The Manifestation of New Birth, 1 Jno. 2. 29
5. The Security of New Birth, - 1 Jno. 5. 18
6. The Effect of New Birth, - - 1 Jno. 5. 1
7. The Rank of New Birth, - - Jno. 1. 12

## The Holy Spirit.

1. The Comfort, Acts 9. 31
2. The Power, - Rom. 15. 13
3. The Temple, 1 Cor. 6. 9
4. The Communion, 2 Cor. 13. 14
5. The Joy, - 1 Thess. 1. 6
6. The Gifts, - Heb. 2. 4
7. The Renewing, Titus 3. 5. H.K.D.

## The Christian Life.

1. Confession of Christ, - - John 12. 42
2. Cleansing by Christ, - - John 13. 10
3. Communion with Christ, - - John 13. 23
4. Chastening unto Christ, - - John 15. 2
5. Comfort in Christ, - - John 16. 33
6. Consecration to Christ, - - John 15. 14
7. Conflict for Christ, - - John 15. 19

## Seven Positions
### Which Christ holds for His people.

1. Above Me, Heb. 6. 20
2. Beneath Me, Deut. 33. 27
3. Behind Me, Isa. 52. 12
4. Before Me, John 10. 4
5. Beside Me, Psa. 16. 8
6. Around Me, S. of S. 2. 6
7. Within Me, Gal. 2. 2

R.L.B.

## How to Raise the Dead.

In the picture of the raising of the Shunammite's son we have the qualifications of the worker (2 Kings 4).

1. WEAKNESS—"A young man and an ass," - verse 22
2. ZEAL—"Drive and go forward, slack not," - ,, 24
3. FAITH—The brokenhearted husband, indifferent, child dead—"It is well," - ,, 26
4. PRAYER—"He went in, shut the door, prayed unto the Lord," - - - ,, 33
5. ADAPTATION—Man and child made to fit, mouth upon mouth, eyes upon eyes, hands upon hands, - - - - ,, 34
6. PATIENCE—Walked to and fro, sneezed seven times, wailed, - - - - ,, 35
7. VICTORY—"Opened his eyes. Take up thy son," - - - - v. 35, 36 HYP.

## Three Stages of Apostasy.

1. The way of Cain, - Natural apostasy, - - Jude 11
2. The error of Balaam, Sacrificial apostasy, - - Jude 11
3. Gainsaying of Core, Ecclesiastical apostasy, - Jude 11

T. B.

## Blessings of Obedience.

1. Plenty, - - - Lev. 26. 5
2. Peace, - - - „ 26. 6
3. Power, - - - „ 26. 7
4. Presence, - - „ 26. 8

H. K. D.

## Three Stages.

1. Saved by grace, - Eph. 2. 8
2. Sealed with the Spirit,
Eph. 1. 13
3. Seated with Christ, Eph. 2. 6

T. B.

## Cain and Abel Contrasted.

1. Cain was a scorner,
Gen. 4. 9
2. Cain was a persecutor,
Gen. 4. 8
3. Cain was a leader, Jude 11

1. Abel was an acceptable
offerer, - - - Heb. 11. 4
2. Abel was a martyr, Gen. 4. 8
3. Abel was a speaker,
Heb. 12. 24 Js. Fs.

## What the Christian Should Avoid.

Resist the devil, - - - James 4. 7; 1 Peter 5. 9
Flee fornication, - - - - - 1 Cor. 6. 18
Flee idolatry, - - - - - 1 Cor. 10. 7
Flee love of money, - - - - 1 Tim. 6. 11
Flee youthful lusts, - - - 2 Tim. 2. 22 W W.F.

## Seven-fold Perfection.

1. The Perfect Sacrifice, - - - - Heb. 10. 12
2. The Perfect Priest, - - - - „ 5. 9
3. The Perfect Captain, - - - - „ 2. 10
4. The Perfect Tabernacle, - - - - „ 9. 11
5. The Perfect Object, - - - - „ 6. 1
6. The Perfect Worshipper, - - - - „ 10. 22
7. The Perfect State, - - - - - „ 11. 40

Js. Fs.

## The Gospel of God
(Rom. 1. 1). It is

1. A predicted Gospel, ver. 2
2. A glorious Gospel, „ 3
3. A universal Gospel, „ 5
4. A soul-captivating
Gospel, - - - - „ 9
5. An all-powerful Gospel, „ 16
6. It will be a condemning
Gospel, - - - - „ 18

G. H.

## The Master's Command
(Matt. 21. 28).

1. Son, - - - Unity
2. Go, - - - Authority
3. Work, - - Activity
4. To-day, - - Opportunity
5. In, - - - Locality
6. My, - - - Dignity
7. Vineyard, - Prosperity

J. M. H.

# SUBJECTS FOR SPEAKERS AND STUDENTS.

## God for Us.

Reconciled to Himself, - - - - Col. 1. 20
Subdued to Himself, - - - - Phil. 3. 21
Purified to Himself, - - - - Titus 2. 14
Presented to Himself, - - - Eph. 5. 29 R.L.B.

## Pictures of Prosperity,
#### As seen in Restored Israel, Hosea 14.

1. LILY, - Purity, thorns, blossom, - verse 5
2. OLIVE, - Beauty. "Go," spread, - ,, 6m
3. CEDAR, - Fragrance (unnamed), - - ,, 7
4. CORN, - Revive, substance, strength, - ,, 7
5. VINE, - Growth, fruit, abiding, - - ,, 7
6. WINE, - Memorial, mirth, - - - ,, 7
7. FIR TREE,- Evergreen, Heavenwards, - ,, 8

HyP.

## Looking.

1. BACKWARD we can say, *Ebenezer* (Hitherto hath the Lord helped us).

2. FORWARD - we can say, *Jehovah-Jireh* (The Lord will provide).

3. UPWARD - we can say, *Jehovah-Nissi* (The Lord our Banner).

4. AROUND - we can say, *Jehovah-Shalom* (The Lord send Peace). F.K.

## A Type of Whole-hearted Love,
#### As seen in David and Jonathan.

Jonathan "*loved* David as his own soul," - 1 Sam. 18. 1
Jonathan "*covenanted*" with David, - 1 Sam. 18. 3
Jonathan "*stripped* himself of his robe, garments, sword, bow and girdle" for David, - - - - - 1 Sam. 18. 4
Jonathan *delighted* much in David, - - 1 Sam. 19. 2
Jonathan "*spake good* of David," - - 1 Sam. 19. 4
especially concerning "a great salvation," - - - v. 5
Jonathan gave everything and went anywhere. "*Whatsoever* thy soul desireth," 1 Sam. 20. 4
Jonathan *encouraged* David.—"Fear not,... thou shalt be king over Israel," - 1 Sam. 23. 17
Yet Jonathan died with his father among the enemies of David, 1 Sam. 31. 2,6 HyP.

## Three Notable Things.

1. A notable prisoner, Matt. 27. 16
2. A notable miracle, Acts 4. 16
3. A notable day, - Acts 2. 20

Js. Fs.

## Three Precious Things.

1. Our character—Holy brethren, - - Heb. 3. 1
2. Our calling—Heavenly, Heb. 3. 1
3. Our consideration—Jesus Christ, - Heb. 3. 1 H. K. D.

## " Counsel."

1. Precept—Hear counsel, and receive instruction, Prov. 19. 20
2. Possession—The Lord hath given me counsel, Psa. 16. 7
3. Prayer—The Lord fulfil all thy counsel, - Psa. 20. 4
4. Partnership—We took sweet counsel together, Psa. 55. 14
5. Prospect—Thou shalt guide me with Thy counsel, and afterward receive me to glory, - - - - - Psa. 73. 24 W. T. R.

## The Manna and its Meaning.

1. Its taste, - - - Sweet, - - Exod. 16. 31
   If ye have tasted, - - - - 1 Peter 2. 3
2. Its price, - - - Free, - - Exod. 16. 4
   Freely ye have received, - - - Matt. 10. 8
3. Its colour, - - - White, - - Exod. 16. 31
   Christ without sin, - - - - Heb. 4. 15
4. Its size, - - - Small, - - Exod. 16. 14
   Christ in the manger, - - - Luke 2. 16
5. Its form, - - - Round,- - Exod. 16. 14
   Christ for Jew and Greek, - - Rom. 1. 16
6. Its name, - - - What is it? - Exod. 16. 15
   Christ unknown, - - - - John 1. 10
7. Its quantity, - - Sufficient, - Exod. 16. 18
   Christ able to save,- - - - Heb. 7. 25
8. Where from, - - Heaven, - Exod. 16. 4
   Christ from heaven, - - - John 6. 38
9. Where it came to, - The ground,- Exod. 16. 14
   Christ in the world, - - - John 17. 18
10. Who for, - - - The People, - Exod. 16. 4
    Christ for the world, - - - John 6. 51
11. Who gathered it, - - Every man, - Exod. 16. 16
    As many as received Him, - - John 1. 12
12. When not found, - - On the Sabbath, Exod. 16. 25
    While ye have it, - - - - John 12. 36
13. When overstored, - Corrupted, - Exod. 16. 20
    **Christ came for judgment,** - John. 9. 39 Js. Fs.

# SUBJECTS FOR SPEAKERS AND STUDENTS.

## Three Things the Believer Should "Lay Up."

1. Lay up, - God's Commandments, - Prov. 7. 1
2. Lay up, - Knowledge, - - - Prov. 10. 14
3. Lay up, - Treasure in Heaven, - Matt. 6. 20

T.B.

## A Talk about Trees.

Adam and Eve *amongst* the trees (Gen. 3. 8),- *Hiding*.
Zacchaeus *up* the tree (Luke 19. 4), - - *Seeking*.
Nathaniel *under* the tree (John 1. 47, 48), - *Confessing*.
*Jesus on* the tree (1 Peter 2. 24),- *Suffering*. W.J.M.

## God's Seven Gifts.

1. God gives rest to labouring ones, - - Matt. 11. 28
2. God gives life to dead ones, - - - Rom. 6. 23
3. God gives righteousness to guilty ones, - Rom. 9. 30
4. God gives His Spirit to obedient ones, - Acts 5. 32
5. God gives salvation to lost ones, - - Luke 19. 9
6. God gives suffering to favoured ones, - Phil. 1. 29
7. God gives consolation to sorrowing ones, 2 Thess. 2. 16

Js. Fs.

## Health Rules.

These seven rules are not only good for the health of
the soul, they are good for the body as well.

1. Healthy appetite—Hunger after Righteousness, - - - - - Matt. 5. 6
2. Best food—The Living Bread, - - John 6. 51
3. Pure atmosphere—In Him we live, - Acts. 17 28
4. Regular habits—The Scriptures daily, - Acts 17. 11
5. Clean living—Adorn the doctrine - - Titus 2. 10
6. Proper exercise—Resist the devil, - James 4. 7
7. Rest awhile—Wait on the Lord, - - Psa. 27. 14

H. H. MARTIN.

## Ministry of Angels.

Delivered Lot, - - - - - Gen. 19. 15
Delivered from Egypt, - - - - Num. 20. 10
Strengthened Elijah, - - - - 1 Kings 19. 5
Saved His people, - - - - - Isa. 63. 9
Delivered His servants, - - - - Dan. 3. 28
Shut lion's mouth, - - - - - Dan. 6. 22
Ministered unto Christ, - - - - Mark 1. 13
Delivered Peter, - - - - - Acts 12. 11
   Heb. 1. 14. R.L.B.

# SUBJECTS FOR SPEAKERS AND STUDENTS.

## Bethany and its Lessons.

1. Death and resurrection, - - - - John 11
2. Service and instruction, - - - - Luke 10. 38
3. Worship and communion, - - - John 12. 1
4. Blessing and ascension, - - - Luke 24. 50 H.K.D.

## Four Points in Psalms 25 and 61.

| | |
|---|---|
| 1. A Friend, - Psa. 25. 2 | 1. Prayer, - - Psa. 61. 1 |
| 2. A Guide, - „ 25. 5 | 2. Protection, - „ 61. 3, 4 |
| 3. A Teacher, - „ 25. 8, 9, 12 | 3. Preservation, „ 61. 6 |
| 4. A Preserver, „ 25. 15, 21 | 4. Praise, - - „ 61. 8 |

W. J. M.

## Lot's Seven Wrong Steps.

1. Lot looks toward Jordan, - - - - Gen. 13. 10
2. Lot chooses Jordan's plains, - - - Gen. 13. 11
3. Lot journeys East, - - - - Gen. 13. 11
4. Lot dwells in cities of the plain, - - Gen. 13. 12
5. Lot pitches his tent toward Sodom, - - Gen. 13. 12
6. Lot dwells in Sodom, - - - - Gen. 14. 12
7. Lot sits in Sodom's gate, - - - Gen. 19. 1 Js. Fs.

## What Sin Has Done.

1. Made man a transgressor, - - - Rom. 5. 14
2. Made Satan a tyrant, - - - - Heb. 2. 14
3. Made God a worker, - - - - - Isa. 5. 17
4. Made Christ a sufferer, - - - - 1 Peter 3. 18
5. Made earth a wilderness, - - - Rom. 8. 22
6. Made punishment a necessity, - - - Matt. 25. 46
7. Made hell a reality, - - - - Luke 16. 23 T. B.

## David's Mighty Men
### had seven characteristics. They were:

1. *Attracted* by David, - - - - 1 Sam. 16. 12, 13
2. Separated unto David, - - - 1 Chron. 12. 8
3. Loyal servants of David. "To turn the
   kingdom of Saul to him," - - 1 Chron. 12. 23
4. Wholly devoted to David. "They were not
   of double heart," - - - 1 Chron. 12. 33

These are *moral.* There were also three characteristics
of their *service.*

5. *United* in service. "They could keep rank," 1 Chron. 12. 33
6. *Expert* in service. "They could use *both*
   hands," - - - - - - 1 Chron. 12. 2
7. *Intelligent* in service. "They had understanding," - - - - 1 Chron. 12. 32 W. B.

# SUBJECTS FOR SPEAKERS AND STUDENTS.

## Three Systems of Cure.

1. Man's,   -   -  To *tame* him,   -   Mark 5. 4
2. The World's   -  To *chain* him,   -   ,, 5. 4
3. The Lord's,   -  To *change* him,   -   ,, 5. 8
It was a wonderful change,   -   -   ,, 5. 15

HyP.

## Two Lovely Scenes
### For moments of meditation.

1. Jesus Slept,  Matt. 8. 24
2. Jesus Wept,  John 11. 35

HyP.

## "Joy"
### Phil. 4. 4.

1. The Salvation = Rejoice
2. The Limitation = In  the  Lord
3. The Continuation = Alway  H.K.D.

## Doxologies.

Twofold,   -  Rev. 1. 6
Threefold,  -  Rev. 4. 9-11
Fourfold,   -  Rev. 5. 13
Sevenfold, Rev. 7. 12  R.L.B.

## Three Relationships.

1. My sheep,  -  John 10. 14
2. My friends, -  John 15. 14
3. My brethren, Psa. 22. 22

W.L.

## Thus Saith the Lord.

1. Stand,     Jer. 6. 16
2. See, -   -   ,, 16
3. Ask,   -   ,, 16
4. Walk,    ,, 16 HyP.

## What a Supply
### For the thirsty and needy (Isa. 55. 1).

1. Water of life,  Isa. 55. 1
2. Wine of joy,    ,, 1
3. Milk of sustenance, ,, 1 HyP.

## Salvation.

1. Its author,   Jonah 2. 9
2. The way of, Rom. 10. 8-13
3. The knowledge of
         1 John 5. 13
4. The joy of,   1 Pet. 1. 8
5. The season of, 2 Cor. 6. 2
6. The duration of,
        Heb. 5. 9  F.F.

## Equipment for Teachers.

1. PRAYER,  -   -   -   Acts 6. 4; Col. 4. 12
2. PREPARATION,     -   1 Tim. 4. 13-16
3. PUNCTUALITY,  -   -   Luke 2. 38; 22. 14
4. PATIENCE,     -    2 Tim. 2. 24; James 1. 3, 4
5. PEACEABLENESS,  -   1 Thess. 5. 16; Col. 3. 15
6. PURITY,  -   -   -   1 Tim. 4. 12; 5. 22; 2 Cor. 6. 3
7. PERFECTNESS,  -    Luke 6. 40; Col. 3. 14  L-W.

## Delightful Pastures.
### As seen in the Song of Solomon 1. 7.

1. PERSONAL COMMUNION—"Thou whom my soul loveth."
2. DIVINE NOURISHMENT—"Where Thou feedest."
3. QUIETNESS AND REST—"To rest at noon."   HyP.

78

# SUBJECTS FOR SPEAKERS AND STUDENTS.

## "He and I."

1. Past—"I *have* loved you, saith the Lord," - Mal. 1. 2
2. Present—"The Lord *taketh* pleasure in His
    people," - - - - - Psa. 149. 4
3. Future—"The Lord *will* give grace and glory,"
    Psa. 84. 11 W.T.R.

### The Beloved.

1. Leaning on the Beloved,
    S. of Sol. 8. 5
2. Listening to the Beloved,
    S. of Sol. 2. 8
3. Longing for the Beloved,
    S. of Sol. 8. 14
    H. K. D.

### Christ's Sufferings.

1. Christ's sufferings from
    men—Hatred, - Isa. 53. 3
2. Christ's sufferings with
    men—Sympathy, Isa. 53.4
3. Christ's sufferings for
    men—Atonement, Isa 53.5
    W. W. F.

### The Breaking of Bread.

1. The Cross anticipated, "He brake it," - Luke 22. 19
2. The Cross accomplished, "Blessed it and brake,"
    Luke 24. 30
3. The Cross remembered, "As often as ye eat,"
    1 Cor. 11. 26 J. H.

### A Study in Emphasis.

1. We *must* be born again,
    John 3. 7
2. We *may* be blameless
    and harmless, Phil. 2. 15
3. We *should* be holy,
    Eph. 1. 4
4. We *shall* be like Him,
    1 John 3. 2 W.T.R.

### A Study in Summaries.

1. A solemn declaration,
    Isa. 1.4
2. A touching lamentation,
    Isa. 1. 5
3. A gracious invitation,
    Isa. 1.18
4. A divine conclusion,
    Isa. 1. 19,20 G. H.

### Moses, the Man of Purpose and Power
(Hebrews 11. 24-30).

1. Refusing, - verse 24, what he refused, - Honour
2. Choosing, - ,, 25, what he chose, - Suffering
3. Esteeming, ,, 26, what he esteemed, Reproach
4. Respecting, ,, 26, what he respected, Recompense
5. Forsaking, ,, 27, what he forsook, - Egypt
6. Enduring, ,, 27, what he endured, - Wrath
7. Keeping, - ,, 28, what he kept, - The Passover
8. Overcoming, ,, 29, 30, what he overcame, All obstacles
    The secret of his success, "By Faith."

The Christian is *saved* (Eph. 2. 8; 1 Peter 1. 9), *lives* (Heb.
10. 38), *walks* (2 Cor. 5.7), and *overcomes* (1 John 5. 4)
"By Faith." J. M. K.

# SUBJECTS FOR SPEAKERS AND STUDENTS.

## "Up from the Wilderness."

WHO?            -    -    Lost, enemies, -    - S. of S. 8. 5
WHERE FROM?    - "The wilderness,"  -    ,,    ,,
WHAT DOING?     - "Leaning, loving,"  -    ,,    ,,
WHERE GOING?   - "Up" to Glory,     -    ,,    ,, HYP.

## "Of Faith."
### Gal. 3. 9.

1. The Word of Faith,    -    -    •    - Rom. 10. 8
2. The Work of Faith,    -    -    •    - 1 Thess. 1. 3
3. The Walk of Faith,        -    •    - 2 Cor. 5. 7
4. The Door of Faith,    -    -    -    - Acts 14. 27
5. The Prayer of Faith, -    -    -    - Jas. 5. 15
6. The Breastplate of Faith,    -    - 1 Thess. 5. 8
7. The Shield of Faith,  -    - Eph. 6. 16    JS. FS.

## God's Cautions.

1. Beware lest thou forget God,    -    - Deut. 6. 12
2. Beware lest He take thee away, -    - Job 36. 18;
   1 Cor. 11. 30
3. Beware of hypocrisy, -    -    •    - Luke 12. 1
4. Beware of covetousness,    -    -    - Luke 12. 15
5. Beware lest any man spoil you,  -    - Col 2. 8
6. Beware of being led away, -    2 Peter 3. 17   F.F.

## What Jesus Did for Us.

1. Made us whole, -    -    -    -    - Matt. 9. 22
2. Made peace for us,    -    -    -    - Col. 1. 20
3. Made us accepted,    -    •    -    - Eph. 1. 6
4. Made us free,    -    -    •    -    - Rom. 8. 2
5. Made us to rest,    -    •    -    - Eph. 2. 6
6. Made us to prosper,    -    •    - 2 Chron. 26. 5
7. Made us kings, -    -    -    -    - Rev. 1. 6 F.

## Walked with God.
### Genesis 5. 22.   To walk with God involves

1. Separation and self-denial, 1 Kings 8. 53; Matt. 16. F
2. Holiness and moral purity, Heb. 12. 14; Matt. 5. 8 2
3. Grace and gentleness, -    -Acts 4. 33; 1 Thess. 2. 7
4. Humility and tenderness, -Acts 20. 19; Eph. 4. 32
5. Zeal and energy,    -    -Psa. 119. 139; Phil. 2. 30
6. Patience and longsuffering, Col. 1. 11
7. Faithfulness and uncom-
   promising decision,    -Heb. 3. 2; Dan. 3. 18 F.F.

# SUBJECTS FOR SPEAKERS AND STUDENTS.

## A Three-fold Joy.

1. At Saviour's birth, - - - - - Luke 2. 10
2. At Saviour's resurrection, - - - - Luke 24. 41
3. At Saviour's ascension, - - - Luke 24. 51 W.J.M.

## Separation: Positives and Negatives.

| | |
|---|---|
| 1. Be ye clean, - Isa. 52. 11 | 1. Be not, - - - Rom. 12. 2 |
| 2. Be ye holy, - 1 Peter 1. 15 | 2. Love not, - 1 John 2. 15 |
| 3. Be ye separate, 2 Cor. 6. 17 | 3. Touch not, - -2 Cor. 6. 17 |

W. T. R.

## A Three-fold Call.

1. "Come unto Me," - Grace, - - - Matt. 11. 28
2. "Come after Me," - Guidance, - - Luke 14. 27
3. "Come away," - Glory, - - - S. of Sol. 2. 10

W. J. M.

## After His Resurrection.

### The ministry of Christ to His disciples after His resurrection.

1. Bereavement—Mary, "Taken away my Lord," John 20. 13
2. Disappointment—Cleopas, "We trusted that it had been He," - - - - Luke 24. 21
3. Fear—The Twelve, "For fear of the Jews," John 20. 19
4. Doubt—Thomas, "Except I shall see," - John 20. 25
5. Backsliding—Peter, "I go a fishing," - John 21. 3
6. Commissioning—Disciples, "Go ye into all the world,"- - - - - Matt. 28. 19
7. Blessing—His own, "He lifted up His hands," Luke 24. 50

J. H.

## What God says to Believers—"Ye Are."

1. Ye are of purification, - - - - 1 Cor. 6. 11
2. Ye are of sanctification, - - - - „ 6. 11
3. Ye are of justification, - - - - „ 6. 11
4. Ye are of union with Christ, - - - „ 6. 15
5. Ye are of possession by Christ, - - - „ 6. 19
6. Ye are of purchase by Christ, - - - „ 6. 20
7. Ye are of a life like Christ, - - - „ 6. 20

G. H.

## Grace Reigning (Rom. 5. 20).

Ye are saved, - - Eph. 2. 8
Wherein we stand, Rom. 5. 2
Find grace to help, Heb. 4. 16
My grace is sufficient, 2 Cor. 12. 9
Teaching us, - - Titus 2. 12
Brought unto us (coming), 1 Peter 1. 13 J.H.

## Four Steps.

1. Separation—Went forth, Gen. 12. 5
2. Failure—Went down, Gen. 12. 10
3. Restoration—Went up, Gen. 13. 1
4. Progress—Went on, Gen. 13. 3 W.W.F.

# SUBJECTS FOR SPEAKERS AND STUDENTS.

## Naaman's Mistakes.

NAAMAN WENT TO

1. Wrong person  - in the     Right way,  - 2 Kings 5.  6
2. Wrong spirit   - to the     Right person,      ,,      9
3. Word given     - wasn't     Received,    -      ,,     10
4. Wanted show    - outward    Religion,    -      ,,     11
5. Wanted to wash - in wrong   Rivers,      -      ,,     12
6. Went away -    - in a       Rage,        -      ,,     12

CURE CAME AS THE RESULT OF

1. Wise (His servant's advice) Reasoning, - 2 Kings 5. 13
2. Without (dipped seven times) Reserve,    -      ,,     14
3. Wonderful (clean as a little
     child) -    -    -    Result,     -      ,,     14

W.R.

## Be Likeminded (Rom. 15. 5).

1. A Right Mind, -    -    -    -    - Luke 8. 35
2. A Sound Mind, -    -    -    -    - 2 Tim. 1. 7
3. A Pure Mind,  -    -    -    -    - 2 Peter 3. 1
4. A Spiritual Mind,  -    -    -    - Rom. 8. 6
5. A Girded Mind,     -    -    -    - 1 Peter 1. 13
6. A Garrisoned Mind, -    -    -    - Phil. 4. 7
7. A Renewed Mind,    -    -    -    - Rom. 12. 2

JS. FS.

## The Manifestation of Faith (Hebrews 11).

1. Faith's Worship—
     "A more excellent sacrifice,"    -    -    - v. 4
2. Faith's Witness—
     "Enoch pleased God" (translated),    -    - v. 5
3. Faith's Work—
     "Noah prepared an ark,"   -    2 Peter 2. 5; v. 7
4. Faith's Walk—
     "Abraham went out,"    -    -    -    - v. 8
5. Faith's Waiting—
     "He looked for a city,"    -    -    -    - v. 10
6. Faith's Willingness—
     "Sarah received strength,"  -    -    - vv. 11, 12
7. Faith's Welcome—
     These all "were persuaded"—confessed
          ... a better country,  -    -    - vv. 13-16

DR. GRIFFITH THOMAS.

# SUBJECTS FOR SPEAKERS AND STUDENTS.

## The Immensity of God's Love.

I. THE TRUE ORIGIN OF SALVATION,   -   God so loved
    God's love was—1, Infinite; 2, Eternal; 3, Immeasurable

II. THE INFINITE SACRIFICE FOR THE WORLD,
                  He gave His only begotten Son

   1. A Free Gift,   -   -   -   -   He gave
   2. A Precious Gift, -   -   -   - only begotten Son
   3. The Unworthy Objects of the Gift,   -   the world

III. THE DESIGN OF LOVE,   -   -   whosoever, etc.
   1. The Channel of Divine Life,   -   -   believeth
   2. The Evil Averted,   -   -   -   not perish
   3. The Benefit Received, -   -   - Everlasting Life

                            T. CROSKERY.

## Seven Three Sixteens.

1. The love of God,   -   -   -   - John 3. 16
2. The work of God,   -   -   -   - 1 John 3. 16
3. The people of God (O. T.), -   -   - Mal. 3. 16
4. The people of God (N. T.), -   -   - Col. 3. 16
5. The Son of God,   -   -   -   - Matt. 3. 16
6. The Word of God,   -   -   -   - 2 Tim. 3. 16
7. The judgment of God,   -   - Eccles. 3. 16.   J. Mk.

## The Believer's Heirdom.

1. Heirs of promise,   -   -   -   - Heb. 6. 17
2. Heirs of salvation,   -   -   -   - Heb. 1. 14
3. Heirs of righteousness,   -   -   - Heb. 11. 7
4. Heirs of life,   -   -   -   -   - 1 Peter 3. 7
5. Heirs of the world,   -   -   -   - Rom. 4. 13
6. Heirs of the promised kingdom,   -   - James 2. 5
7 Heirs of God,   -   -   -   - Rom. 8. 17   Js. Fs.

## Things Concerning Himself
(Luke 24. 27).

1. Humbled Himself, Phil. 2. 8
2. Committed Himself,
           1 Peter 2. 23
3 Offered Himself, Heb. 9. 14
4. Gave Himself, Gal. 1. 4; 2. 20
5. Pleased not Himself,
          Rom. 15. 3
6. Glorified not Himself,
          Heb. 5. 5
7. He cannot deny Himself,
    2 Tim. 2. 13   J. Mk.

## Attributes of Jesus.

1. Jesus the atoning Victim,
          Heb. 10. 9
2. Jesus the Priest, Heb. 4. 14
3. Jesus the Mediator,
          Heb. 12. 24
4. Jesus the Sanctifier,
          Heb. 13. 12
5. Jesus the Surety, Heb. 7. 22
6. Jesus the Leader,
          Heb. 12. 2
7. Jesus the Forerunner,
          Heb. 6. 20   Js. Fs.

# SUBJECTS FOR SPEAKERS AND STUDENTS.

## Things Opened.

1. The Opened Heaven, - - - Luke 3. 21
   The Father's commendation of the Son.
2. The Opened Scriptures, - - - Luke 24. 32
   The Son's revelation of Himself.
3. The Opened Books, - - - Rev. 20. 12
   The sinner's condemnation.
4. The Opened Prison, - - - - Isa. 61. 1
   The captive's liberation.     H.K.D.

### For Times of Need.

When tried, - Isa. 40. 29, 31
When hungry, ,, 40. 11
When thirsty, ,, 41. 18
When fearful, ,, 41. 10, 13
When troubled, ,, 66. 13
When tempted, ,, 59. 19
When fighting, ,, 54. 17
Whatever state, ,, 49. 16
"All your need."   F.F.

### Blackness of

1. Sin, - - Lam. 4. 8
2. Sickness, - Job 30. 30
3. Sorrow, - - Jer. 8. 21;
4. Want, - - Lam. 5. 10
5. Service, - Cant. 1. 5
6. Youth, - - Matt. 5. 36;
       cf. Cant. 5. 11
7. Judgment,   Isa. 1. 3;
       Jude 13.   S.E.H.

## "Fruit Unto God."
### Read John 15. 1-6; Song of Solomon 4. 12-16.

The production of "fruit unto God" is wholly dependent on the existence of spiritual life in the soul: there can be no fruit whatever without it. But even where that life exists, the fruit varies. There is—

1. Fruit - - John 15. | 4. Thirtyfold - Matt. 13. 23
2. More fruit - John 15. | 5. Sixtyfold - Matt. 13. 23
3. Much fruit - John 15. | 6. Hundredfold Matt. 13. 23
    G.M.T.

## God and Satan Working.
### Acts 5. 18-21.

SATAN'S WORK.—"Laid their hands on the Apostles, and put them in the common prison."

GOD'S WORK.—"The angel of the Lord"
1. "By night"
2. Removed hindrances, "Opened the prison doors."
3. Delivered: "Brought them forth."
4. Commanded: "Go, stand...speak...all the words of this life."

They obeyed—"They *heard...entered...early...taught*."
"Our God *is* able to deliver us."     W.H.K.

# SUBJECTS FOR SPEAKERS AND STUDENTS.

## Three Classes at the Cross.

1. Apathy—sitting down, - - - - Matt. 27. 36
2. Antipathy—passing by, - - - - Mark 15. 29
3. Sympathy—standing by, - - - John 19.25 H.K.D.

## "I Have Enough."

1. The man of the world, "I have much,"Gen. 33.9
2. The man of faith, "I have all," - Gen. 33. 11

(Two different Hebrew words used.) w.w.f.

## Five Solemn Negatives

in John 5. 40-47.

1. Ye will not, - - verse 40
2. Ye have not, - - „ 42
3. Ye receive not, - „ 43
4. Ye seek not, - - „ 44
5. Ye believe not, - „ 47

G. H.

## Some Better Things in Hebrews.

1. A better name, - - - - - Heb. 1. 4
2. A better persuasion, - - - - „ 6. 9
3. A better hope, - - - - - „ 7. 19
4. A better testament, - - - - „ 7. 22
5. A better promise, - - - - „ 8. 6
6. A better sacrifice, - - - - „ 9. 23
7. A better substance, - - - - „ 10. 34
8. A better resurrection, - - - „ 11. 35
9. A better country, - - - - „ 11. 16
10. A better provision, - - - - „ 11. 40
11. A better testimony, - - - - „ 12. 24

Ja. Fs.

## Prayer (Acts 16. 25).

### I. PRAYER POSSIBLE AT ALL TIMES.

1. In time of prosperity, - - 1 Kings 8. 22; Acts 10. 1
2. In time of adversity, - - - - James 5. 13
3. In time of danger, - - Luke 22. 42; Matt. 14. 28-33
4. In time of dense darkness, - Jonah 2. 1; Luke 23. 42

### II. PRAYER PROFITABLE AT ALL TIMES.

1. It puts us into contact with God, - - Dan. 9. 23
2. It acquaints God with what we need, - Phil. 4. 4-7
3. It makes it possible for God to help us,

1 Kings 18. 36-39; Acts 4. 31

4. True prayer is always crowned with success,

John 14. 13; James 1. 5, 6

### III. PRAYER POWERFUL AT ALL TIMES.

1. It starts God's machinery, - - Dan. 10. 10-21
2. It makes Satan tremble, - Eph. 6. 10-20; James 4. 7
3. It frees man from sin, - - - - Luke 22.40
4. It enables God to move foundations, Matt. 17.19-21 L.D.

# SUBJECTS FOR SPEAKERS AND STUDENTS

## Links of Fellowship.

1. Fellow-heirs—of one inheritance,   - Eph. 3. 6
2. Fellow-members—of one body,   - Eph. 3. 6, R.V.
3. Fellow-partakers—of one calling,   - Eph. 3. 6, R.V.
4. Fellow-citizens—of one home,   - Eph. 2. 19
5. Fellow-labourers—of one Master,   - Phil. 4. 3
6. Fellow-soldiers—in one warfare,   - Phil. 2. 25
7. Fellow-prisoners—with one hope,   - Rom. 16. 7

F.F.

### Believers Are

Labourers with
  God, - - 1 Cor. 3. 9
Husbandry of God,  ,,  9
Building of God,  ,,  9
Temple of God,  ,,  16
Property of God,  ,,  22

H.K.D.

### In the Lord

1. Everlasting salvation,
    John 10. 28
2. Righteousness, Jer. 23. 6
3. Strength, Zech. 10. 6-12
4. Justification, Rom. 5. 1
5. Glory, - - Jer. 9. 23, 24

F.F.

## Simple Setting of the Prodigal Son (Luke 15).

1. The Prodigal's CONSIDERATION of his position and prospects.
2. The Prodigal's CONVICTION of his sin.
3. The Prodigal's CONTRITION for his wickedness.
4. The Prodigal's CONFESSION of his wrong-doing and ruin.
5. The Prodigal's CONVERSION through his Father's forgiving and restoring mercy.    C.R.H.

## Thoughts on Pleasing God.

1. Impossibility of Pleasing God—
   They that are in the flesh cannot,   - Rom. 8. 8
   Without faith it is impossible,   - Heb. 11. 6
2. Power for Pleasing God, - Phil. 2. 13; Heb. 13. 20, 21
3. Examples of Pleasing God,
   Christ - Matt. 3. 17; 17. 5; - John 8. 29
   John, - - - - - 1 John 3. 22
   Paul, - - - - - 1 Thess. 4. 1
   Enoch, - - - - - Heb. 11. 5
4. Evidences of Pleasing God—
   Separation, - - - - 2 Tim. 2. 2
   Stewardship, - - - - 1 Thess. 2. 4
   Fellowship, - - - - Phil. 4. 19
   Obedience, - - - - Col. 3. 20

H.H.

# SUBJECTS FOR SPEAKERS AND STUDENTS.

## Very Personal.

| | | |
|---|---|---|
| 1. My heart, | - | - Psa. 26. 2 |
| 2. My eyes, | - - | - Psa. 26. 3 |
| 3. My hands, | - | - Psa. 26. 6 |
| 4. My voice, | - | - Psa. 26. 7 |
| 5. My feet, | - - | Psa. 26. 12 |

F. F.

## Isaiah 43.

| | | |
|---|---|---|
| 1. Purchased, | - - | verse 1 |
| 2. Preserved, | - - - | ,, 2 |
| 3. Precious, | - - - | ,, 4 |
| 4. Provided for, | - - | ,, 20 |
| 5. Pardoned, | - - - | ,, 25 |

W. J. M.

## The Faith of the Thessalonians.

| | | |
|---|---|---|
| 1. Your work of faith, - - - - - | - 1 Thess. | 1. 3 |
| 2. In every place your faith ... is spread abroad, | ,, | 1. 8 |
| 3. Sent Timotheus ... to comfort you concerning your faith, - - - | ,, | 3. 2 |
| 4. I sent to know your faith, - - | ,, | 3. 5 |
| 5. Timotheus ... brought us good tidings of your faith, - - - - - | ,, | 3. 6 |
| 6. We were comforted ... by your faith, - | ,, | 3. 7 |
| 7. We might perfect that which is lacking in your faith, - - - - - | ,, | 3. 10 |
| 8. Putting on the breastplate of faith, - - | ,, | 5. 8 |
| 9. We ... thank God that your faith groweth exceedingly, - - - - | - 2 Thess. | 1. 3 |
| 10. We glory ... for your faith in all your persecutions and tribulations that ye endure, - - - - - - | ,, | 1. 4 |
| But the Lord is faithful, - - - - | ,, | 3. 3 |

J. 8N.

## Time (2 Cor. 6. 2).

### I. GOD'S TIME.

| | | |
|---|---|---|
| 1. Time for repentance, | - - - | - Acts 17. 30 |
| 2. Time for humiliation, | - - - | - James 4. 5-10 |
| 3. Time for confession, - | - - | - Rom. 10. 9 |
| 4. Time for asking, | - - - | - Matt. 7. 7 |
| 5. Time for receiving, - | - - | - Heb. 3. 7 |

### II. THE DEVIL'S TIME.

| | |
|---|---|
| 1. To resist God, - - - | Job 1. 7; Acts 13. 10 |
| 2. To rob men, - - - - | 1 Peter 5. 8 |
| 3. To bring upon himself and his eternal ruin, | Rev. 20. 10-15 |
| 4. To fill hell with men and women, - | Luke 16. 19-31 |

### III. MAN'S TIME.

| | |
|---|---|
| 1. To escape from hell, - - | Heb. 2. 3; Isa. 55. 6 |
| 2. To know or love God, - - | - 1 John 4. 7, 8 |
| 3. To become an heir of heaven, - - | - Rom. 8. 14-18 |
| 4. To receive everlasting life, - | John 3. 36 L. D. |

# SUBJECTS FOR SPEAKERS AND STUDENTS.

## The Fear of the Lord.

1. Is wisdom, - - - - - Job 28.28
2. Is to hate evil, - - - - - Prov. 8.13
3. Is strong confidence, - - - - Prov. 14.26
4. Is a fountain of life, - - - Prov. 14.27
5. Is true riches, honour, and life, - - Prov. 22.4
6. Is quick understanding, - - - Isa. 11.3
                                                    N.Z.T.

## "Blessed"

IN THE PSALMS FOR THE

1. Forgiven one,   Psa. 34.1
2. Satisfied one,   ,,   65.4
3. Chastened one,   ,,   94.12
4. Fearing one,   ,,   128.1
5. Obedient one,   ,,   119.2
6. Abiding one,   ,,   84.4
7. Trusting one, Psa.34.8 w.h.

## Illustration of New Creature.

(Gen. 21. 7-10)

1. Born, - - 1 Pet. 1. 23
2. Grew, - - 1 Pet. 2. 2
3. Weaned, - 1 Pet. 2. 11
4. Great feast, - Rev. 3. 20
5. Mocking, - Matt. 5. 11
6. Heir, Rom. 8. 17   F.F.

## The Triune God in John 3. 16.

| God | - | - | - Ruler | - | - | - Micah 5. 2 |
|---|---|---|---|---|---|---|
| so | - | - | - Benefactor | - | | - Psalm 68. 19 |
| loved | - | - | - Lover | - | - | - 1 John 4. 9 |
| the | - | - | - Creator | - | - | - Genesis 1. 1 |
| world, | - | | - Maker | - | - | - Psalm 95. 6 |
| that | - | - | - Purposer | | - | - Ephesians 3. 11 |
| He | - | - | - Governor | - | | - Matthew 2. 6 |
| gave | - | - | - Giver | - | - | - 1 Timothy 6.17 |
| His | - | - | - Father | - | - | - Isaiah 9. 6 |
| only | - | - | - Saviour | - | | - Luke 2. 11 |
| begotten | - | | - Mediator | - | - | - 1 Timothy 2. 5 |
| Son, | - | - | - Redeemer | - | - | - Job 19. 25 |
| that | - | - | - Intercessor | - | | - Isaiah 53. 12 |
| whosoever | | | - Provider | - | - | - Genesis 22. 8 |
| believeth | | | - Counsellor | - | | - Isaiah 9. 6 |
| in | - | - | - Revealer | - | - | - Daniel 2. 22 |
| Him | - | - | - Messenger | - | | - Malachi 3. 1 |
| should | - | | - Commander | - | - | - Isaiah 55. 4 |
| not | - | - | - Comforter | - | - | - John 14. 26 |
| perish, | - | - | - Deliverer | - | | - Romans 11. 26 |
| but | - | - | - Restorer | - | - | - Ruth 4. 15 |
| have | - | | - Bestower | - | - | - Isaiah 63. 7 |
| everlasting | | - | - Keeper | - | - | - Psalm 121. 5 |
| life, | - | - | - Preserver | - | - | - Psalm 37. 28 |

# SUBJECTS FOR SPEAKERS AND STUDENTS.

## God's Love to the World.

1. The OBJECT of His Love,  -  -  -   the world
2. The GIFT of His Love,  -   -  His only begotten Son
3. The DESIGN of His Love,  -  -  should not perish

## God's Love Story.

1. A SACRED Person,  -  -  -  -  -  -  God
2. A STRONG Passion,  -  -  -  -  so loved
3. A SINFUL People,  -  -  -  -  -  the world,
4. A STRIKING Proof,  -  gave His only begotten Son,
5. A SIMPLE Plan,  -  -  -  whosoever believeth
6. A SURE Pledge,  -  -  -  -  should not perish,
7. A STERLING Possession,  -  have Everlasting Life.

H. K. DOWNIE.

## A Pointed Address.

WHO?  "His own self"—The Lord Jesus, the Son of God.
WHAT?  "Bare our sins in His own body."
WHEN?  "On the tree."
WHY?  "That we, being dead to sins, should live unto righteousness."
THE RESULT.  "By whose stripes ye were healed"
(1 Peter II. 24).          N. B.

## Pointed Precepts.

P ray without ceasing,  -  -  -  -  1 Thess. 5. 17
R ejoice evermore,  -  -  -  -  ,, 5. 16
E dify one another,  -  -  -  -  ,, 5. 11
C omfort the feeble-minded,  -  -  -  ,, 5. 14
E ver follow that which is good,  -  -  ,, 5. 15
P rove all things,  -  -  -  -  -  ,, 5. 21
T herefore, let us not sleep, as do others,  -  ,, 5. 6
S ee that none render evil for evil,  -  -  ,, 5. 15

W. T. R.

## Beware . . and . . Consider.

1. Despising the Gospel,     | 1. Christ,  -  Heb. 3. 1; 12. 3
     Acts 13. 41 | 2. Lilies and ravens,
2. False prophets,  - Matt. 7. 15 |          Matt. 6. 28
3. Hypocrisy,  - Luke 12. 1 | 3. Scripture,  -  - 2 Tim. 2. 7
4. Covetousness,   Luke 12. 15 | 4. One another, -   Heb. 10. 24
5. Philosophy,  -  Col. 3. 8 | 5. Thyself,  -  -  Gal. 6. 1
6. Evil workers,  - Phil. 3. 2 | 6. The beam,  - - Matt. 7. 3
7. The error of wicked,      | 7. Your way,  -  Hag. 1. 5-7
     2 Peter 3. 17 |            T. B.

# SUBJECTS FOR SPEAKERS AND STUDENTS.

## Ten Golden Keys
UNLOCKING PRECIOUS TRUTH ABOUT GOD HIMSELF.

1. His Will, - - Ep. 1. 5
2. His Grace, - ,, 6
3. His Blood, - ,, 7
4. His Good Pleasure, ,, 9
5. His Glory, - - ,, 12
6. His Calling, - ,, 18
7. His Inheritance, ,, 18
8. His Power, - ,, 19
9. His Feet, - - ,, 22
10. His Body, - ,, 23

F.-T.

## The Believer's Calling.
1. High, - - Phil. 3. 14
2. Holy, - - 2 Tim. 1. 9
3. Heavenly, - Heb. 3. 1.
4. Of God in Christ Jesus, - Phil. 3. 14
5. To life, - 1 Tim. 6. 12
6. To liberty, - Gal. 5. 13
7. Into light, - 1 Pet. 2. 9
8. To peace, - Col. 3. 15
9. To holiness, 1 Thess. 4. 7
10. To eternal glory, - 1 Pet. 5. 10

W. H. S.

## The Cross in Heaven.

Turn to the Book of Revelation and sum up in a few sentences the presence and importance of the Cross in Heaven. John beholds in the very midst of the Throne of God Himself, "A Lamb standing as though it had been slain." This title of Christ—the Lamb—used twenty-eight times in Revelation, presents our Lord in His sacrificial aspect, and thus constitutes wherever it is used a direct reference to the Cross. Thus:

1. The Cross is our only title to Heaven and Glory, - - - - Rev. 7. 9-15
2. The Cross is the centre of Heaven's Government, - - - - ,, 4. 2; 5. 6
3. The Cross is the source of Heaven's Life, ,, 22. 1
4. The Cross is the brilliance of Heaven's Light, - - - - - ,, 21. 23
5. The Cross is the scene of Heaven's Worship, - - - - ,, 21. 22
6. The Cross is the theme of Heaven's Song, ,, 5. 9
7. The Cross is the incentive of Heaven's Service, - - - - - ,, 22. 3
8. The Cross is the basis of Heaven's Triumph, - - - - ,, 12. 11
9. The Cross is the subject of Heaven's Rejoicing, - - - - ,, 19. 7
10. The Cross will be the terror of Heaven's Enemies, - - - ,, 6. 12-17

R. J. G. VOISIN.

# SUBJECTS FOR SPEAKERS AND STUDENTS.

## A Threefold Headship.

1. Abraham, Israel's lineal head, - - - Gen. 17. 7
2. Aaron, Israel's priestly head, - - - Heb. 5. 4
3. David, Israel's royal head, - - - Psa. 89. 3, 4

## Seven Continual Things.

1. Continual offering,
   Exod. 29. 38
2. Continual praise,
   Heb. 13. 15
3. Continual feast,
   Prov. 15. 15
4. Continual service,
   Dan. 6. 16
5. Continual sorrow,
   Rom. 9. 2
6. Continual guidance,
   Isa. 58. 11
7. Continual association,
   2 Sam. 9. 13

## Seven Incorruptible Things.

1. The incorruptible seed,
   1 Peter 1. 23
2. The incorruptible price,
   1 Peter 1. 18
3. The incorruptible inheritance, - - 1 Peter 1. 4
4. The incorruptible body,
   1 Cor. 15. 53
5. The incorruptible crown,
   1 Cor. 9. 25
6. The incorruptible
   behaviour, - 1 Peter 3. 4
7. The incorruptible language,
   Eph. 4. 29

## Seven Aspects of Christ's First Coming.

1. Christ come to fulfil the law, - - - Matt. 5. 17
2. Christ come to call to repentance, - - Matt. 9. 13
3. Christ come to make division, - - - Matt. 10. 34
4. Christ come to give life, - - - - John 10. 10
5. Christ come in His Father's name, - - John 5. 43
6. Christ come to give light, - - - - John 12. 46
7. Christ come for judgment, - - - John 9. 39

## Seven Reasons why the Blood of Christ is Precious.

1. Because it cleanses the
   conscience, - Heb. 9. 14
2. Because it redeems us to
   God, - 1 Peter 1. 19
3. Because it procures
   forgiveness, - Eph. 1. 7
4. It justifies, - - Rom. 5. 9
5. It sanctifies, - Heb. 13. 12
6. Because it is the pass-
   port to heaven, Heb. 10. 19
7. Because it gives us the
   victory, - Rev. 12. 11

## Seven Things Old and New.

1. The old and new creation,
   2 Cor. 5. 17; Col. 3. 10
2. The old and new head,
   Rom. 5. 17
3. The old and new covenants,
   Heb. 8. 13
4. Old and new man, Col. 3. 10
5. The old and new com-
   mandment, - 1 John 2. 7
6. The old and new treasures,
   Matt. 13. 52
7. The old and new heavens,
   2 Peter 3. 5-13 Jr. Fs.

# SUBJECTS FOR SPEAKERS AND STUDENTS.

## Seven Things We are to Follow.

1. In the footsteps of Christ, - - - 1 Peter 2. 21
2. Follow righteousness, - - - - 1 Tim. 6. 11
3. Follow peace, - - - - - Heb. 12 .14
4. Follow holiness, - - - - Heb. 12. 14
5. Follow, to apprehend that which you are
    apprehended of in and by Christ, - Phil. 3. 12
6. Follow charity (love), - - - 1 Cor. 14. 1
7. Follow that which is good, - - 1 Thess. 5. 15

F.E.M.

## The Gospel.

1. Power of, - Rom. 1. 16
2. Blessing of, Rom. 15. 29
3. Truth of, - Gal. 2. 5
4. Faith of, - Phil. 1. 27
5. Hope of, - Col. 1. 23
6. Afflictions of, 2 Tim. 1. 8
7. Bonds of, - Philem. 13

H. K. D.

## Open Thy Mouth
(Psa. 81. 10)

IN

1. Prayer, - John 15. 7
2. Praise, - - Heb. 13. 15
3. Proclamation, Acts 13. 38
4. Propagation, Mark 16. 20
5. Presentation, Rom. 12. 1

W. J. G.

## The New Song.
### As given in the Book of Revelation 5. 8.

1. The highest note, - - =Thou art worthy.
2. The greatest sacrifice, - - =Thou wast slain.
3. The sweetest theme, - - =Redeemed by Blood.
4. The widest result, - - =Kindred, tongue, etc.
5. The newest relationship, - =Kings and priests.
6. The brightest hope, - - =We shall reign.

H.K.D.

## A New Setting of "Cities of Refuge."

1. RELIABLE—not deliver the slayer up (Josh. 20. 5); so
    the refuge in Christ (John 10. 27-30).
2. EXHIBITED—Mount Naphtali, etc. (v. 7); so Cross on
    Mount Calvary (John 3. 14).
3. FREE—*gave* him a place (v. 4); so we have nothing to
    pay (Rom. 5. 15-21).
4. UNBOUNDED—for Israelite, stranger, whosoever (v. 9);
    so salvation alike free to all (Rom. 3. 22).
5. GOD'S REMEDY—"*the Lord* also spake" (vv. 1, 2);
    *God* sent His Son (1 John 4. 9).
6. EVER OPEN—might flee thither (v. 3. 9); so sinner ever
    welcome (Rev. 22. 17).                    F.F.

# SUBJECTS FOR SPEAKERS AND STUDENTS.

## Micaiah.

### A Faithful Servant.

1. Hated, - - 1 Kgs. 22. 8
2. Despised, - ,, 22.18
3. Persecuted, - ,, 22.24
4. Imprisoned, - ,, 22.26
5. Afflicted, - ,, 22.27

N.L.K.

## "He that heareth My Voice."

1. Hearing and heeding,
   Ezek. 33. 4
2. Hearing and doing,
   Matt. 7. 24
3. Hearing and receiving,
   Matt. 13.19   W.T.R.

## Some Counterfeits.
### 1 Kings 12. 26-33.

1. Counterfeit God, - - - - - - ver. 28
2. Counterfeit Priesthood, - - - - ver. 31
3. Counterfeit Sacrifice, - - - - - ver. 32
4. Counterfeit Worship, - - - - - ver. 32
5. Counterfeit Feast, - - - - - ver. 33

F. M'L.

## Some "Looks" of the Word.

1. Searching Look of the Lord, - - - Psa. 14. 2, 3
2. Saving ,, ,, ,, Sinner, - - Isa. 45. 22
3. Satisfying ,, ,, ,, Saint, - - Heb. 12. 2
4. Steadfast ,, ,, ,, Pilgrim, - - Prov. 4. 25
5. Solemn ,, ,, ,, Worldling, - Gen. 19. 26
6. Sorrowing ,, ,, ,, Christ Rejecters, - John 19. 37
   Rev. 1. 7
7. Saints ,, for ,, Coming One, - Phil. 3. 20
   Titus 2. 13
8. Saints ,, of Endless Joy, - 1 Thess. 4. 17
   Psa. 17. 15

W.J.M.

## "The Riches of His Grace."
### Outline of sermon on Ephesians 1. 7.

1. The greatest wonder in the world, - "Redemption."
2. The blessed Redemption brings, "Forgiveness of sins."
3. The Person through whom it comes,
   "Our Lord Jesus Christ...in WHOM."
4. The means by which it is accomplished,
   "Through His Blood."
5. The way we become possessed of it,
   "United to Him, in whom ye also trusted."
6. The great fountain-head of all,
   "The riches of His GRACE."   PROF. JAMES ORR.

# SUBJECTS FOR SPEAKERS AND STUDENTS.

## Very Personal.

1. Reckon *yourselves* dead to sin, - - Rom. 6. 11
2. Yield *yourselves* to God, - - - Rom. 6. 13
3. Arm *yourselves*, - - - - - 1 Peter 4. 1
4. Keep *yourselves* from idols, - - 1 John 5. 21
5. Build up *yourselves*, - - - Jude 20.
6. Keep *yourselves* in the love of God,- - Jude 21.
7. Do not forsake the assembling of *yourselves*
    together,- - - - - - Heb. 10. 25
    W.H.

## The Three "Unspeakables."

Unspeakable is only used these three times in N.T.
1. His Unspeakable Gift, - - - 2 Cor. 9. 15
2. Heard Unspeakable Words, - - 1 Cor. 12. 4
3. Rejoice with Joy Unspeakable, - 1 Peter 1. 8

Each word translated "unspeakable" is a totally different
word in Greek. Reconstructing the passages by Liddell
and Scott's Greek Lexicon, we get:

1. Thanks be unto God for His *"indescribable"* gift.
2. Caught up into Paradise and heard *"unpublished"* words.
3. We rejoice with joy *"unutterable"* and full of glory.
LIEUT. G. MASCULL.

## Marvels at a Miracle.

Men of prayer—Peter and John, - - - Acts 3. 1
Man begging—Lame from birth, - - - ,, 2
Monetary difficulty—Silver and gold none, - ,, 6
Miracle performed—Feet and ankles strong, - ,, 7
Manifestation—Leaping—Praising God, - ,, 8
Multitude—All the people—Ran together, - ,, 9
Message—Look not on us—See the exalted One, ,, 12-26
Man whom ye slew—Made Lord and Christ, - ,, 12 26
W.H.

## A Sevenfold Unity

GIVEN US, THE BASIS OF ALL OTHERS:

1. I was crucified with Christ, - - - Gal. 2. 20
2. I was buried with Him, - - - - Rom. 6. 4
3. I was quickened with Him, - Eph. 2. 16; Col. 13
4. I was raised with Him, - Eph. 2. 6; Col. 3. 1
5. I am seated in Heaven in Him, - - Eph. 2. 6
6. I am suffering with Him, - - - Rom. 17
7. I shall be glorified and reign with Him, - Rev. 20. 4
"Christ is all and in all." DR. W. P. MACKAY.

# SUBJECTS FOR SPEAKERS AND STUDENTS.

## The Kingdom.

1. The kingdom come, - - - - - Rom. 14. 17
2. The kingdom coming, - - - - Luke 23. 42
   The characteristics of each; (1) Righteousness;
   (2) Joy; (3) Peace.    w.w.f.

## Christ's Love-marks.

1. Divine love, - - Corrects, - - Mark 10. 21
2. Divine love, - Chastens, - - John 11. 5
3. Divine love, - Cleanses, - - John 13. 14
4. Divine love, - Claims, - John 13. 23 w.

## Seven Aspects of Christian Service.

1. The pattern for service, - - - Matt. 20. 28
2. The sphere for service, - Gal. 5. 13; 1 Cor. 9. 19
3. The motive for service, - - - - 2 Cor. 5. 13
4. The power for service, - - - - Acts 1. 8
5. The object for service, - - - - Acts 27. 23
6. The condition for service. - - - - Luke 9. 48
7. The reward for service, - - - 1 Cor. 9. 25 js.fs.

## His Presence.

1. The Lord thy God *hath been* with thee, - Deut. 2. 7
2. The Lord thy God *is* with thee, - - Josh. 1. 9
3. The Lord God, even my God, *will be* with thee,
   1 Chr. 28. 20

## *His Presence with Israel Assured.*

1. Food—Manna, angel's food, - - - Deut. 8. 16
2. Drink—Water (out of flinty rock), not wine
   or strong drink, - - - Deut. 8. 15; 29. 6
3. Raiment—Clothes and shoes waxed not old, Deut. 29. 5
4. Care of bodies—Feet did not swell, - Deut. 8. 4
5. Every need met—Ye lacked nothing, Deut. 2. 7 hyp.

## Adam, a Type of Christ.

1. God put Adam to sleep, - - - - Gen. 2. 21
   Christ laid down His life, - - - John 10. 18
2. Eve owed her being to his sleep, - - Gen. 2. 22
   The Church owes existence to death of Christ, Eph. 5. 25
3. Eve not breathed into—only Adam, - Gen. 2. 7
   The Church has the life of Christ, - John 17. 2
4. Eve a companion for Adam, - - - Gen. 2. 20
   The Church a companion for Christ, - John 15. 15
5. Eve builded out of the rib, - - - Gen. 2. 22
   "I will build My Church," - - - Matt. 16. 18
6. God presented Eve to Adam, - - Gen. 2. 22
   Christ presents the Church unto Himself, Eph. 5. 27

j.c.m.d.

# SUBJECTS FOR SPEAKERS AND STUDENTS.

## Some Knotty "Nots" in Hebrews.

1. The "have not" of ignorance,  -  -   Heb. 3. 10
2. The "shall not" of exclusion,  -  -   ,, 3. 11
3. The "harden not" of warning,  -  Heb. 3. 15; 4. 7
4. The "believed not" of barrier,  -  ,,    3. 18
5. The "could not" of inability,  -  -  ,,    3. 19
6. They "did not" of unbelief,  -  -  ,,    4. 2
7. They "entered not" of sin, -  -  -  ,, 4. 6 w-w.

## God is Seen as

1. Redeemer through the Lamb,  -  Exod. 12. 42
2. Leader in the Cloud,  -  -  -  ,,    13. 21
3. Saviour at the Sea,  -  -  -  ,,    14. 13
4. Healer at Marah,  -  -  -  ,,    15. 26
5. Provider in the Manna,  -  -  ,,    16. 15
6. Defender against Amalek,  -  -  ,,    17. 13
7. Ruler in the Tabernacle,  -  -  ,,    40. 16

JS. FS.

## Written Seven Times.

1. Written in the mind—the will made willing to do God's will. This is **Conversation** (Heb. 10. 16).
2. The Christ preached in the Gospel becomes thereby written on the heart—**Salvation** is accepted.
3. And because now accepted in God's family as a child, the Spirit writes on our hearts the assurance of this **Relationship** (Gal. 4. 6; Rom. 8. 16).
4. "I will write upon him the Name of my God." This is a special promise to believers who will keep His Word and not deny His Name. We take it to mean: Consciousness of being in that new relationship given to us as being "**Accepted in the Beloved**" (Rev. 3. 12; Eph. 3. 17).
5. "And the name of the city of My God"—Consciousness given of having received the Heavenly **Vocation**; of belonging to that city which comes down from Heaven (Rev. 3. 12; Eph. 1. 17, 18).
6. "And I will write upon him my New Name"—Consciousness of that **Especial Relationship** to Him as Head and Bridegroom of the Church (Rev. 3. 12; John 14. 20; 2 Cor. 11. 2).
7. The full result manifest in **Glory**. The name now hidden in the heart becomes visible to all, resplendent on the forehead (Rev. 22. 4).    C. H. BRIGHT.

## The Bread of Life.

1. Life given—"the living Bread" which
   "came down," - - - - - John 6. 35, 41
2. Life sustained—"the Bread of that life"
   which "cometh down," - John 6. 48, 50 W.H.H.

## God's Measuring Line.

1. Measures to the *ankles*—walk and testimony, Ezek. 47. 3
   He did not go in head foremost—lip and life.
2. Measures to the *knees*—prayer, - - - Ezek. 47. 4
   The promises of God are as good as ready money any day.
3. Measures to the *loins*—personal purity, - Ezek. 47. 5
   We may not all be clever, but we can all be clean. D.C.

## Restoration and Victory
### As seen in the days of Samuel.

1. The people *lamented*, - - - - - 1 Sam. 7. 2
2. They *put away* strange gods, - - - ,, 7. 3
3. They gathered *together*, - - - - ,, 7. 6
4. *Offered* a sucking lamb, - - - - ,, 7. 9
5. Gained the *victory*, - - - - - ,, 7. 10
6. Set up a *testimony*, - - - - - ,, 7. 12
7  Samuel continued in *circuit* to Bethel, Gilgal,
   and Mizpah, and returned *home* to
   Ramah, - - - - - - ,, 7. 16
                                    SIR ROBT. MATHESON.

## Paul's Voyage and Shipwreck (Acts 27).

1. DIVINE PROTECTION. Julius, although a Roman
   centurion, is kindly disposed toward Paul,
   and brings him safely to Rome. God was
   at the back of the arrangement, - - - verse 1
2. PERILOUS REJECTION. Paul's wise advice to the
   mariners was rejected; like the Gospel
   to-day, - - - - - - verses 10, 11
3. PREVAILING INTERCESSION. During the great
   storm Paul had been praying for the safety
   of the 275 lives on board, - - - verses 21, 22
4. COMPLETE SALVATION. All lives saved, - - verse 22
5. PERSONAL DEVOTION. Whose I am—possession;
   whom I serve—consecration, - - - verse 23
6. PERFECT RESIGNATION. The storm was unabated.
   He did not trust the ship, for it was doomed;
   nor the sailors, a bad lot; but against all
   appearances he trusted God, - - verse 25 J. G.

# SUBJECTS FOR SPEAKERS AND STUDENTS.

## God's People.
### GOD'S PEOPLE ARE
1. A Saved people, - - - - - Deut. 33. 29
2. A Unique people, - - - ,, ,,
3. A Happy people, - - - - - ,, ,,
4. A Sheltered people, - - - ,, ,,
5. A Defended people, - - - ,, ,,
6. A Persecuted people, - - - . ,, ,,
7. Will be a Triumphant people, - - ,, ,,

G.H.

## Six Heavenly Things.
1. Heavenly RELATIONSHIP, - John 1. 12, 13; John 3. 3;
      see Matt. 6. 14, 26, 32
2. Heavenly POSITION, - Eph. 1. 3; 2. 6-8; Phil 3. 20
3. Heavenly CALLING, - - Heb. 3. 1; Phil. 3. 14
4. Heavenly COUNTRY, - Heb. 11. 16.
     No sin, sorrow, conflict, tears, want, or death.
5. Heavenly IMAGE, - - 1 Cor. 15. 49; Rom. 8. 29;
      1 John 3. 3
6. Heavenly KINGDOM, - - 2 Tim. 4. 16-18; 2 Peter
      1. 11; ct. John 18. 36

H.H.

## Declension or Imitation ?
### REAL CAUSES FOR EXAMINATION OF HEART.
1. Savourless Salt, - - - - - Matt. 5. 13
2. Foundationless Builders, - - - Luke 6. 49
3. Fruitless Branches, - - - - John 15. 6
4. Covered Candles, - - - - Luke 8. 16
5. Tares instead of Wheat, - - - Matt. 13. 30
6. Broken Bottles, - - - - Luke 5. 37
7. Bastards and not Sons, - - - Heb. 12. 8

JS. FS.

## A Simple Gospel Message.
1. "COME unto Me, and I will give you rest" (Matt. 11. 28).
Enlarge on the meaning of "come." Illustrate
"coming" by child taking first step.
2. "TAKE My yoke upon you and learn of Me" (Matt.
11. 28; Rev. 22. 17). Illustrate by acceptance of
New Year, birthday, and other *gifts*.
3. "HAVE Eternal Life" (John 5. 24; 1 John 5. 13).
Present possession. "Have" means "I've got it."
4. "TELL." "Go tell" (Matt. 28. 10). Tell of Jesus the
crucified, risen, willing Saviour.    HYP.

98

# SUBJECTS FOR SPEAKERS AND STUDENTS.

## Christ in John 1.

1. Christ the Word, John 1. 1
2. Christ the Light, John 1. 8
3. Christ the Lamb, John 1.29
4. Christ, Son of God, John 1.49

J. O. M. D.

## Redemption.

##### We are Redeemed by the Death of Christ from the

1. Curse of the law, - - - - - Gal. 3. 13
2. Tradition of the fathers, - - - - 1 Peter 1. 18
3. Spirit of the present age—lawlessness, Titus 3. 9 J.G.

## The Master's Calls.

1. Come unto Me, - Salvation and Security, - Matt. 11. 28
2. Learn of Me, - Sanctification and Satisfaction, ,, 11. 29
3. Come after Me, - Self-Surrender, - - - ,, 16. 24
4. Abide in Me, - Succour and Strength, - John 15. 4
5. Follow Me, - - Schooling and Service, Matt. 4. 19 J.M.H.

## Faith and its Actings.

1. The Operation of Faith—"through faith unto salvation, - - - - - 1 Peter 1. 5
2. The Probation of Faith—"that the trial of your faith," - - - - - 1 Peter 1. 7
3. The Exultation of Faith—"believing, ye rejoice with joy unspeakable," - - 1 Peter 1. 8
4. The Consummation of Faith—"receiving the end of your faith," - - 1 Peter 1. 9 W.E.V.

## Some Exhortations in Hebrews.

1. Let us fear, - - Heb. 4. 1
2. Let us labour, - ,, 4. 11
3. Let us hold fast, ,, 4. 14
4. Let us come boldly, ,, 4. 16
5. Let us go on, - ,, 6. 1
6. Let us draw near, ,, 10. 22
7. Let us consider, ,, 10. 24
8. Let us lay aside, ,, 12. 1
9. Let us run, - - Heb. 12. 1
10. Let us have grace, ,, 12. 28
11. Let brotherly love continue, - - ,, 13. 1
12. Let conversation be without, - ,, 13. 5
13. Let us go forth, ,, 13. 13
14. Let us offer, - ,, 13. 15

Js. Fs.

## As the Centre of Seven Circles.

##### Jesus in the Midst in Seven Characters.

1. Jesus in the midst as the Listening One, - Luke 2. 46
2. Jesus in the midst as the Suffering One, - John 19. 18
3. Jesus in the midst as the Risen One, - - John 20. 19
4. Jesus in the midst as the Gathering One, - Matt. 18. 20
5. Jesus in the midst as the Praising One, - Heb. 2. 12
6. Jesus in the midst as the Judging One, - Rev. 1. 13
7. Jesus in the midst as the Throned One, - Rev. 5. 6

# SUBJECTS FOR SPEAKERS AND STUDENTS.

## Upon Christ's Shoulders.

1. As High Priest—the names of the tribes, Exod. 28. 12
2. As King—the government, -    -    - Isa. 9. 6
3. As Shepherd—the lost sheep,    -    - Luke 15. 5

F.F.

## God and The World.
### THREE GREAT FACTS.

God made,    -    - Gen. 1. 1
God loved,    -    John 3. 16
God will judge, Acts 17. 38

H.K.D.

## A Crooked Woman.

Bound by Satan, Luke 13. 16
Bent by Disease,    ,,    11
Blessed by Christ,    ,,    13
Brought glory to
   God,    Luke 13.   W.J.G.

## Ready When He Comes.

"Blessed is that servant . . . found watching" (Matt. 24. 33. 44. 46).

1. Doing His will (obedient), -    -    - John 14. 23
2. Not defiling our separation,    -    - 2 Cor. 6. 14
3. Not forsaking pilgrim character,    - John 17. 13
4. Going forth without the camp, -    - Heb. 13. 13
5. Witnessing for Christ,    -    - Acts 1. 8
6. Affections on things above, -    -    - Col. 3. 1
7. Laying up treasure in Heaven, -    - Matt. 6. 19

F.F.

## Seven "L's"
### OF REAL VALUE TO ALL WHO LOVE THE LORD.

1. Looking unto Jesus,    -    -    - Heb. 12. 2
2. Love to Person of Jesus,    -    - 1 John 4. 19
3. Learning the mind of Jesus,    -    - Matt. 11. 29
4. Lying at feet of Jesus,    -    - Psa. 23. 2
5. Leaning on the arm of Jesus,    - Sol. Song 8. 5
6. Living for the glory of Jesus,    - Phil. 1. 21
7. Longing to behold the face of Jesus,    - Rev. 22. 20

G.H.

## Meditation on Psalm 17.

1. "Hear the right,"    -    - v. 1, - Supplication
2. "I am purposed,"    -    - v. 3, - Resolution
3. "The word of Thy lips,"    - v. 4, - Inspiration
6. "Keep me,"    -    -    - v. 8, - Protection
5. "I will behold,"    -    - v. 15, - Expectation
6. "I shall be satisfied, -    - v. 15, - Satisfaction
7. "When I awake,"    -    - v. 15, - Resurrection

JS. FS.

# SUBJECTS FOR SPEAKERS AND STUDENTS.

## Habakkuk.

Chap. I. Desolation—"Spoiling and violence before me."
Chap. II. Revelation—"Write the vision, make it plain."
Chap. III. Exaltation—"Revive Thy work. . . . God came.
. . . His glory covered the heavens. . . . I will joy in the
God of my salvation.                                    H. B.

## Psalm 16.

1. Confidence in God—"I put my trust,"     -     - verse 1
2. Rule—"Thou art my Lord,"     -     -     -     ,,   2
3. Portion—"The portion of mine inheritance,"   -  ,,   5
4. Counsellor—"Who hath given me counsel,"   -   ,,   7
5. Object—"I have set the Lord always before me,"  ,,  8
                                                      W. D.

## Our Calling.

1. The Christian's calling. (1) Individual—"Blessed with
   all spiritual blessings"(Eph. 1. 3). (2) Collective—
   "One body" (Eph. 2. 16), "builded together"
   (verse 21).
2. A man who came short of his calling (Gen. 28). Jacob
   was called to (1) the land; (2) east, west, north,
   south; (3) the earth. He was satisfied with the
   common necessaries of life—"food to eat, and
   raiment to put on." How many are Jacob-like
   to day, satisfied with "beggarly elements?"
3. A man who rose above his calling (Heb. 11. 8-10).
   Abram was called unto an inheritance below—
   Canaan. He looked for an inheritance above "a
   city which hath foundations—God." The Christian
   cannot rise above his "heavenly calling."   W. W. F.

## "Reserved."

1. Inheritance for saints,     -     -     -   1 Peter 1. 4
2. Judgment for angels,     -     -     -   - 2 Peter 2. 4
3. Punishment for men,     -     -     -   - 2 Peter 2. 9
4. Catastrophe for world,     -     -     -   2 Peter 3. 7
5. Black darkness for professors, -   -   - Jude 13  T. B.

## Paul's Service was—

1. Devoted, "At all seasons,"     -     -   - Acts 20. 18
2. Humble, "Humility of mind,"   -   -   -   ,,  20. 19
3. Real, "With tears,"     -     -     -   -   ,,  20. 19
4. Faithful,"Kept nothing back that was profitable," ,, 20. 20
5. Thorough, "Taught publickly, and from
   house to house,"     -     -     -   Acts 20. 20  J. G.

# SUBJECTS FOR SPEAKERS AND STUDENTS.

## Five Gospel R's.

WHAT IS IN THE BIBLE?

Ruin, - - - 1 Cor. 15. 52
Redemption, - Luke 23. 33
Regeneration, - John 3. 7
Reception, - - Luke 8. 12
Rejoicing, - - Acts 8. 39

HYP.

## Divine Milestones.

1. Submission, - Acts 9. 6
2. Remission, - Acts. 10. 43
3. Admission, - Heb. 10. 19
4. Transmission, 2 Tim. 2. 2
5. Commission, Mark 16. 15
6. Permission, - 1 Cor. 7. 6
7. Omission, - Matt. 23. 23

IS. FS.

## Superlative John 3. 16.

1. For God - - - - - ETERNAL LOVER
2. so loved - - - - - MEASURELESS LOVE
3. the world, - - - - - UNWORTHY OBJECT
4. that He gave His only begotten Son, GREATEST GIFT
5. that whosover - - - - LARGEST NUMBER
6. believeth in Him - - - - SIMPLEST WAY
7. should not perish, - - - MIGHTIEST RESULT
8. but have Everlasting Life, - RICHEST POSSESSION

ANON.

## The Great Salvation Text.

1. The Author of Salvation, - - - - GOD
2. The object of Salvation, - - - THE WORLD
3. The Procurer of Salvation, HIS ONLY BEGOTTEN SON
4. The offer and condition of Salvation,

   THAT WHOSOEVER BELIEVETH IN HIM

5. The Blessings of Salvation, { SHOULD NOT PERISH
                                { HAVE EVERLASTING LIFE
6. The Assurance of Salvation, - THE WORD OF GOD

JAS. STEPHEN.

## Salvation for the Worst
### as revealed in Acts 3. 26.

1. THE WORST FIRST, - - - " Unto *you* first."
   Rebels red with blood three weeks after the crucifixion.
2. THE WORST BLESSED, - " Sent Him to *bless* you."
   They cursed—He blessed instead of " blasting "
                    (Deut. 28. 22).
3. THE WORST TURNED, - " By turning away every one
   of you from his iniquities."
   Not blessed *in* sin, but by being turned *from* sin—
         " born again " (John 3. 3). HYP.

# SUBJECTS FOR SPEAKERS AND STUDENTS.

## What We Have.

1. Our Preserver, - - - - - - Psalm 16. 1
2. Our portion, - - - - - - „ 16. 5
3. Our path, - - - - - - - „ 16. 11
4. Our prospect, - - - - Psalm 16. 11 W. J. M.

## Behold, What Manner of Love.

1. Unparalleled love, - - - - - 2 Sam. 1. 26
2. Unmerited love, - - - - - Rom. 5. 8
3. Unmistakable love, - - - - - John 3. 16
4. Unending love, - - - - - Jer. 31. 3 H. K. D.

## Threefold Prayer in Psalm 143.

1. Cause me *to hear* Thy loving kindness, - - verse 8
2. Cause me *to know* the way wherein I should walk, „ 8
3. Teach me *to do* Thy will, - - - - - „ 10

## And the Threefold Reason.

1. For in Thee do I trust, - - - - - - „ 8
2. For I lift up my soul unto Thee, - - - „ 8
3. For Thou art my God, - - - verse 10. H. P., Jun.

## Go, Speak to that Young Man (Zech. 2. 4).

1. Speak to the Thoughtless young man, - Eccles. 11. 9
2. Speak to the Foolish young man, - Prov. 7. 7
3. Speak to the Deserted young man, - - 1 Sam. 30. 13
4. Speak to the Ungrateful young man, - - 2 Sam. 18. 5
5. Speak to the Self-Righteous young man, - Matt. 19. 20
6. Speak to the Fearful young man, - - 2 Kings 6. 17
7. Speak to the Diligent young man, - 1 Kings 11. 28 G. H.

## Motto for the Lord's People.
### *Our Past*—Lost and Guilty.

1. Astray like lost sheep, - - - - Psa. 119. 176
2. All the world . . . guilty, - - - - Rom. 3. 19

### *Our Present*—Saved and Justified.

1. God, who hath saved us, - - - - 2 Tim. 1. 8, 9
2. It is God that justifieth, - - - - Rom. 8. 33

### *Our Future*—Christ and Glory.

1. To be with Christ, - - - - - Phil. 1. 23
2. Ye shall appear with Him in glory, - Col. 3. 4
3. Jesus Christ the same yesterday (*past*),
      to-day (*present*), and for ever (*future*), - Heb 13. 8
4. I have loved you, John 13. 34 (*past*), I will
      never leave thee, Hebrews 13. 5 (*present*),
   I will come again and receive you, John
   14. 3 (*future*).                                    HYP.

# SUBJECTS FOR SPEAKERS AND STUDENTS.

## A Setting in Metre of John 3. 16.
1. The greatest *kindness* ever shown.
2. The greatest *offering* to atone.
3. The greatest *welcome* ever known.
4. The greatest *blessing* for your own. T.R.C.

## Points About Power (Psa. 62. 11).
1. Searching Power of the Word, ..    ..    Heb. 4. 12
2. Saving Power of the Gospel,   ..    ..    Rom. 1. 16
3. Keeping Power of God,     ..    ..    1 Peter 1. 5
4. Energising Power of the Spirit,    ..    Acts 1. 8
5. Resurrection Power of the Lord,    ..   1 Cor. 15. 43
W.J.M.

## Why Glory in the Cross?
1. It is the measure of man's guilt,   ..    Acts 3. 13-15
2. The manifestation of God's love,   ..    Rom. 5. 6-8
3. The means of salvation,    ..    ..   John 3. 14, 15
4. The mark of separation,    ..    ..    Gal. 6. 14
5. The motive to service, ..    ..   2 Cor. 5. 14, 15
6. The melody of Heaven,    ..    ..   Rev. 5. 8-10
F.F.

## Some Things About Myself.
1. My sin troubleth,    ..    ..    ..    Psa. 38. 3
2. My wounds stinketh,   ..    ..    ..    ,,    5
3. My heart panteth,    ..    ..    ..    ,,    10
4. My strength faileth,    ..    ..    ..    ,,    10
5. My friends forsaketh,    ..    ..    ..    ,,    11
6. My sorrow continueth, ..    ..    ..    ,,    17
7. MY LORD SAVETH,    ..    ..    ..    ,,    22
W.J.M.

## "Whom say ye?" (Matt. 16. 15).
1. "Thou art My beloved Son"—The Father,    ..    ..    ..    Mark 1. 11
2. "I am the Son of God"—The Lord Jesus, ..    ..    ..    ..    John 10. 36
3. "This is the Son of God"—The Baptist,   John 1. 34
4. "Thou art the Son of God,"—Nathaniel,   John 1. 49
5. "Thou art the Son of God"—Simon Peter,   John 6. 69
6. "Thou art the Son of God"—Martha,    John 11. 27
7. "This was the Son of God"—The Centurion,    ..    ..    ..    Matt. 27. 54
8. "Thou Son of God"—The Demons,    ..    Matt. 8. 29
Js. Fs.

# SUBJECTS FOR SPEAKERS AND STUDENTS.

## Three Phases of Acquaintance.

1. Christ's acquaintance with grief, - - Isa. 53. 3
2. Our acquaintance with God, - - - Job 22. 21
3. God's acquaintance with our ways, - Psa. 139. 3

T. B.

## A Study in Opposites.

1. Great trial of affliction, - - - - 2 Cor. 8. 2
2. Abundance of joy, - - - - - ,,
3. Deep poverty, - - - - - - ,,
4. Rich liberality, - - - - - ,,

H. K. D.

## "His Own."

1. His own will, - - - - - Eph. 1. 11
2. His own Son, - - - - - Rom. 8. 32
3. His own body, - - - - - 1 Peter 2. 24
4. His own blood, - - - - - Heb. 9. 12
5. His own sheep, - - - - - John 10. 3
6. His own servants, - - - - Matt. 25. 14
7. His own power, - - - - 1 Cor. 6. 14

G. H.

## Figures of the Word of God.

1. Compared to a hammer—to break, - - Jer. 23. 29
2. Compared to a fire—to melt, - - - Jer. 23. 29
3. Compared to a lamp—to shine, - - Psa. 119. 105
4. Compared to a sword—to smite, - - Heb. 4. 12
5. Compared to a mirror—to reveal, - - 2 Cor. 3. 12
6. Compared to food—to sustain, - - 1 Peter 2. 2
7. Compared to water—to cleanse, - Psa. 119. 9

Js. Fs.

## Threefold Power.

1. Of the Spirit, - - - - - Luke 4. 14
2. Of the Word, - - - - - Luke 4. 32
3. Of the Lord, - - - - - Luke 4. 36

W. J. M.

## A Threefold Doxology and Its Motives.

Blessed be the God and Father of our Lord Jesus Christ,
(1) 1 Peter 1. 3; (2) Ephesians 1. 3; (3) 2 Corinthians 1. 3,
R.V., who—

1. Hath begotten us, - - - - Regeneration
2. Hath blessed us, - - - - Beautification
3. Comforteth us, - - - - Consolation
1. Foundation, - - - The Resurrection of Christ
2. Source, - - - - Our Election *in* Christ
3. Purpose, - - - Sympathy with others, *by*
   Christ (verse 5). W. E. V.

# SUBJECTS FOR SPEAKERS AND STUDENTS.

## The Risen Christ.
### As seen in Matthew 28. 17-20.

1. An Important Fact—"He is Risen," - - v. 17
2. A Blessed Truth—"All power is given," - - v. 18
3. A Glorious Commission—"Go ye therefore," - v. 18
4. A Public Confession—"Baptising them," - v. 19
5. A Growing Experience—"Teaching them," - v. 20
6. A Divine Promise—"Lo, I am with you," - v. 20

G.H.

## The Ark.
A TYPE OF CHRIST.

Admitted free, Gen. 7. 1
Right welcome, Isa. 55. 1
Kept secure, - Gen. 7. 16

HYP.

## 4 "R's" in Phil. 4.

Registered, - - - v. 3
Rejoicing, - - - v. 4
Restful, - - - - v. 7
Rewarded, - - - v. 9

G.H.

## Nine Things Ready.

1. The sinner is ready to perish, - - Isa. 27. 13
2. Day of darkness is ready, - - - Job 15. 23
3. Destruction is ready, - - - - Job 18. 12
4. Christ is ready to judge quick and dead, 1 Peter 4. 5
5. God is ready to pardon, - - - Neh. 9. 17
6. Ready to forgive, - - - - Psa. 86. 5
7. Ready to save, - - - - Isa. 38. 20
8. The feast is ready, - - - - Luke 14. 17
9. They that were ready went in, - - Matt. 25. 10

N-B.

## A Christian's Exercise—Running.

1. A holy determination—
   "I will run," - - - - Psa. 99. 32
2. Personal attractions—
   "Draw me, we will run," - - Cant. 1. 4
3. Encouragement in the race—
   "Run and not weary," - - - Isa. 40. 31
4. Patience in the race—
   "Run with patience," - - - Heb. 12. 1
5. A safe place to run to—
   "A strong tower," - - - Prov. 18. 10
6. Some may run in vain—
   "Labouring in vain," - - - Phil. 2. 16
7. Reward to the runner—
   "So run," - - - - - 1 Cor. 9. 24

"That ye may *obtain.*"          HERBERT R. FRANCIS.

# SUBJECTS FOR SPEAKERS AND STUDENTS.

## Seven Signs of the Times.

1. Departure from the faith, - - - 1 Tim. 4. 1
2. Disobedience to parents, - - - 2 Tim. 3. 2
3. Despisers of good, - - - - 2 Tim. 3. 2
4. Devotion to pleasure, - - - 2 Tim. 3. 4
5. Denial of power of godliness, - - 2 Tim. 3. 5
6. Distress among nations, - - - Luke 21. 25
7. Downtrodden Jews arising, - - Luke 21. 24, 30

H.K.

## Three Glasses.

THE GLASS OF
1. Nature, - - James 1. 24
2. Knowledge, 1 Cor. 13. 12
3. Glory, - - 1 Cor. 3. 18

T. B.

## Hands.

Saviour's hand, Psa. 22. 16
Scarred hand, John 20. 27
Stretched hand, Prov. 1. 24
Shepherd's hand, John 10. 28

HYP.

## Scenes of Distress.

WHICH HAPPENED AFORETIME FOR OUR INSTRUCTION.

1. Moses with Israel, - - - - Num. 11. 15
2. Elijah with Jezebel, - - - - 1 Kings 19. 4
3. Job with Satan, - - - - Job 3. 3
4. David with Saul, - - - - 1 Sam. 27. 1
5. Jeremiah with Judah - - - Jer. 20. 14
6. Paul with the Gentiles, - - - 2 Cor. 1. 8
7. Christ in Gethsemane, - - - Mark 14. 34

JS. FS.

## The King and the Cripple.

HOW DAVID WELCOMED MEPHIBOSHETH (1 Sam. 9).

Worked out as an "Eyegate" Lesson on "*How to Make and Show* 100 *Eyegate Lessons*," page 17

1. The SOURCE.—He went in and sat before the Lord.
   (1) "According to Thine own heart" (2 Sam. 7. 18).
   (2) "For Jonathan's sake" (2 Sam. 9. 1).
2. The SUBJECT.—He was (1) Lost. David has to hunt for him. (2) Lame on both feet. (3) "Left." Well-nigh left altogether.
3. The STYLE.—(1) Powerfully. He sent and fetched him. (2) Peacefully. He said, "Fear not." (3) Perpetually. "Thou shalt eat bread of my table always."
4. The SEQUEL.—Two Mephibosheths. (1) Spared. (2) Hanged (1 Sam. 21. 7, 9). Which shall *you* be in Eternity?

HYP.

# SUBJECTS FOR SPEAKERS AND STUDENTS.

## The Compassion of Christ.

1. As "the good Samaritan," - - Luke 10. 30
2. The man with an unclean spirit, - Mark 5. 19
3. The leper, - - - - - Mark 1. 41
4. All that were sick, - - - - Matt. 14. 14
5. The blind men, - - - - Matt. 20. 30
6. Feeding the multitudes, - - - Matt. 15. 32
7. In caring for His people, - - Matt. 9. 36
8. To backsliders, - - - - Luke 15. 20

W.H.

## "I Wills" (Exod. 3).

1. The Lord's Proposal, - I will send thee, - - v. 10
2. The Lord's Presence, - I will be with thee, - v. 12
3. The Lord's Purpose, - I will bring you out, - v. 17
4. The Lord's Power, - I will stretch out my hand,
   v. 20
5. The Lord's Provision,- I will give this people favour,
   v. 21 H.K.D.

## The Perpetual Exercises of the Believer.

1. Set the Lord *always* before you, - - Psa. 16. 8
2. To be praying *always*, - - - Eph. 6. 18
3. *Always* triumphing in Christ, - - 2 Cor. 2. 14
4. *Always* magnifying Christ, - - - Phil. 1. 20
5. *Always* obeying the truth, - - - Phil. 2. 12
6. *Always* rejoicing in the Lord, - - Phil. 4. 4
7. *Always* ministering or adding to faith, 2 Peter 1. 15

A precious promise—"Lo, I am with you *alway*"
(Matt. 28. 20). F-T.

## "Right was the Pathway."

"So He bringeth them unto their desired haven," Psalm 107. 30.

Through the waters, - - - - Isa. 43. 2
Through the rivers, - - - - Isa. 43. 2
Through the fire, - - - - - Isa. 43. 2
Through the flood, - - - - Psa. 66. 6
Through the depths, - - - - Psa. 106. 9
Through the deserts, - - - - Isa. 48. 21
Through the darkness, - - - Job 29. 3
Through the great wilderness, - - Deut. 2. 7
Through the valley of the shadow of death, Psa. 23. 4

"With gladness and rejoicing shall they be brought:
they shall enter into the King's Palace" (Psa. 45. 15;
cp. 107. 30). N-B.

### Gifts in John.

1. Life—Salvation, - - John 10.11
2. The Spirit—Consolation, ,, 14. 16
3. Glory—Consummation, ,, 17. 22

W.T.R.

### Nehemiah.

1. Commissioned by the King, Neh. 2. 6
2. Chided by the Enemy, - ,, 2. 19
3. Constrained by his God , 2. 20

W.J.M.

### "That I may know Him."
(Phil. 3. 10).

1. We will run after Thee, - S. of S. 1. 4
2. We will rejoice in Thee, ,, ,,
3. We will remember Thy love, ,, ,,
4. I know whom I have believed, 2 Tim. 1. 12 W.J.M.

### Remember! Remember!

1. The Believer in Christ, - Luke 22. 19
2. The Backslider from Christ, Rev. 2. 5
3. The Stranger to Christ, - Luke 17. 32
4. The Banished from Christ, Luke 16. 25

G.H.

### Three Different Altars.

1. The Transgressor's Altar, - - - Exod. 20. 24
2. The Worshipper's Altar, - - - - Exod. 27. 1
3. The Backslider's Altar, - - 1 Kings 18. 30 JS. FS.

### Sent Ones.

I. The waiting one—"I heard the voice of the Lord saying, Whom shall I send?"

1. The ready one—Here am I, send me, - Isaiah 6. 8
2. The word to the sent one—Go, - - - Isa. 6. 8, 9

II. The waiting one is sent—"Go work."

1. His place appointed—In My vineyard, - Matt. 21. 28
2. His time arranged—To-day, - - - Matt. 21. 28

III. Workers must be—

1. Competent, - - - - 1 Chron. 9. 13; 12. 33
2. Wholehearted, - - - - Neh. 4. 6; 6. 3
3. Men of valour, - - - - 2 Chron. 32. 7, 8
4. Diligent, - - - - Ezra 7. 23; Neh. 4. 21
5. Vigilant, - - - - - Neh. 4. 11, 18
6. Not discouraged, - - - - Neh. 4. 11-14
7. Must look to God for results, - - Neh. 4. 20
8. Keep His honour in view, - - Neh. 5. 9; 6. 15
9. Give Him the glory, - - - Neh. 12. 27, 43

E. A. H.

# SUBJECTS FOR SPEAKERS AND STUDENTS.

## True Friendship for Christ.

Working for - - HIM - - Luke 10. 38, 40
Waiting upon - HIM - - Luke 10. 39, 42
Worshipping - - HIM - - John 12. 3 F. ss.

## "Hitherto" (1 Sam. 7. 12).

"EBENEZER—Hitherto hath the Lord helped us."

1. Divine Forbearance, - - - - Exod. 7. 16
2. Divine Forgiveness, - - - - Num. 14. 19
3. Divine Blessing, - - - - - Josh. 17. 14
4. Persevering Prayer, - - - - 1 Sam. 1. 16
5. Divine Help, - - - - - 1 Sam. 7. 12
6. Divine Guidance, - - - - - 2 Sam. 7. 18
7. Divine Support in Testing, - - - Psa. 71. 7

G.H.

## "Henceforth" (2 Tim. 4. 8).

"HENCEFORTH there is laid up for me a crown—and unto all."

1. Living for Christ, - - - - 2 Cor. 5. 15
2. Communion with Christ, - - - John 15. 15
3. Walking before Christ, - - - - Eph. 4. 17
4. Growth in Christ, - - - - - Eph. 4. 14
5. Service for Christ, - - - - Rom. 6. 6
6. Used by Christ, - - - - - Luke 5. 10
7. Rewarded by Christ, - - - - 2 Tim. 4. 8

G.H.

## Christ's Superiority.

No fewer than seven things are said about Christ in proof of His superiority.

1. Christ, the Heir—
   "Heir of all things," - - - - Heb. 1. 2
2. Christ, the Creator—
   "Through whom . . . made worlds," - ,, 2
3. Christ, the Revealer—
   "The effulgence—the very image," - ,, 3
4. Christ, the Sustainer—
   "Upholding all things," - - - ,, 3
5. Christ, the Redeemer—
   "Made purification for sins," - - ,, 3
6. Christ, the Ruler—
   "Sat down on the right hand," - - ,, 3
7. Christ, the Supreme—
   "Much better . . . more excellent," - ,, 4

"In all things Pre-eminent." DR. GRIFFITH THOMAS.

# SUBJECTS FOR SPEAKERS AND STUDENTS.

## "God for Us" (Rom 8. 31).

1. Loved by the Father, - - - 2 Thess. 2. 16
2. Blessed by the Father, - - - Eph. 1. 3
3. Chosen by the Father, - - - Eph. 1. 4
4. Predestinated by the Father, - - Eph. 1. 5
5. Drawn by the Father, - - - John 6. 44
6. Begotten by the Father, - - - 1 Peter 1. 3
7. Delivered by the Father, - - - Col. 1. 13

JS. FS.

## "Only."

1. Sinner's "only,"
   Mark 2. 7
2. Saviour's "only,"
   Mark 5. 36
3. Backslider's "only,"
   Psa. 51. 4
4. Worker's "only,"
   1 Sam. 7. 3
5. Soul's "only,"
   Psa. 62. 5
6. Devotion "only,"
   Acts 21. 13
7. Safety ''only,''
   Psa. 4. 8    S.E.B.

## Fullness of Power

1. Creating power,
   John 1. 3
2. Controlling power,
   Heb. 1. 3
3. Forgiving power,
   Matt. 9. 6
4. Sustaining Power,
   2 Tim. 4. 17
5. Preserving power,
   John 10. 28
6. Reigning Power,
   1 Pet. 3. 22
7. Coming power,
   Rev. 1. 7    S.E.B.

## The Better Ministry of Christ.

1. A Better Priest—
   "High Priest of good things," - - Heb. 9. 11
2. A Better Sanctuary—
   "A greater and more perfect tabernacle, ,, 11
3. A Better Sacrifice—
   "Not blood of goats and calves . . . His
   own blood, - - - - - ,, 12
4. A Better Method—
   Offering "once for all," - - - ,, 12
5. A Better Blessing—
   Having "obtained eternal redemption," ,, 12
6. A Better Guarantee—
   "The Eternal Spirit," - - - ,, 14
7. A Better Result—
   "Purge conscience . . . serve the living
   and true God," - - - - ,, 14

DR. GRIFFITH THOMAS.

# SUBJECTS FOR SPEAKERS AND STUDENTS.

## Things Done Quickly.

1. Turned aside quickly, - - - - Exod. 32. 8
2. Perish quickly, - - - - - Deut. 28. 20
3. Go out quickly, - - - - - Luke 14. 21
4. Behold, I come quickly, - - - Rev. 22. 12

N.B.

| **Four Similes** | **The Rock** | |
|---|---|---|
| Blacker than coal, Lam. 4.8 | Reliable, | - Heb. 13. 8 |
| Red as crimson, Isa. 1. 6 | Old, - | - 1 Cor. 10. 4 |
| White as wool, Isa. 1. 6 | Cleft, - | - 1 Cor. 2. 2 |
| Bright as gold, Rev. 21. 18 | Keeps - | - Jude 24 |

HYP.　　　　　　　　　　　HYP.

## The Holy Spirit of God.

He is called the Spirit of life, of truth, of grace, of adoption, of power, of comfort, and of holiness.

He strives with sinners, - - - Gen. 6. 3
He reproves (convicts) of sin, - - John 16. 8
He helps our infirmities, - - - Rom. 8. 26
He comforts - - - - - Acts 9. 31
He teaches, - - - - - John 14. 26
He guides, - - - - - John 16. 13
He sanctifies, - - - - - Rom. 15. 16
He testifies of Christ, - - - John 15. 26
He glorifies Christ, - - - - John 16. 14
He searches all things - - - 1 Cor. 2. 10
He worketh according to His own will, 1 Cor. 13. 11
He dwells in saints - - - - John 14. 17
He may be grieved, - - - - Eph. 4. 30
He may be vexed, - - - - Isa. 63. 10
He can be resisted, - - - - Acts 7. 51
He can be tempted, - - - - Acts 5. 9
He can be quenched, - - - 1 Thess. 5. 19

D. WARD

## "Before God"

1. Sinner's Condition before God, - Rom. 3. 19
2. Sinner's Plea before God, - - Lev. 4. 16
3. Believer's Sitting before God, - 2 Sam. 8. 17
4. Believer's Standing before God, - Gen. 18. 22
5. Believer's Walking before God, - Gen. 17. 1
6. Believer's Speaking before God, - Judges 11. 11
7. Believer's Appearing before God, - Psa. 84. 7

G.H.

# SUBJECTS FOR SPEAKERS AND STUDENTS.

## Even So.

1. Of submission, Matt. 11. 26
2. Of resurrection, 1 Thes. 4. 14
3. Of expectation, Rev. 22. 20
4. Of lamentation, - Rev. 1. 7
5. Of retribution, Rev. 16. 7
6. Of commission, John 20. 21
7. Of sustentation, 1 Cor. 9. 14

T. B.

## Things to Continue In.

1. His Word, - - John 8. 31
2. His love, - - John 15. 9
3. His grace, - - Acts 13. 42
4. The faith, - - Acts 14. 22
5. Prayer, - - - - Col. 4. 2
6. Brotherly love, Heb. 13. 1
7. Following the Lord,
1 Sam. 12. 14 W. J. M.

## Seven Precious Things for the Believer.

1. Saved, - - Acts 16. 31
2. Forgiven, - - Acts 13. 38
3. Justified, - - Acts 13. 39
4. Peace, - - - Rom. 5. 1
5. Eternal life, - 1 John 5. 11
6. Sealing by Holy Spirit, Eph. 1. 13
7. Glory with Christ, Col. 3. 4

If all the "shalls" in Scripture meant "perhaps,"
And all the "haths" meant simply "hope to have,"
I well might doubt.
But since the loving God means what He says, and cannot lie,
I trust His faithful word, and know that I
Shall surely dwell throughout eternity
With Him I dearly love, e'en Christ Himself.  J. W. H. N.

## My Saviour.

Luke 1. 47.

1. A personal Saviour,
Psa. 55. 16
2. A present Saviour,
Jer. 15. 20
3. A powerful Saviour,
Heb. 7. 25 W.

## Seven Things to Flee From.

1. Wrath to come, - Matt. 3. 7
2. Fornication, - 1 Cor. 6. 8
3. Idolatry, - - 1 Cor. 10. 14
4. Youthful lusts, 2 Tim. 2. 22
5. Strangers, - - John 10. 5
6. Mammon, - - 1 Tim. 6. 11
7. Persecution, Matt. 10. 23 T. B.

## Seven "I Wills" of Jehovah in Exodus 6.

1. I will bring you, - verse 6
2. I will rid you, - „ 6
3. I will redeem you, „ 6
4. I will take you, - „ 7
5. I will be to you, - „ 7
6. I will bring you, - „ 8
7. I will give to you, „ 8

Jehovah then signs His name as a guarantee of His grace to these wonderful promises, "I am the Lord."  G. S.

## Sins Against the Holy Spirit.

1. Despising Him,
Heb. 10. 28, 29
2. Resisting Him, -Acts 7. 51
3. Hardening heart against
Him, - - - Heb. 3. 7, 8
4. Lying to Him, - Acts 5. 3
5. Tempting Him, - Acts 5. 9
6. Grieving Him, Eph. 4. 30
7. Quenching Him, 1 Thes. 5. 19
"Take heed."  I-C.

# SUBJECTS FOR SPEAKERS AND STUDENTS.

## Christ's Complete Ministry.

### IN ITS THREEFOLD ASPECT ON EARTH AND IN HEAVEN.

1. The Sacrificial Work of Christ, - - Heb. 9. 23
2. The Priestly Work of Christ, - - ,, 24-26
3. The Kingly Work of Christ, - - ,, 27, 28

W.H.G.T.

## David "Giving Instruction"
### (*margin*),
### in Psalm 32 speaks of

1. Decline—"My bones waxed old," - - - v. 3
2. Discipline—"Thy hand was heavy upon me," v. 4
3. Decision—"I will confess my transgression," - v. 5
4. Deliverance—"In a time when Thou mayest be found," - - - - - - v. 6
5. Dependence—"Thou art my hiding-place," - v. 7

*The Witness.*

## The Course of Every Believer.

| | | | | | |
|---|---|---|---|---|---|
| ONCE | | | | | |
| Ruined, | - | - | - Col. 1. 13, | - | - In darkness |
| NOW | | | | | |
| Rescued, | - | - | - ,, 1. 13, | - | - Delivered |
| Redeemed, | - | - | - ,, 1. 14, | - | - By His Blood |
| Reconciled, | - | - | - ,, 1. 21, 22, | | - Through death |
| Rich, | - | - | - ,, 2. 2, | - | - All riches |
| Rooted, | - | - | - ,, 2. 7, | - | - In Him |
| Risen, | - | - | - ,, 2. 12; 3. 1, | - | - With Christ |
| FINALLY | | | | | |
| Rewarded, | | - | - ,, 3. 24, | - | - Ye shall receive |

S.E.D.

## A New Start.

1. A NEW MASTER.—"Ye call Me Master and Lord, and ye say well, for so I am" (John 13. 13).
2. A NEW POWER.—"Ye shall receive power" (Acts 1. 8).
3. A NEW OBJECT.—"He died for all, that they which live should not henceforth live unto themselves, but unto Him which died for them, and rose again" (2 Cor. 5. 15).
4. NEW DESIRES.—"Walk in the Spirit, and ye shall not fulfil the lusts of the flesh" (Gal. 5. 16).
5. NEW COMPANY.—"And being let go they went to their own company" (Acts 4. 23). W. B. WESTCOTT.

# SUBJECTS FOR SPEAKERS AND STUDENTS.

## Price—Proof—Possession.

1. The Blood of Jesus Christ, the Price of all, 1 Pet. 1. 2
2. The Resurrection of Jesus Christ, the Proof of all, - - - - - - 1 Pet. 1. 3
3. The Appearing of Jesus Christ, the Possession of all, - - - - - 1 Pet. 1. 7 G.H.

## Four Blessed Men.

1. Blessed is the man whose sins are forgiven, Psa. 32. 1
2. Blessed are the undefiled who walk in the way of the Lord, - - - - - Psa. 119. 1
3. Blessed are the dead who die in the Lord, - Rev. 14. 13
4. Blessed is he who hath part in the first resurrection, - - - - Rev. 20. 6 J.B.

## Four "Beholds."
### (Gen. 28.)

1. Behold a ladder, verse 12—God's only way, John 14. 6
2. Behold the angels, verse 12—God's active servants, - - - - - - Heb. 1. 14
3. Behold the Lord, verse 13—God's exalted Son, - - - - - - - Phil. 2. 9
4. Behold I am with thee, verse 15—God's precious promise, - - - Heb. 13. 5 W.J.M.

## God's Lamb in Evidence.

Where is the Lamb? - - - - - Gen. 22. 7
God will provide a Lamb, - - - - Gen. 22. 8
Behold the Lamb of God, - - - - John 1. 29
A Lamb without blemish, - - - - 1 Pet. 1. 19
A Lamb as it had been slain, - - - Rev. 5. 6
Elders fell down before the Lamb, - - Rev. 5. 8
Worthy is the Lamb that was slain, - - Rev. 5. 12
The Lamb opened one of the seals, - - Rev. 6. 1
Hide us from the wrath of the Lamb, - - Rev. 6. 16
A great multitude stood before the Lamb, - Rev. 7. 9
Salvation unto the Lamb, - - - - Rev. 7. 10
Washed their robes in the blood of the Lamb, Rev. 7. 14
Lamb slain from the foundation, - - - Rev. 13. 8
A Lamb stood on the Mount Sion, - - Rev. 14. 1
They follow the Lamb, - - - - Rev. 14. 4
Firstfruits unto God and the Lamb, - - Rev. 14. 4
And the Lamb shall overcome them, - - Rev. 17. 14
The marriage of the Lamb is come, - Rev. 19. 7
The Bride the Lamb's Wife, - - Rev. 21. 9 J.A.

# SUBJECTS FOR SPEAKERS AND STUDENTS.

## God First.
1. As a Sinner against God,   -  -  - Psa. 51. 4
2. As a Saint from God,   -  -  - - Psa. 5. 3
3. As a Servant toward God,   -  - - Acts 24. 16

JS. FS.

## A Sevenfold Spring of Christian Joy.
1. Joy in Believing,   -  -  -  - - 1 Pet. 1. 8
2. Joy in Abiding, -  -  -  -  - - John 15. 11
3. Joy in Asking,  -  -  -  -  - John 16. 24
4. Joy in Listening,  -  -  -  - John 17. 13
5. Joy in Obeying,  -  -  -  - John 13. 17
6. Joy in Suffering,   -  -  -  - Acts 5. 41
7. Joy in Finishing Well,   -  -  - Acts 20. 24

G-H.

## The Lesson of Elijah and Elisha.
Elijah and Elisha are taking the last walk together. Elijah is about to be taken. Elisha will carry on the work. But what leads to him getting the power (2 Kings 2).?
1. PREPARATION.—Gilgal, 1; Bethel, 2; Jericho, 4; Jordan, 6. These places gave a fitness, a moral preparation for the power.
2. PRAYER.—"Ask what I shall do for thee before I be taken from thee" (v. 9).
3. PROMISE (v. 10).—"If ye see me when I am taken from thee."
4. POSSESSION (vv. 14, 15). Spirit rests on Elisha. S.E.D.

## Perfect Salvation.
### Hebrews 7. 25.
1. ABILITY—"He is able to save" (7. 25); able to sympathise (4. 15); to succour (2. 18); make stand (Rom. 14. 4); to stablish (Rom. 16. 25); to keep from falling, to present faultless (Jude 24); build up (Acts 20. 32); to subdue (Phil. 3. 21); to do exceedingly abundantly (Eph. 3. 20).
2. ACTIVITY—"able to keep on saving" (*literal translation*, past—present—future).
3. ASSURANCE—"He ever liveth to make intercession. For unsaved, His work on *earth*; for saved, His work in Heaven.
4. APPROACH—"Them that come to God by Him" (*literally*, "them that draw near," or, "them that come right up.")

DR. GRIFFITH THOMAS.

# SUBJECTS FOR SPEAKERS AND STUDENTS.

## What Peniel was to Jacob and is to us.

### Power with God and man (Gen. 32. 24).

1. The place of solitude, - - - Gen. 32. 24
2. The place of subjection, - - - Gen. 32. 25
3. The place of supplication, Gen. 32. 26; Hosea 12. 4 H. K. D

## The Servant of Jehovah.

### "The Son of Man came not to be ministered unto, but to minister" (Mark 10. 45).

1. He made Himself of no reputation, - - Phil. 2. 7
2. He was obedient unto death, - - - Phil. 2. 8
3. He was faithful in His preaching, - - Luke 13. 3
4. He was fervent in prayer, - - - Mark 14. 35
5. He honoured the Word of God, - - Luke 4. 14
6. He was substitutionary in His doctrine, - John 10. 11
7. His supreme aim was the salvation of precious souls, - - - - John 4. 10 R. L.

## "Hopelessly Incurable."

1. THE HEAD—The whole head is sick - Isa. 1. 5
2. THE EYES—Which have eyes, and see not, Jer. 5. 21
3. THE EARS—Which have ears, and hear not, Jer. 5. 21
4. THE THROAT—Their throat is an open sepulchre, - - - - - Rom. 3. 13
5. THE TONGUE—With their tongue they have used deceit, - - - - Rom. 3. 13
6. THE LIPS—The poison of asps is under their lips, - - - - - Rom. 3. 13
7. THE MOUTH—Whose mouth is full of cursing and bitterness, - - - Rom. 3. 14
8. THE NECK—Stiffnecked, - - - Acts 7. 51
9. THE HEART—Deceitful above all things, and desperately wicked, - - - Jer. 17. 9
10. THE HANDS—Wicked, - - - - Acts 2. 23
11. THE LEGS—Not equal, - - - - Prov. 26. 7
12. THE FEET—Swift to shed blood, - - Rom. 3. 15
13. THE GENERAL CONSTITUTION—From the sole of the foot even unto the head there is no soundness in it; but wounds, and bruises, and putrifying sores : they have not been closed, neither bound up, neither mollified with ointment, - - Isa. 1. 5, 6 J. H. E.

# SUBJECTS FOR SPEAKERS AND STUDENTS.

## Judgments of the New Testament.

1. Judgment of the Sinner, predicted (Heb. 9. 27; Eccles. 11. 9; 2 Peter 2. 2-4; Heb. 10. 27).
2. Judgment of the Believer, past (John 5. 24, R.V.; Rom. 8. 1; Gal. 2. 20).
3. Judgment of the Servant, future (2 Cor. 5. 10; Rev. 22. 12; Col. 3. 24, 25; 1 Cor. 4. 1-5).
4. There is no such thing as a general judgment taught in Scripture.                                                  N.Z.T.

## On Taking.

1. Take the *cup*, - - - - - Psa. 116. 13
      Implying Salvation.
2. Take *My yoke*, - - - Matt. 11. 29
      Implying Service.
3. Take *away* the stone, - - John 11. 39
      Implying Stumbling-blocks.
4. Take *up* the Cross, - - - Matt. 16. 24
      Implying Suffering.
5. Take *hold* of My strength, - - Isa. 27. 5
      Implying Sufficiency.
6. Take *with* your words, - - Hosea 14. 2
      Implying Prayer.
7. Take *no* thought for your life, - - Matt. 6. 25
      Implying Faith.                                                    J.S.

## Moses, the Man of Faith.

Note some of his characteristics in Hebrews 11—
1. Courageous Love—
      "They saw he was a proper child, - - - v. 23
2. Definite Refusal—
      "When he was come to discretion," - - v. 24
3. Deliberate Preference—
      "To suffer affliction," - - - - - v. 25
4. Careful Consideration—
      "The reproach of the Messiah," - - - v. 26
5. Clear Prospect—
      "The recompense of the reward," - - v. 26
6. Wholehearted action—
      "He forsook—he endured," - - - - v. 27
7. Simple obedience—
      "He kept the Passover," - - - - v. 28
                                        DR. GRIFFITH THOMAS.

# SUBJECTS FOR SPEAKERS AND STUDENTS.

## Onesimus, the Slave.

1. A runaway slave,    -    -    -    -    -Phile. 11-15
2. A regenerated man, -    -    -    -    -Phile. 10
3. A reliable servant,  -    -    -    -    -Phile. 13
4. A respected brother,-    -    Phile. 16; Col. 4. 9.  W. J. M.

| A Threefold Confession. | The Four Leprous Men. |
|---|---|
| 1. The sinner of his sins, Prov. 28. 13 | Consultation, -    - 2 Kings 7. 3 |
| | Consideration,    - 2 Kings 7. 4 |
| 2. The saint of his Saviour, Rom. 10. 9 | Decision, -    -    - 2 Kings 7. 5 |
| | Salvation, -    -    - 2 Kings 7. 8 |
| 3. The servant of his sovereign, Matt. 10. 32  G. H. | Proclamation,    - 2 Kings 7. 9 |
| | H. K. D. |

## The King and the Cripple.

SEVEN STEPS, or the Kindness of God (2 Sam. 9).

1. Fallen,    -    -    -    -    -    -    - 2 Sam. 4. 4
2. Fatherless,    -    -    -    -    -    - 1 Sam. 31. 2
3. Friendless,    House of Saul, -    -    - 2 Sam. 9. 1
4. Famished,    Lo-debar (Place of no    2 Sam. 9. 4
         pastime).
5. Fetched, -    Then King David sent and    2 Sam. 9. 5
         fetched him.
6. Favoured,    I will surely show thee kind-    2 Sam. 9. 7
         ness for Jonathan thy
         Father's sake.
7. Fed for his {He did eat continually at}2 Sam. 9. 7-13
   Father's sake { the King's table. }
                                             J. M.

## Wisdom for the Worried.

A poetical study for repeating in home or meeting.

Why should I "careful" be, when God has
    said to me    -    -    -    -    -    - Phil. 4. 6
That everything is working for the best ?  - Rom. 8. 28
Though He my faith may try, He shall my
    need supply :    -    -    -    -    - Phil. 4. 19
His promise gives me solid, perfect rest,    - Heb. 10. 23
Relying on *His* care, He will my sorrows
    share,    -    -    -    -    -    -    - 1 Pet. 5. 7
And "good things" He will surely send
    along,    -    -    -    -    -    -    - Psa. 84. 11
Each day I'm bound to tell, He "doeth *all*
    things well :"    -    -    -    -    - Mark 7. 37.
He only is my Comfort and my Song, Psa. 118. 14  W. T. R.

# SUBJECTS FOR SPEAKERS AND STUDENTS.

## The Forgiveness of Sins.

1. The Message, - - - - - Acts 13. 38
2. The Source, - - - - - Acts 5. 31
3. The Ground, - - - - - 1 John 2. 12
4. The Means, - - - - - Col. 1. 14
5. The Condition, - - - - - 1 John 1. 9
6. The Extent, - - - - - Col. 2. 13
7. The Measure, - - - - - Eph. 1. 7
8. The Result, - - - - - Eph. 4. 32

I.W.P.

## "Kept by the Power of God"
### (1 Peter 1. 5).

If we are kept by the power of God we shall be—

| | | | |
|---|---|---|---|
| Kept safe | - Deut. 32. 10 | Kept always | - Isa. 27. 3 |
| Kept up | - Psa. 91. 11 | Kept for Christ | Jude 1, R.V. |
| Kept back | - Psa. 19. 13 | Kept in - | - Psa. 31. 20 |
| Kept on | - 1 Sam. 2. 9 | Kept under | - 1 Cor. 9. 27 |
| Kept through | - Luke 8. 15 | Kept shut | - Psa. 141. 3 |
| Kept clean | - John 17. 11 | Kept quiet | - Isa. 26. 3 |
| Kept in order | - Jer. 31. 10 | Kept separate | John 17. 15 |

W-W.

## Preaching Christ.

"Christ Jesus came into the world to save sinners" (1 Tim. 1. 15).

1. WHO.
   (1) Luke 2. 11, *Christ*—Jehovah—Anointed One, Creator, I am, Exodus 3. 14. Yesterday, to-day, etc. Genesis 12. 8. Joel 2. 32.
   (2) Luke 1. 31, *Jesus*. Saviour—Name of Man— Jesus of Nazareth.
2. WHERE.
   (1) *"Came . . . world."* Planet—Society of Men.
   (2) Condescension. Glory. Birth Manger.
   (3) Truth of Statement. Effects of. Importance of.
3. WHY.
   (1) *"To Save"* . . . call Name Jesus. Bodily— Health and Spiritual salvation—went about doing good.
   (2) Cause of Journey of 2.
4. WHAT. *Sinners*—not righteous, seek and save lost.
5. WHEN. Make appeal—recapitulate 1-4 and make Personal.

G.H.H.

# SUBJECTS FOR SPEAKERS AND STUDENTS.

## Little Things, and their Lessons.

1. The ants—The wisdom of preparation,   - Prov. 30. 25
2. The coney—The necessity for precaution, - Prov. 30. 26
3. The locusts—The secret of power,   -   - Prov. 30. 27
4. The spider—The fruits of perseverance,   - Prov. 30. 28

H. K. D.

## Love and Hate in Psalm 119.

1. I love Thy law,   -   -   -   - verses 97, 113, 163
2. I love Thy testimonies, -   -   -   ,,   119, 167
3. I love Thy commandments,   -   - verse 127
4. I love Thy precepts,   -   -   -   ,,   159
5. I hate the double-minded,   -   -   ,,   113, R.V.
6. I hate every false way, -   -   -   ,,   128
7. I hate falsehood,   -   -   - verse 163, R.V.   W. W. F.

## A Gospel Study of Zacchæus.

1. A rich man unsatisfied,   -   -   -   - Luke 19. 2
2. An anxious man hindered,   -   -   - Luke 19. 3
3. An earnest man in a hurry,   -   -   - Luke 19. 4
4. An obedient man brought down,   -   - Luke 19. 6
5. A genuine convert—He received Jesus,   - Luke 19. 6
6. A happy man—" Joyful in the Lord,"   - Luke 19. 6
7. A real man—He owns Jesus as Lord and
   manifests a change,   -   -   Luke 19. 8   W. J. M

## The Father's Seven Gifts to His Son.

1. John 17. 2, Authority or power over all—
   His position,   -   -   - Matt. 11. 27
2. John 17. 4, The work to do—His Mission,   John 1. 8
3. John 17. 6, The men out of the world—
   His people,   -   -   - John 6. 37-40
4. John 17. 7, All things whatsoever — His
   endowments,   -   -   - John 3. 35
5. John 17. 8, Sayings or words to give unto
   them—His message -   - John 7. 16
6. John 17. 22, The glory of Redemption
   Work—His reward,   -   - 2. Thess. 1. 10
7. John 17. 24, The glory of Eternal Creator-
   ship—His pre-eminence,   - Col. 1. 18

As the Obedient Son He acquired a glory which He shares with His own.

As the Co-Eternal Son He has an essential glory which is incommunicable.   F. S. B.

# SUBJECTS FOR SPEAKERS AND STUDENTS.

## The Result of Being Faithful.

1. Abraham was BLESSED,    ..    ..    Gen. 24. 35
   "A faithful man shall abound with
   blessings" (Prov. 28. 20).
2. Daniel was PRESERVED,    ..    ..    Dan. 6. 22
   "The Lord preserveth the faithful"
   (Psa. 31. 23).
3. Paul will be REWARDED,    ..    ..    Matt. 25. 21
   "There is laid up for me a crown"
   (2 Tim. 4. 8).
   Be thou faithful (Rev. 2. 10).      W.J.M.

## Wonderful Openings.

SURE PURPOSE—"To open blind eyes," ..    Isa. 42. 7
SWEET PROMISE—"Open the windows of
     Heaven,"    ..    ..    ..    ..    Mal. 3. 10
SOLEMN PROSPECT—"I will open your
     graves,"    ..    ..    ..    ..    Ezek. 37. 12
SAD PRAYER—"Lord, Lord, open to us,"   Matt. 25. 11
     W.T.R.

## Three Characters in Acts 12.

| | | |
|---|---|---|
| Herod | Stretched out his hand, .. | Acts 12. 1 |
| | Slew James, .. .. .. | Acts 12. 2 |
| | Sentenced the soldiers, .. | Acts 12. 19 |
| The Angel | Shined in the prison, .. .. | Acts 12. 7 |
| | Smote Peter, .. .. .. | Acts 12. 7 |
| | Spoke to Peter, .. .. | Acts 12. 8 |
| Peter was | Prisoner, .. .. .. | Acts 12. 4 |
| | Prayed for, .. .. .. | Acts 12. 5 |
| | Preserved, .. .. .. | Acts 12. 19 |

Js.Fs.

## God's Great Love.

ANOTHER SETTING OF IMMORTAL JOHN 3. 16.

1. For God   ..    ..    ..    God is love.
2. so loved   ..    ..    ..    Fact of His love.
3. the world,..    ..    ..    Object of His love.
4. that He gave   ..    ..    Proof of His love.
5. His only begotten Son, ..   Son of His love.
6. that whosoever   ..    ..    Scope of His love.
7. believeth in Him..    ..    Simple term of His love.
8. should not perish,    ..    Prevention of His love.
9. but have everlasting life.    Provision of His love.
     J.B.G.

# SUBJECTS FOR SPEAKERS AND STUDENTS.
## Three Days.
1. DEATH—Unknown, - - - - - Gen. 27. 2
2. SALVATION—Now, - - - - - 2 Cor. 6. 2
3. JUDGMENT—Appointed, - - Acts 26. 28 H. K. D.

## Seven Trumpets.
1. Law, - - - Exod. 19. 16
2. Gathering, - - Num. 10. 2
3. Journeying, - Num. 10. 5
4. Victory, - - Josh. 6. 4;
Num. 10. 9; Judges 7. 18
5. Joy, Psa. 98. 6; Num. 10. 19;
2 Chron. 29. 2
6. Warning, - - Ezek. 33. 3
7. Christ's coming, 1 Cor. 15. 52;
1 Thess. 4. 16 N.

## Jeremiah's Questions.
1. RUIN—*How* canst thou say I am not polluted? - - - - - - Jer. 2. 23
2. REDEMPTION—*How* shall I pardon thee? - Jer. 5. 7
3. REGENERATION—*How* shall I put thee among the children? - - - - Jer. 3. 19
4. RETRIBUTION—*How* wilt thou do in the swelling of Jordan? - - Jer. 12. 5 W. J. M.

## Threefold Deliverance.
1. Deliverance from demons, - - - Mark 5. 1-20
Sin utterly shameless. No outward chain could bind him; deliverance must come from inside. Legalism cannot save.
2. Deliverance from disease, - - - -Mark 5. 25-34
The touch of faith brought deliverance immediately, - - - - -Mark 5. 27-29
3. Deliverance from death, - - Mark 5. 22-24, 35-43
Contact with Christ means life. W. R.

## God's Five Calls to Repentance.
1. Lack of necessities—Yet have ye not returned unto Me, - - - - - Amos 4. 6
2. Envious surroundings—Yet have ye not returned unto Me, - - - - Amos 4. 7-8
3. Reversal of prosperity—Yet have ye not returned unto Me, - - - - Amos 4. 9
4. Bereaving visitation—Yet have ye not returned unto Me, - - - - Amos 4. 10
5. Marvellous providences—Yet have ye not returned unto Me, - - - - Amos 4. 11
Finally, " PREPARE TO MEET THY GOD." F. S. B.

# SUBJECTS FOR SPEAKERS AND STUDENTS.

## Peter's Three Sleeps.

1. The sleep of unripe experience,      ..      Luke 9. 32
2. The sleep of unfaithful life,    ..    ..    Mark 14. 37
3. The sleep of unquestioning trust,    ..    Acts 12. 6

W. H. GRIFFITH THOMAS.

## "Abounding."

What *shall* abound?—"*Iniquity* shall abound," Matt. 24. 12
What *should* abound?—"Increase, and abound
     in *love*,    ..    ..    ..    ..    1 Thess. 3. 12
What *does* abound?—"God is able to make
     all *grace* abound,"    ..    ..    2. Cor. 9. 8

W.T.R.

## Daily Grace for Daily Living.

1. Grace that bringeth salvation,    ..    Titus 2. 11
2. Grace that teaches us how to live,    ..    Titus 2. 12
3. Grace that gives us a song,    ..    ..    Col. 3. 16
4. Grace that gives strength and courage,    2 Tim. 2. 1
5. Grace to enable us to serve God with
     acceptance,    ..    ..    ..    Heb. 12. 28
6. Grace that makes us grow,    ..    ..    2 Peter 3. 18
7. Grace in abundance to make us victors, Rom. 5. 20, 21

T.H.

## The Scriptures.

1. The Lord Jesus OPENING,    ..    ..    Luke 24. 32
2. The Lord Jesus EXPOUNDING, ..    ..    Luke 24. 27
3. The Lord Jesus FULFILLING,    Luke 4. 21; John 19. 36
4. The Lord Jesus COMMENDING, ..    ..    John 10. 35
5. Saints SEARCHING,    ..    ..    ..    Acts 17. 11
6. Servants KNOWING,    ..    ..    ..    2 Tim. 3. 15
7. Sinners IGNORING,    ..    ..    ..    2 Peter 3. 16

W.J.M.

## "The True Sayings of God"
### (Rev. 19. 9; 22. 6).

1. The True God, John 17. 3; 1 John 5. 20..The SOURCE.
2. The True Grace of God, 1 Peter 5. 12..The SALVATION.
3. The True Riches, Luke 16. 11    ..    The SUPPLIES.
4. The True Bread, John 6. 32      .. The SUSTENANCE.
5. The True Light, John 1. 9; 1 John 2. 8..The SUNSHINE.
6. The True Tabernacle, Heb. 8. 2..The SECRET PLACE.
7. The True Worshippers, John 4. 23..The SONGS OF SAINTS.
8. The True Heart, Heb. 10. 22..The SPRINKLED HEART.
9. The True Holiness, Eph. 4. 24..The SPIRITUAL CON-
     DITION.      J.M.

# SUBJECTS FOR SPEAKERS AND STUDENTS.

## Three Onlys.

1. He only, - - Psa. 62. 2
2. They only, - Psa. 62. 4
3. Thou only, - Psa. 62. 5

W. J. M.

## Three States of Grace.

1. Past, - - - 2 Cor. 1. 10
2. Present, - - 2 Cor. 1. 10
3. Future, - - 2 Cor. 1. 10

W. J.

## Exhortations and Answers.

THREE EXHORTATIONS TO CHOOSE.

1. Whom will ye serve?
   Josh. 24. 15
2. How long halt ye?
   1 Kings 18. 21
3. Whether of the two will ye?
   Matt. 27. 21

AND THE THREE ANSWERS.

1. We will serve the Lord,
   Josh. 24. 17
2. The people answered him
   not a word, 1 Kings 18. 21
3. They said, "Barabbas,"
   Matt. 27. 21 H. P., Jr.

## Bible Robes.

1. A scarlet robe (Matt. 27. 28), - A rejected king
2. A long robe (Luke 20. 46), - - A religious hypocrite
3. The best robe (Luke 15. 22), - - A returned prodigal
4. A white robe (Rev. 7. 9), - - A redeemed person
5. A clean robe (Rev. 19. 7), - - A rejoicing bride
6. A red robe (Rev. 19. 13), - - A ruling king H. K. D.

## The Bride.

1. Before the kingdom,
   Rev. 19. 7
2. During the kingdom,
   Rev. 21. 9
3. After the kingdom,
   Rev. 21. 2 W. W. F.

## I Shall Not Be Moved.

1. The sinner's false confidence, - - - Psa. 10. 6
2. The saint's false confidence,
   Psa. 30. 6
3. The saint's true confidence,
   Psa. 16. 8 W. W. F.

## The Lord was Anointed Three Times, each Time by a Woman.

FIRST—In Simon the Pharisee's house, the early part of His ministry. His feet anointed, - - - - - - Luke 7. 37

SECOND—Six days before the Passover at Bethany by Mary, the sister of Lazarus and Martha. His feet, - - - - Thess. 12

THIRD—Two days before the Passover at Bethany, the house of Simon the leper, by a woman (no name given, might have been Mary first at the temple). His head, His body, - - - - - - Mark 14 D. M.

125

# SUBJECTS FOR SPEAKERS AND STUDENTS.

## A Memorable Text
" There they crucified Him" (Luke 23. 33).

There - The PLACE, - - Calvary.
They - The PEOPLE, - Hebrew, reek and Roman
Crucified The PUNISHMENT, Gentile form.
Him - The PERSON, - Immanuel. JS. FS.

## The Satan-Bound Woman.

1. Her condition, Mark 5.25
2. Her concern, - ,, 26
3. Her conviction, ,, 28
4. Her cure, - - ,, 29
5. Her confession, ,, 33
6. Her comfort, ,, 34

D. WARD.

## Names of God.

1. God of Patience,
   Rom. 15. 5
2. God of Hope,
   Rom. 15. 13
3. God of Love,
   2 Cor. 13. 11
4. God of All Comfort,
   2 Cor. 1. 3
5. God of Peace,
   Phil. 4. 9
6. God of All Grace,
   1 Peter 5. 10
7. God of Glory,
   Acts 7. 2   H.K.D.

## Seven Very Great "Blessings."

GOD HATH

1. Forgiven us, Eph. 4. 32
2. Chosen us, 2 Thess. 2. 13
3. Made us meet,
   Col. 1. 12, 13
4. Translated us,
   Col. 1. 12, 13
5. Delivered us,
   Col. 1. 12, 13
6. Made us accepted,
   Eph. 1. 6
7. Sent the spirit of His
   Son into our hearts,
   Gal. 4. 6

Look these verses up, "name them" again and again until they are your own, and then you will be able to sing with heart and understanding:

" Count your many blessings,
Name them one by one,
And it will surprise you
What the Lord hath done." S.T.

## "Thine are we David"
(1 Chron. 12. 18) indicates

1. Decision of heart—"Thine are we." Creation and Redemption urge us to like surrender.

2. Definite choice of sides—"on thy side." Two sides then; two to-day—no compromise. Do not only enjoy the grapes brought home by Caleb and Joshua; go and gather some for yourself.

3. Deliberate adhesion to David—"Thou son of Jesse." " Who is on the Lord's side?" A. MACE.

# SUBJECTS FOR SPEAKERS AND STUDENTS.

## What God Does.

1. Searches us, - Psa. 17. 2
2. Sustains us, - Psa. 17. 5
3. Saves us, - Psa. 17. 7
4. Shelters us, - Psa. 17. 8
5. Satisfies us, - Psa. 17. 15

H. K. D.

## Jesus Turned

1. To a following multitude,
   Luke 14. 25
2. To a backsliding disciple,
   Luke 22. 61
3. To an impulsive disciple,
   Matt. 16. 23
4. To a trembling believer,
   Mark 5. 30  C.

## Six Cities of Refuge.

Joshua 20. 7, 8.

1. Kedish—holy, 2 Cor. 5. 21
2. Shechem—shoulder,
   Luke 15. 5
3. Hebron—friendship,
   Prov. 18. 24
4. Bezer—stronghold,
   Psa. 31. 3
5. Ramoth—high place,
   Hab. 3. 19
6. Golan—happy,
   Prov. 16. 20  J. R. B.

## Witnesses to Christ.

1. The Father, - John 8. 18
2. The Son, - - ,, 8. 18
3. The Holy Spirit, ,, 15. 26
4. The Holy Scrip-
   tures, - - - , 5. 39
5. The Baptist, - ,, 1. 15
6. The Works of
   Christ, - - ,, 5. 36
7. The Prophets, - Acts 10. 43
8. The Believer, - ,, 1. 8

J. M. H.

## The Godly.

THREE REFERENCES TO THE
GODLY IN PSALMS.

1. The Godly set apart, - 4. 3
2. The Godly at prayer, 32. 6
3. The Godly translated, 12. 1

T. B.

## "It is Good."

FIVE TIMES "IT IS GOOD" IN
THE PSALMS,

1. God's Name, - - 52. 9
2. To draw near to God, 73. 28
3. To give thanks, - - 92. 1
4. To have been afflic-
   ted, - - - 119. 71
5. To sing praises, - 147. 1

T. B.

## Five Downward Steps.

1. They soon for-
   got His works, Psa. 106. 13
2. They forgot God, ,, 21
3. They joined them-
   selves also unto
   Baalpeor, - - ,, 28
4. They learned their
   works, - - - ,, 35
5. They were defiled
   with their own
   works, - - - ,, 39

H. C. H.

## Andrew, i.e., Manly.

A LIFE STUDY.

1. His occupation, Mark 1. 16
2. His call, - - ,, 1. 17
3. His discipleship, John 1. 37
4. His ordination, Mark 3. 14
5. His first service, John 1. 14
6. His desire to learn,
   Mark 13. 31
7. His activity, John 6. 8, 9
8. His fellowship, John 12. 22
9. His continuance, Acts 1. 14
10. His joint testimony,
    Acts 2. 14  S. J. S.

# SUBJECTS FOR SPEAKERS AND STUDENTS.

## A Great Salvation.
### Psalm 18. 16-19.

1. The original source,   -  -   Above
2. The loving method,   -  -   Took and drew
3. The personal aspect,   -  -   Me
4. The grand end,   -  -  -   A large place H.K.D.

## Daily Hints.
### Well worth noting by all the Lord's people.

Do all the Good you can,  - - -  - Eccles. 9. 10
In all the Ways you can,  - - -  - Matt. 5. 16
To all the People you can, -  - -  Gal. 6. 10
In every Place you can,  - - -  Acts 10 38
At all the Times you can, -  - -  - 1 Cor. 15. 58
In the Quietest way you can,  - -  - Matt. 6. 34
As Long as ever you can,  - - -  Rev. 2. 10 v.

## Seven Things about "His Son."

1. The nearness of His relationship,  -  Heb. 1. 2, 5, 8
2. The word of His power, -  - - - -  - 3
3. The excellence of His name,  - - -  - 4
4. The duration of His throne,  - - - -  - 8
5. The sceptre of His kingdom,  - - - -  - 8
6. The unchangeableness of His person,  - -  - 11
7. The triumph of His cause,  - -  - 13 H. K. D.

## The Sin Question in 1 John.

1. A bold profession, 1 John 1. 8—No sin.
2. A self-deceiver, 1 John 1. 8—Deceive ourselves.
3. A false position, 1 John 1. 8—Truth not in us.
4. A necessary confession, 1 John 1. 9—Confess our sin.
5. A complete absolution, 1 John 1. 9—Forgive and cleanse
6. An important admonition, 1 John 2. 1—Sin not.
7. A gracious provision, 1 John 2. 1—If we sin. H.K.D.

## Seven Great Clusters.

1. The Great GOD,  - - - - -  God
2. The Great LOVE,  - - - - -  so loved
3. The Great COMPANY,  - - -  the world
4. The Great GIFT,  - -  His only begotten Son
5. The Great INVITATION, - -  whosoever believeth
6. The Great DELIVERANCE,  -  - should not perish
7. The Great INHERITANCE,  -  - Everlasting Life

# SUBJECTS FOR SPEAKERS AND STUDENTS.

## Threefold Glory of Christ.

Dayspring (Luke 1), - - - - Incarnation
Daysman (Job 33), - - - - Reconciliation
Daystar (2 Peter 1), - - - - Satisfaction G. H.

## Three Great Facts.

The Word in the beginning, - - - John 1. 1
The Light in the world, - - - - John 1. 9
The Son in the bosom, - - John 1. 18 W. J. M.

## Sound Doctrine concerning

1. Salvation of sinners, - - - - 1 Tim. 1. 15
2. Inspiration of Bible, - - - - 2 Tim. 3. 16
3. Incarnation of Christ, - - - - 1 Tim. 3. 16
4. Condition of last days, - - - - 1 Tim. 4. 1
5. Intercession for all men, - - - - 1 Tim. 2. 1
6. Position of women, - - - - - 1 Tim. 2. 9
7. Qualifications of overseers, - 1 Tim. 3. 1 H. K. D.

Avoid "any other thing that is contrary to sound doctrine" (1 Tim. 1. 10).

## Acquaintance with God.
(Job. 22. 21.)

1. Present, - Now.
2. Personal, - Thyself.
3. Peaceful, - Be at peace.
4. Profitable, - Good shall come. H. K. D.

## Eight Simons.

1. Simon Peter, Matt. 10. 2
2. Simon the Canaanite, Matt. 10. 4
3. Simon of Mary and Joseph, - Matt. 13. 55
4. Simon of Cyrene, Matt. 27. 32
5. Simon the Leper, Mark 14. 3
6. Simon the Pharisee, Luke 7. 40
7. Simon the Sorcerer, Acts 8. 9
8. Simon a Tanner, Acts 9. 43 T. B.

## Characteristics of God.

1. Slow to anger, Neh. 9. 17
2. Ready to forgive, Psa. 86. 5
3. Mighty to save, Isa. 63. 1
H. K. D.

## A Full Salvation.

Sin covered, - - Psa. 32. 1
Sinner clothed, - Isa. 61. 10
Saint crowned, - Zech. 3. 5

## Examples of Prayer.

1. The Pharisee's, Luke 18. 11, 12
2. The Publican's, Luke 18. 13
3. The Penitent's, Luke 23. 42
4. The Poor-Rich Man's, Luke 16. 24
5. The Professor's, Luke 13. 25, 26
6. The Pig-feeder's, Luke 8. 28
7. A Possessor's, Luke 8. 33

# SUBJECTS FOR SPEAKERS AND STUDENTS.

## No Difference, and Yet a Difference.

| | | | |
|---|---|---|---|
| No difference declared, | - | - | - - Rom. 3. 23 |
| A great difference made, | - | - | - - Exod. 8. 23 |
| A vast difference seen, | - | - | - Exod. 11. 7 G. H. |

| Our Calling as | Love that is |
|---|---|
| Sons, - - - - 1 John 3. 1 | Commended, - Rom. 5. 8 |
| Saints, - - - Rom. 1. 7 | Changeless, - - John 13. 1 |
| Servants, - - - 1 Pet. 2. 16 | Continuous, - - Jer. 31. 3 |
| Sufferers, - - - 1 Pet. 2. 21 | Constraining, - 2 Cor. 5. 14 |
| W. T. R. | W. T. R. |

## Things Which May Be Despised.

1. The riches of God's goodness, - - - Rom. 2. 4
2. The chastening of the Lord, - - - Heb. 12. 5
3. One of Christ's little ones, - - - Matt. 18. 10
4. The Church of God, - - - - 1 Cor. 11. 22
5. Prophecy, - - - - - - 1 Thess. 5. 20
6. Self-righteous people despise others, - Luke 18. 9
7. Servants may despise masters, - - 1 Tim. 6. 2 T. B.

| Seven Mary's. | Living Things. |
|---|---|
| 1. The Virgin Mary, Luke 1. 26, 27 | 1. Living Water, John 4. 10, 11 |
| 2. Mary Magdalene, John 20. 1 | 2. Living Way, - Heb. 10. 20 |
| 3. Mary of Bethany, John 11. 1 | 3. Living Word, Heb. 4. 12; 1 Pet. 1. 23 |
| 4. Mother of James, Matt. 27. 56 | 4. Living Stone, - 1 Pet. 2. 4 |
| 5. Wife of Cleophas, John 19. 25 | 5. Living Stones, 1 Pet. 2. 5 |
| 6. Mother of Mark, Acts 12. 12 | 6. Living Sacrifice, Rom. 12. 1 |
| 7. Mary of Rome, Rom. 16. 6 | 7. Living Epistles, 2 Cor. 3. 3 |
| T. B. | H. K. D. |

## A Model Young Man.

Timothy, whose name means Honoured of God, is an example as to his

1. Childhood, - - - - - - 2 Tim. 3. 15
2. Relatives, - - - - - - 2 Tim. 1. 5
3. Conversion, - - Acts 16. 1; 2 Tim. 1. 5; 1 Tim. 1. 2
4. Testimony, - - - - Acts 16. 2; 1 Cor. 16. 10
5. Unselfishness, - - - - - Phil. 2. 20
6. Ability to work with others, 1 Thess. 3. 2; Rom. 16. 21
7. Bravery, - - - - - - Heb. 13. 23
8. Charge, - - - - - 1 Tim. 1. 18; 6. 20
9. Honoured, - - - Phil. 1. 1; Cor. 1. 1 S. J. S.

# SUBJECTS FOR SPEAKERS AND STUDENTS.

## A Remarkable Contrast.

1. Four women filled with the Spirit,   Acts 21. 9
2. Four men filled with religion,   -  Acts 21.23 w. w. f.

### The Christian's Looks.

1. Looking unto Jesus (Heb. 12. 2), - - The Upward
2. Looking upon fields (John 4. 33), - - The Outward
3. Looking for a Saviour (Phil. 3. 20), - - The Onward

H. K. D.

### Saul of Tarsus.

1. Subdued,   -   Acts 9. 4
2. Saved,  - -   „  9. 5
3. Submissive,    „  9. 6
4. Strengthened,   „  9. 19-22
5. Served,  - -   „  9. 20
6. Suffered,  -   „  9. 16
7. Separated,  -   „  9. 26-28

W. J. M.

### Wonderful.

1. Wonderful works, Psa. 40. 5
   Towards Israel, Exod. 14. 31; Psa. 78. 11-16
   Towards us, Eph. 1. 19, 20; 2. 4-7
2. Wonderful thoughts, Psa. 40. 5
   Towards Israel, Jer. 29. 11; Rom. 11. 25-36
   Towards us, Rom. 8. 29, 30; Eph. 1. 3-6

W. W. F.

### Healed by Faith of Others.

1. A man carried on bed by four friends, - - Matt. 9. 1, 2
2. A Canaanitish mother's daughter, - - - Matt. 15. 28
3. A nobleman's servant, - Matt. 8. 5-13
4. A ruler's daughter, Matt. 9. 18, 19, 23-26
5. A nobleman's son, John 4. 46-50 R. G.

## Remarkable Units.

1. One thing lacking,  -  -  -  -  - Mark 10. 21
   To take up the Cross and follow Christ.
2. One thing certain,  -  -  -  -   John 9. 25
   Once I was blind, but now I see.
3. One thing needful,  -  -  -  -  - Luke 10. 42
   To sit at Jesus' feet and hear His word.
4. One thing predominant,  -  -  -   Phil. 3. 13, 14
   I press toward the mark of the high calling.
5. One thing remembered,  -  -  -   2 Peter 3. 8, 9
   The Lord is not slack concerning His promise.
   One day is with the Lord as a thousand years.
6. One thing desired,  -  -  -  -  - Psalm 27. 4
   That I may dwell in the house of the Lord for ever.
7. One thing not discovered,  -  -   Joshua 23. 14
   Not one thing hath failed of all the good things
   which the Lord your God spake.     W. R.

# SUBJECTS FOR SPEAKERS AND STUDENTS.

## Ittai. A STUDY.

1. He was tested, 2 Sam. 15.19
2. He was devoted, ,, 15.21
3. He was promoted,
   2 Sam. 18. 2

## Innumerable Things.

1. God's thoughts of grace,
   Psa. 40. 5
2. My iniquities, Psa. 40. 12
   W. W. F.

## Four Points in Galatians 6. 9.

"And let us not be weary in well-doing, for in due season we shall reap if we faint not."

1. A life to be lived, - - Well doing
2. A danger to be feared, - Getting weary
3. A promise to be claimed, - In due season ye shall reap
4. A condition to be fulfilled, Faint not       R. M.

## Six Comes.

Come down, - - Luke 19. 5, - Conviction.
Come unto Me, - Matt. 11. 28, - Conversion.
Come with Me, - S. of S. 4. 8, - Communion.
Come ye after Me, - Mark 1. 17. - Consecration.
Come away, - - S. of S. 2. 10, - Consummation.
Ye will not come, - John 5. 40, - Condemnation.
                                                    W. J. M.

## The "Seeing" Chapter (Matt. 9).

1. Jesus saw their faith, - - - - Verse 2
2. Multitudes saw miracles, - - - - ,, 8
3. Jesus saw Matthew, - - - - - ,, 9
4. Pharisees saw Jesus dining with sinners, - ,, 11
5. Jesus saw cured woman, - - - - ,, 22
6. Jesus saw minstrels, - - - - - ,, 23
7. Jesus saw multitudes, - - - - - ,, 36
8. Blind men receive their sight, - - - ,, 30
9. It was never so seen in Israel, - - - ,, 33
                                                    H. K. D.

## Arise.

1. Conversion, - Arise, get thee out, - Gen. 31. 13
2. Sanctification, ,, go up to Bethel, ,, 35. 1
3. Inheritance, ,, go over, - - Josh 1. 2
4. Service, - ,, be doing, - - 1 Chron. 22. 16
5. Food, - ,, and eat - - 1 Kings 19. 7
6. Warfare, - ,, anoint, shield, &c., Isa. 21. 5, 6
7. Testimony, - ,, and shine, - Isa. 60. 1
8. Intercession, ,, cry out, - Lam. 2. 19
9. Communion, ,, come away, - S. of S. 2. 13
10. Home-call, ,, ye and depart, - Micah 2. 10
                                                    A. M. P.

132

# SUBJECTS FOR SPEAKERS AND STUDENTS.

## Four Judgments.

1. Man—at the Cross, - - - - - John 12. 31
2. The Judgment-seat of Christ, - - 2 Cor. 5
3. The Nations, - - - - - - Matt. 25. 31
4. All the "dead," - - - - - - Rev. 20. 11

DR. OWLES.

## Names of Believers.

1. Sons, - - 2 Tim. 2. 1
2. Soldiers, - ,, 2. 3
3. Athletes, - ,, 2. 5
4. Husbandmen, ,, 2. 6
5. Workmen, - ,, 2. 15
6. Vessels, - ,, 2. 21
7. Servants, - ,, 2. 24

H.K.D.

## Three Musts of John 3.

The Sinner's Must—
"Ye must be born
again," - - - v. 3
The Saviour's Must—
"So must the Son of
Man be lifted up," v. 14
The Sovereign's Must—
"He must reign," v. 30

HYP.

## "At All Times."

A Blessed Fact, - - - - - Prov. 17. 17
An Important Exhortation, - - - Psa. 62. 8
A Glorious Outcome, - - - - Psa. 34. 1
A Growing Desire, - - - - - Psa. 119. 20
Heaven's Benediction, - - - - Psa. 106. 3

G.H.

## God Loves the Whole World.

1. GOD'S ATTITUDE TOWARDS THE WORLD,
   Loved the world
2. GOD'S ATTITUDE TOWARDS US, - - Hates sin
3. GOD'S ATTITUDE TOWARDS HIS SON, Gave His only
   begotten Son, the object of God's delight; given for
   the world—you and me.
4. GOD'S ATTITUDE TOWARDS BELIEVERS,
   Have Everlasting Life
5. GOD'S ATTITUDE TOWARDS UNBELIEVERS, Perish

DR. TORREY.

## The Stream of Eternal Bliss.

1. THE FOUNTAINHEAD, - God so loved the world,
2. THE STREAM, - He gave His only begotten Son,
3. The Act of DRINKING, - - whosoever believeth
4. The DRAUGHT, - - - - - Everlasting Life.

# SUBJECTS FOR SPEAKERS AND STUDENTS.

## Peter on the Water.

1. The Person, - - It is I, - - - Matt. 14. 27
2. The Word, - - Come, - - - ,, 29
3. The Power, - - He walked to go, - ,, 29

S.E.D.

## "As For Me."

1. Personal Resolution, - - - - Josh. 24. 15
2. Childlike Dependence, - - - - Psa. 55. 16
3. Individual Temptation, - - - - Psa. 73. 2
4. Earnest Intercession, - - - - 1 Sam. 12.33
5. Self-forgetfulness, - - - - Dan. 2. 30
6. Rendering Good for Evil, - - - Psa. 35. 13
7. Eternal Satisfaction, - - - - Psa. 17. 15

G.H.

## Bible Alarms,
### AND THEIR LESSONS FOR US.

1. Babel, - Against, - - - Gen. 11. 8
2. Sodom, - Loss, - - - - Gen. 19. 24
3. Egypt, - - Attend, - - - Exod. 12.29
4. Jerus, - - Rebels, - - - Ezek. 9. 5
5. Capen, - Must, - - - - Matt. 11. 23
6. World, - Suffer, - - - Rev. 20. 11

JS. FS.

## "Conversation" in Peter.
### AS A MODEL FOR THE SAINTS TO-DAY.

1. Vain Conversation, - - - - 1 Peter 1. 18
2. Holy Conversation, - - - - ,, 1. 15
3. Honest Conversation, - - - - ,, 2. 12
4. Chaste Conversation, - - - - ,, 3. 2
5. Good Conversation, - - - - ,, 3. 16
6. Heavenly Conversation, - - - 2 Peter 3. 11

G.H.

## The Peril of Drifting.

Need of the appeal, "The more earnest need," Heb. 2. 1
Basis        ,,        "Therefore," - ,, 1
Urgency, ,,        "We ought," - ,, 1
Solemnity ,,        "Lest haply we drift," ,, 1
Reason        ,,        "Through the Lord," ,, 3
Justification,,        "If we neglect," - ,, 3
Conclusion ,,        "How shall we escape," ,, 3
"Escape is impossible."    DR. GRIFFITH THOMAS.

# SUBJECTS FOR SPEAKERS AND STUDENTS.

## Seven "I Wills" of God.

1. "I will make My covenant," - - - Gen. 17. 2
2. "I will multiply thee exceedingly," - ,, 2
3. "I will make thee exceeding fruitful," - ,, 6
4. "I will make nations of thee," - - ,, 6
5. "I will establish My covenant," - - ,, 7
6. "I will give unto thee . . . the land," - ,, 8
7. "I will be their God," - - - - ,, 8

F.F.

## The Christian's Walk.

1. Past, - - Eph. 2. 2
2. Present, (R.V.) ,, 2. 10
3. Ideal, - - ,, 4. 1
4. Separate, - ,, 4. 17
5. Pattern, - ,, 5. 2
6. Influence, - ,, 5. 8
7. Manner, (R.V.) ,, 5. 15
8. Peace, (R.V.) ,, 6. 15

S.E.B.

## Pride Before Destruction.

SOME EXAMPLES.

Nebuchadnezzar, Dan. 6. 20
Belshazzar, Dan. 5. 23, 24
Amaziah, 2 Kings 14. 10
Uzziah, - 2 Chron. 26. 16
Hezekiah, 2 Chron. 32. 25
Prince of Tyrus,
Ezek. 28. 2, 17
Herod, - Acts 12. 22, 23

R.C.B.

## On Following Christ.

1. In service, - Matt. 4. 19; Mark 2. 14; Luke 5. 27; John 1. 43
2. In cross-bearing, - Matt. 16. 24; Mark 8. 34; Luke 9. 23
3. In daily life, - - - - - John 12. 26
4. In willing obedience, - - - John 10. 27
5. Without questioning, - - - John 21. 22
6. Where we are yet to follow Him, - John 13. 36
7. Lacking decision to do so, - Matt. 8. 22; Matt. 19. 21; Mark 10. 21; Luke 9. 59

F.E.M.

## A Full Redemption.

1. "LOOK," - - that is receiving with the eyes.
2. "HEAR," - - that is receiving with the ears.
3. "TAKE," - - that is receiving with the hands.
4. "TASTE," - - that is receiving with the mouth.
5. "COME," - - that is receiving with the feet.
6. "TRUST," - - that is receiving with the heart.
7. "CHOOSE," - - that is receiving with the will.

From an address by DR. PIERSON at Keswick.

# SUBJECTS FOR SPEAKERS AND STUDENTS.

## Concerning the Faith.
### Acts 24. 24.

1. The Ground of Faith,
   Rom. 10. 17
2. The Object of Faith,
   Acts 20. 21
3. The Activity of Faith,
   Gal. 5. 6
4. The Trial of Faith,
   1 Peter 1. 7
5. The Fight of Faith,
   1 Tim. 6. 12
6. The Victory of Faith,
   1 John 5. 4
7. The Rest of Faith,
   Heb. 4. 3  T-H.

## Thou Hast

1. Lifted me,      Psa. 30. 1
2. Healed me,              ,,    2
3. Brought me,            ,,    3
4. Kept me,                ,,    3
5. Strengthened me,   ,,    7
6. Changed me,          ,,   11
7. Girded me,            ,,   11

## Last Words. W·J·M·

1. Jacob,    ..  Gen. 49. 33
2. Moses,    ..  Deut. 33. 1
3. David,    ..  2 Sam. 23. 1
4. Joshua,   ..  Josh. 24. 29
5. Peter,    ..  2 Peter 1. 14
6. Paul,     ..  2 Tim. 4. 6
7. Christ,   ..  Rev. 22. 20
                    JS. FS.

## A Creation Study.

THE FIRST CREATION A TYPE OF THE NEW, as mentioned
in 2 Cor. 5. 17; Gal. 6. 15; Eph. 2. 10; Eph. 4. 24.

**1st Day**—"Let there be light," ..    .. ILLUMINATION.
Compare Heb. 10. 32; 2 Cor. 4. 6; Eph. 5. 8.

**2nd Day**—"Let there be a firmament,"    SEPARATION.
Compare Gal. 1. 4; John 17. 16; 2 Cor. 6. 14.

**3rd Day**—"Let the dry land appear,"    RESURRECTION.
Compare Eph. 2. 5; Col. 3. 1; Phil. 3. 10, 11.

**4th Day**—"Let there be light," ..    .. IMPARTATION.
(Light never shines for its own sake, but for the benefit
of others.)
Compare the Sun and Mal. 4. 2; John 9. 5.
Compare the Moon and S. of S. 6. 10; Matt. 5. 14.
Compare the Stars.    Phil. 2. 15; 1 Cor. 15. 41; Dan. 12. 3.

**5th Day**—"Let the waters bring forth," MANIFESTATION.
Compare the Believer's Progress through the World.
1 Peter 2. 11; Phil. 3. 12-14; Psa. 84. 7.
Compare the Believer's Ability to rise above the World.
Exod. 19. 4; Isa. 40. 31; Col. 3. 1.

**6th Day**—"Let us make men," ..    .. CONFORMATION.
Compare Rom. 8. 29; Phil. 3. 21; 1 John 3. 2.

**7th Day**—"And God rested," ..    .. SATISFACTION.
Compare Psa. 103. 5; Psa. 36. 8; Psa. 17. 15.   G. H.

136

# SUBJECTS FOR SPEAKERS AND STUDENTS
## The Threefold Shield of Faith.

1. Against DANGER.—The shield of thy *salvation*, - - - - - Psa. 18. 35
2. Against DOUBT.—His *truth* shall be thy shield, - - - - - Psa. 91. 4
3. Against DESPONDENCY.—With *favour* wilt Thou compass him (the righteous) as with a shield, - - - - Psa. 5. 12

T.

## "Arise."

FOR
1. Salvation,     Luke 15. 18
2. Confession,    Acts 22. 16
3. Separation,    Micah 2. 10
4. Fellowship,    John 14. 31
5. Testimony,    Isa. 60. 1
6. Service,    1 Chron. 22. 4
7. Home,   Sol. Song 2. 12

G.H.

## Our Lord

1. Precedes all things, Col. 1. 17
2. Creates,    ,,    Col. 1. 16
3. Upholds,   ,,    Heb. 1. 3
4. Fills,     ,,    Eph. 4. 10
5. Subdues,   ,,    Phil. 3. 21
6. Reconciles ,,    Col. 1. 20
7. Owns,    ,,    Heb. 1. 2; 2. 10 H.K.D.

## The Great Work of Grace
### Read Jeremiah 52. 31-34

1. Brought him forth, - - - Psa. 107. 14
2. Spake kindly unto him, - - - Isa. 40. 1, 2
3. Set his throne above, - - - Eph. 2. 6
4. Changed his prison garments, - - Isa. 61. 10
5. Did continually eat bread, - - John 12. 1, 2
6. Every day a portion, - - Exod. 16. 4, 16-18

F.F.

## "All Taught of God" (John 6. 45).

1. Learn what this meaneth, - - Matt. 9. 13
   —The sinner's lesson.
2. Learn to do well, - - - - Isa. 1. 17
   —The backslider's lesson.
3. Learn of Me, - - - - Matt. 11. 29
   —The saint's lesson.
4. Learn in silence, - - - - 1 Tim. 2. 11
   —The woman's lesson.
5. Learn to show piety, - - - 1 Tim. 5. 4
   —The children's lesson.
6. Learn honest trades, - - - Titus 3. 14
   —The servant's lesson.
7. Learn to fear God, - - - Deut. 31. 12
   —Everybody's lesson.

JS. FS.

# SUBJECTS FOR SPEAKERS AND STUDENTS.

## Abiding.

1. Declaration—I must *abide*, - - - - Luke 19. 5
2. Invitation—*Abide* with us, - - - Luke 24. 29
3. Consolation—He may *abide* with you, - John 14. 16

W. T. R.

## The Greatest Gift in the World.

1. The Author of the Gift, - - - - - God
2. The Incentive to the Gift, - - - so loved
3. The Content of the Gift, - - His only begotten Son
4. The Universality of the Gift, - - - whosoever
5. The Means of Appropriation, - - - believeth
6. The Benefits in the Gift—(1) *negative*, not perish; (2) *positive*, have Everlasting Life. V. A. BARTON.

## The Love of God.

1. Unmerited in its Object, - world, sinners (1 John 4. 10)
2. Unsought in its Action, - God so loved (Rom. 5. 9)
3. Universal in its Offer, - - - - whosoever
4. Unbounded in its Gift, - only begotten Son (Rom. 8. 32)
5. Unfathomable in its depth, - so (Eph. 3. 18, 19)
6. Unbroken in its Ministry, shall not perish (Rom. 8. 39)
7. Unending in its Character, - everlasting (Jer. 31. 3)

T. CROSKERY.

## Characteristics of Faith in Hebrews 11.

Wisdom of Faith—Grasping the unseen, - - verse 1
Warrant of Faith—God said, - - - - ,, 3
Worship of Faith (Abel)—Coming Redeemer, - ,, 4
Walk of Faith (Enoch)—Witness of coming glory, ,, 5
Witness of Faith (Noah)—Coming judgment, - ,, 7
Wanderings of Faith (Abraham)—{Obedience, Pilgrimage, } ,, 8
Trial of Faith (Abraham)—Surrendered all in view of resurrection, - - - - ,, 17
Waiting of Faith—Sarah, - - - - ,, 11
Isaac, sonship, - - - ,, 20
Jacob, service, - - - ,, 21
Joseph, suffering and glory, ,, 22
Moses, renunciation and recompense, - - - ,, 24
Success of Faith—Gideon, - - - - ,, 32
Song of Faith—Barak, - - - - - ,, 32
Supplications of Faith—David (Psalms), - ,, 32
Singleness of Faith as made known in Samuel. H.W.

# SUBJECTS FOR SPEAKERS AND STUDENTS.

## The Inquiry.

| | | |
|---|---|---|
| Who is this? (Isa. 63. 1), | - | - Christ as Judge. |
| Who is this? (Matt. 21. 10), | - | - Christ as King. |
| Who is this? (Luke 7. 49), | - | - Christ as Saviour. |

JS. FS.

## Portion and Prospect

OF BELIEVERS IN CHRIST.

1. Chosen to Salvation, 2 Thess. 2. 13
2. Called to Glory, 2 Thess. 2. 14
3. Consoled through Grace, 2 Thess. 2. 16
4. Comfort in service, 2 Thess. 2. 17

H.K.D.

## God's People.

Born again—by the Word of God, - - 1 Pet. 1. 23

Kept—by the power of God. 1 Pet. 1. 5

Living—to the will of God, 1 Pet. 4. 2

Speaking—as oracles of God, 1 Pet. 4. 11

Stewards—of the grace of God, 1 Pet. 4. 10    F.F.

## The Names in the 16th Chapter of Romans

### AND THEIR SPIRITUAL TEACHING.

1. PHOEBE: "Shining and pure."—We are "light in the Lord" (Eph. 5. 8); and, "Let your light so shine before men, that they may see your good works, and glorify your Father which is in Heaven"(Matt.5.16).

2. ANDRONICUS: "A man excelling others."—We are to covet "earnestly the best gifts" (1 Cor. 12. 31).

3. URBANE: "Civil and courteous."—"Let your speech be always with grace, seasoned with salt" (Col. 4. 6).

4. ARISTOBULUS: "The best counsellor."—In our service for Christ in ministering His truth, "Preach the Word" (2 Tim. 4. 2).

5. PHLEGON: "Zealous."—"Zealous of good works" (Titus 2. 14).

6. OLYMPAS: "Heavenly."—"Partakers of the heavenly calling" (Heb. 3. 1); "Not of the world" (John 17. 14).

7. TIMOTHEUS: "Honoured of God".—"Ye are a chosen generation, a royal priesthood, an holy nation, a purchased people; that ye should show forth the praises of Him who hath called you out of darkness into His marvellous light. . . . Ye are now the people of God" (1 Peter 2. 9).    F.F.

# SUBJECTS FOR SPEAKERS AND STUDENTS.
## The Uniqueness of our Lord
### IN HIS
1. Preaching—Never man spake like this Man, John 7. 46
2. Power—We never saw it in this fashion, - Mark 2. 12
3. Person—What manner of Man is this? - Matt. 8. 27

H.K.D.

## The Lamb of God.
### CHRIST IS
1. The Lamb foreordained from times eternal, 1 Pet.1.18-20
2. The object of expectation from the beginning, Gen. 22. 8
3. The subject of typical foreshadowing,
   Exod. 12. 3-13; 1 Cor. 5. 7
4. The theme of prophetic Scriptures, - Isa. 53. 5-7

T.D.W.M.

## The Good Samaritan.
1. His Coming,        Luke 10. 33; compare    1 Tim. 1. 15
2. His Compassion,    ,,   10. 33;     ,,      Matt. 9. 36
3. His Cure,    -     ,,   10. 34;     ,,      Matt. 9. 12
4. His Care,    -     ,,   10. 34;     ,,      1 Peter 5. 7
5. His Coming Again, ,,   10. 35;     ,,      John 14. 3

W.J.M.

## The Rich Man.
1. The Person—A rich man,        -      -   Luke 16. 22
2. The Place—Hell,        -      -      -      ,,    23
3. The Punishment—Tormented,     -          ,,    24
4. The Prayer—Have mercy on me,      -      ,,    24
5. The Petition—Send to my father's house,  ,,    27
6. The Prophets—They have God's Word,       ,,    29
7. The Prospect—A great gulf fixed,    -     ,,    26

J.M.

## The Most Wonderful Thing in the World.
### It is the love of God.
I. THE OBJECTS OF GOD'S LOVE—
   1, The World; 2, Men of all races; 3, Men of all classes.
II. THE CHARACTER OF GOD'S LOVE—
   1, A pardoning love (Isa. 55. 7); 2, A chastening love
   (Heb. 12. 6); 3, A sympathising love (Isa. 63. 9);
   4, A longsuffering love (2 Peter 3. 9); 5, A self-
   sacrificing love (John 3. 16).
III. OUR TREATMENT OF GOD'S LOVE—
   1. Accepting His Love, Eternal Life.
   2. Rejecting His love, perish—incurring (a) awful
   guilt; (b) loss of Eternal Life (John 5. 40); (c)
   awful punishment (Heb. 10. 26).   DR. TORREY.

# SUBJECTS FOR SPEAKERS AND STUDENTS.

## Worship in the Scriptures.

1. The QUALIFICATION for Worship and Priesthood.—
   1 Peter 2. 5, 9.
2. The OBJECTS of Worship.—The Father, John 4. 20;
   The Son, John 9. 35-38.
3. The POWER for Worship.—Holy Spirit, Philippians 3. 3.
4. The PLACE of Worship.—Inside the Veil, Hebrews
   10. 19-22.
5. ACTS of Worship.—
   1. Presentation of the body, Romans 12. 1.
   2. Praise, Psalm 50. 23; Hebrews 13. 15.
   3. Thanksgiving, Psalm 116. 17.
   4. Communication, Hebrews 13. 16, with such
      sacrifices.                                    H.H.

## The Blunders of a Great General.
### As seen in the story of Naaman, 2 Kings 5.

1. WRONG PRICE.—10 talents of silver, 6000 pieces of gold
   (v. 5), about equal to £16,000. Not enough (Luke
   7. 42).
2. WRONG PERSON.—"Send to the *King* of Israel" (v. 5).
   Maid said "prophet." Christ, God's Prophet alone
   can save to-day.
3. WRONG PLACE.—"Stood at the *door*" (v. 9). Almost
   there, but not altogether. So near, yet so far.
4. WRONG PRESCRIPTION.—"I *thought* he would surely
   come out to me" (v. 11). Not thoughts, but acts.
   Prophet said, *"Go."*
5. WRONG PASSION.—"He went away in a *rage*" (v. 12).
   But he turned again, went down, and was cleansed.
                                                      HyP.

## How to Study the Bible.

1. With a regenerate mind,      -    -    1 Cor. 2. 14
2. With a willing mind,         -    -    John 7. 17
3. With an obedient mind,       -    -    James 1. 21, 22
4. With a teachable mind,       -    -    Matt. 11. 25
5. With an unprejudiced mind,   -    -    Exod. 3. 5
6. With open eyes,        -    -    -    Psa. 119. 18
7. Remember it is God's Word,   -    -    1 Thess. 2. 13
   Therefore (1) Submit your judgment always and
   unhesitatingly; (2) bank on its promises without
   discounting; and (3) obey immediately and
   exactly—no questions (Josh. 1. 16).        W.D.

# SUBJECTS FOR SPEAKERS AND STUDENTS.

## At the Beautiful Gate.

| | | |
|---|---|---|
| The cripple, | - | Acts 3. 2 |
| The couple, | - | Acts 3. 3 |
| The cure, | - | Acts 3. 7 |

## Threefold Responsibility.

| | |
|---|---|
| To God, | - 1 Thess. 4. 1 |
| To saints, | - 1 Thess. 4. 9 |
| To sinners, | - 1 Thess. 4. 12 |

H.K.D.

## The "Jehovah" Titles of God (Exod. 6. 3).

Jehovah-jireh, "The Lord will provide," - Gen. 22. 14
Jehovah-nissi, "The Lord my banner," - Exod. 17. 15
Jehovah-shalom, "The Lord send peace," - Judges 6. 24
Jehovah-tsidkenu, "The Lord our righteousness," Jer. 23.6
Jehovah-shammah, "The Lord is there," - Ezek. 48. 35

F.K.

## The Mysteries of the Bible

| | |
|---|---|
| Babylon, - Rev. 17. 5 | Resurrection, 1 Cor. 15. 51 |
| Christ, - - Col. 4. 3 | Salvation, 1 Peter 1. 10-12 |
| Engrafting, | Seven candlesticks, Rev. 1.20 |
| Rom. 11. 25; Eph. 3. 3-6 | Seven stars, - Rev. 1. 20 |
| Faith, - - 1 Tim. 3. 9 | The Gospel, - Eph. 6. 19 |
| God, Col. 2. 2; 1 Cor. 4. 1; | The Kingdom, Matt. 13. 11; |
| Rev. 10. 7 | Mark 4. 11; Luke 8. 10 |
| Godliness, - 1 Tim. 3. 16 | The woman, - Rev. 17. 7 |
| His will, - - Eph. 1. 9 | Union, - - Eph. 5. 32 |
| Iniquity, - 2 Thess. 2. 7 | Christ in you, Col. 1. 27 |
| Marriage, - Eph. 5. 32 | F.P.P. |

## Make Your Companions.

1. Praying Companions like Daniel, - Dan. 2. 17
2. Godly Companions like David, - - Psa. 119. 63
3. Loving Companions like Paul, - - Acts 19. 29
4. Busy Companions like Epaphroditus, - Phil. 2. 25
5. Holy Companions like John, - Rev. 1. 9. L.W.

## The Precious Blood of Christ.

IT IS PRECIOUS BECAUSE IT

1. Redeems us, 1 Peter 1.19
2. Brings us nigh, Eph. 2. 13
3. Blots out our sins, Rev. 1.5
4. Brings peace, Col. 1. 20
5. Justifies, - Rom. 5. 9
6. Cleanses from all sin,
   1 John 1. 7
7. Gives boldness in the day of judgment. D. L. MOODY.

## Threefold Possession.

A Living Hope, 1 Peter 1. 3
A Living Stone, 1 Peter. 2.4
The Living Word,
   1 Peter 1. 23 W.J.M.

## Called—

To Peace—Past, 1 Cor. 7. 15
To Holiness—Present,
   1 Thess. 4. 7
To Glory—Prospective,
   2 Peter 1. 3 W.T.R.

# SUBJECTS FOR SPEAKERS AND STUDENTS.

## The Story of Naaman (2 Kings 5).

1. He was a leper, and - - - - - he knew it
2. He heard of cleansing, and - - - he sought it
3. He disliked the treatment, but - - - he tried it
4. He was immediately cleansed, and - he confessed it
5. He was sincerely grateful, and - - he showed it

L-W.

## A Sign in the Depth and in the Height (Isa. 7. 11).

### IN THE DEPTH.

1. A virgin's Son, Isa. 7. 14
2. Son of Man, -Luke 19. 10
3. Offspring of David,
   Rev. 22. 16
4. He humbled Himself,
   Phil. 2. 8
5. Became poor, - 2 Cor. 8. 9
6. Crowned with thorns,
   Matt. 27. 29
7. Was dead, - - Rev. 1. 18

### IN THE HEIGHT.

1. Emmanuel, - Isa. 7. 14
2. Son of God, - John 1. 34
3. Root of David, Rev. 22. 16
4. God exalted Him, Phil. 2. 9
5. Was rich, - - 2 Cor. 8. 9
6. Crowned with glory,
   Heb. 2. 9
7. Alive for evermore,
   Rev. 1. 18    H. K. D.

## The Climax of the Songs of Degrees.

### IN PSALM 134 WE HAVE

1. A Compendium—As last of the fifteen songs of degrees.
2. A Command—To the watchers in temple.
3. A Competency—They could praise, the servants, the priests, made so by God.
4. A Compliance—They responded.
5. A Comprehension—God as Jehovah and Creator. His great Name and great work. Well able to bless.
6. A Compliment—Bless Thee. They asked much for this one. Yet we have more (Eph. 1. 3).
7. A Channel—Zion. N.T. Analogy
   { Original Christ, John 2
   Secondary and derived Church, - - Eph. 2
   Personal and conditional Christian, - 1 Cor. 6

C. J. R.

## The Saviour and the Saint.

1. Our Position—In Christ, - - - - Phil. 1. 1
2. Our Purpose—Live Christ, - - - ,, 1. 21
3. Our Privilege—Preach Christ, - - - ,, 1. 15
4. Our Prize—Win Christ, - - - - ,, 3. 8
5. Our Prospect—With Christ, - - - ,, 1. 23
6. Our Perfection—Like Christ, - - - ,, 3. 21

W. J. M.

# SUBJECTS FOR SPEAKERS AND STUDENTS.

## A Penitent Prodigal.

1. Halt—And when he came to himself,  -  Luke 15. 17
2. Hope—I will arise and go to my father,  „ 15. 18
3. Humility—Father, I have sinned,  -  „ 15. 18
4. Heartiness—I am no more worthy,  -  „ 15. 19
5. Home—And he arose, and came to his father „ 15. 20
6. Hospitality—Bring hither the fatted calf,  „ 15. 23
7. Happiness—And they began to be merry,  „ 15. 23

T.B.

## A Righteous Man.

1. His way,  -  Psa. 1. 6
2. His inheritance, Psa. 37. 29
3. His gladness,  Psa. 64. 10
4. His flourishing, Psa. 92. 12
5. His remembrance,
   Psa. 112. 6
6. His thanksgiving,
   Psa. 140. 13  F.F.

## Christ Our Life.

1. Bread if Life, - John 6. 35
2. Fountain of Life, Psa. 36. 9
3. Tree of Life,  Rev. 2. 7
4. Light of Life,  John 8. 12
5. Path of Life,  Psa. 16. 11
6. Word of Life,  1 John 1.1
7. Prince of Life,  Acts 3. 15

J.H.B.

## To Young Preachers and Teachers.

"Preaching the Kingdom of God, and teaching those things which concern the Lord Jesus" (Acts. 28. 31).

### WHAT TO PREACH.

His Deity—Godhead,  -  -  - John 1. 1; Rom. 9. 5
His Manhood—Including His birth,
   John 1. 14; Luke 2. 11; Heb. 10. 5
His Life—On the earth,  -  -  -  - Acts 10. 38
His Death—On the tree,  - Acts 10. 39; 1 Peter 2. 24
His Resurrection—By divine power,
   Rom. 1. 4; 6. 4; Acts 13. 30
His Ascension—Into Heaven,
   Heb. 4. 14; Acts 1. 2; Luke 24. 51
His Intercession—Priesthood and advocacy,
   Heb. 5. 6; 8. 1; 1 John 2. 1
His Coming Again—For His own,  John 14. 3; Acts 1. 11
His Reign—Universal peace,
   Isa. 32. 1; 9. 6; Psa. 22. 27, 28; 72. 7. 8, 17
His Glory—For ever and ever,  - John 17. 5; Rev. 5. 13

### HOW TO PREACH.

With all confidence (boldness).
Not with doubts and hesitancy, but that which suggests Stability and certainty (Luke 1. 24).  S.J.S.

# SUBJECTS FOR SPEAKERS AND STUDENTS.

## The Mighty to Save.
### Christ manifest as the Mighty to Save in Mark 5

1. From Power of Sin—Demoniac, - - verse 5
2. From Plague of Sin—Woman with issue of
   blood, - - - - - ,, 29
3. From Penalty of Sin—Dead child, - - ,, 42

A Saviour for man, woman, and child. A Deliverer from
the devil, disease, death.    T.W.

## Give God the Glory.
### WE HAVE HIS

1. Praise sounded, Psa. 34. 1
2. Name exalted, ,, 34. 3
3. Saints exhorted, ,, 34. 9
4. Ears opened, ,, 34. 15
5. Servants comforted,
   Psa. 34. 22

## Christ in Three Characters.

1. Behold the Sower,
   Matt. 13. 3
2. Behold the Lamb,
   John 1. 29
3. Behold the Lion,
   Rev. 5. 5   JS. FS.

## Three Places of Enjoyment.

Yea, He loved [had *on* His bosom or heart] in Thy hand, ... at Thy
feet (Deut. 33. 3)

1. THE PLACE OF LOVE—ON HEART.
   Placed (Exod. 28. 29, 30; Jer. 31. 3), Leaning (John
   13. 23), Showing (1 Peter 2. 9; John 15. 12).
2. THE PLACE OF SECURITY—IN HAND (Isa. 49. 16).
   Held (John 10. 28, 29), Upheld (Isa. 41. 10), Guarded
   (1 Peter 1. 5), Abiding (Jude 21; John 15. 4).
3. THE PLACE OF INSTRUCTION—AT HIS FEET
   (Luke 10. 39; Acts 22. 3).
   Learning (2 Tim. 3. 16, 17), Doing (Luke 6. 47, 48;
   James 1. 22, etc.).    G.G.

## The Excelling Glories of Christ
### In Heb. 1. 1-6

1. Future Ruler, - - - - Heir of all things
2. Past Creator, - By whom also He made the worlds
3. Eternal Son, (*a*) The outspring of God's glory
   (*b*) The die-stamped image of His Person
4. Present Upholder, All things by the Word of His power
5. Great sacrifice, - - By Himself purged our sin
6. Enthroned Prince,
   Sat down on the right hand of the Majesty on high
7. Coming King, - - - When He bringeth *again*
   No longer in lowly form, but in power and glory.   HYP.

# SUBJECTS FOR SPEAKERS AND STUDENTS.
## A Pernicious Prodigal.
1. Haughtiness—Give me the portion of goods
   that falleth to me, - - - -Luke 15. 12
2. Haste—Not many days after, - - ,, 15. 13
3. Habits—Wasted his substance with riotous
   living, - - - - - - ,, 15. 13
4. Hunger—He began to be in want, - - ,, 15. 14
5. Hogs—Into his fields to feed swine, - ,, 15. 15
6. Husks—With the husks that the swine did eat, ,, 15. 16
7. Harlots—Devoured thy living with harlots, ,, 15. 30

## Sentence and Execution.

T.B. Yrs. after

| | |
|---|---|
| 1. Against Egypt (Gen. 15. 14), - B.C. 1920 | Executed - B.C. 1490 430 (Exod. 12. 41), |
| 2. Against Jeroboam's altar (1 Kings 13. 2), - B.C. 975 | Executed - B.C. 677 289 (2 Chron. 34. 5) |
| 3. Against Israel (1 Kings 14. 15), B.C. 956 | Executed - B.C. 740 216 (2 Kings 17. 6) |
| 4. Against the Jews (Isa. 6. 10), - B.C. 760 | Executed - A.D. 31 791 (Matt. 13. 14; John 12. 40) |
| 5. Against Judah (Jer. 25. 9), - B.C. 609 | Executed - B.C. 588 21 (2 Chron. 36. 20) |
| 6. Against Nebuchadnezzar (Dan. 4. 25), - - B.C. 570 | Executed - B.C. 569 1 (Dan. 4. 29) |
| 7. Against Jerusalem (Luke 19. 44; 21. 5, 6), - - A.D. 33 | Executed - A.D. 70 37 (By Titus) |
| 8. Against truth rejecters (2 Thess. 2. 12; Rev. 21. 8), A.D. 96 | Execution in abeyance, 1817 Js. Fs. |

## The Earthly and the Heavenly Contrasted.
THE FIRST MAN (1 Cor. 15. 47)
   1. A Look at the Inside—Altogether Filthy, - Psa. 14. 3
   2. A Look at the Outside—Altogether Vanity, Psa. 39. 5
THE SECOND MAN (1 Cor. 15. 47)
   1. A Look at the Fairest of the Children of
      Men—God over all blessed for ever, Amen, Psa. 45. 2
   2. Altogether Lovely, - - - S. of S. 5. 16
      This is *my* Beloved, and this is *my* Friend (S. of
      S. 5. 16)

J.M.

# SUBJECTS FOR SPEAKERS AND STUDENTS.

## Life of Joseph.

1. His trial,   Gen. 39. 9, 10
2. His sorrows,
   Gen. 40. 20; Psa. 105. 18
3. His joys,  -  Gen. 41. 42
4. His service,   Gen. 50. 20
5. His eyes upward,
   Gen. 41. 16 s.j.s.

## Our Protectors.

1. Kept by power
   of God,   1 Peter 1. 5
2. Kept by peace
   of God,   Phil. 4. 7
3. Kept by pres-
   ence of God, Psa. 31. 20
   H.K.D.

## Milestones on the Way.

1. *Past*—I was chief of sinners,  -   -   -1 Tim. 1. 15
2. *Present*—I am a new creature in Christ Jesus, 2 Cor. 5. 17
3. *Future*—I shall be like Him,  -   -   - 1 John 3. 2
4. *In the meantime*—I press toward the mark,   - Phil. 3. 14
   S.D.

## The Believer's Position.

YE ARE

Dead,  -   -   - Col. 3. 3
Washed, sanctified,
   justified,   1 Cor. 6. 11
A chosen generation,1 Pet.2.9
My witnesses,   Isa. 43. 10
Children of God,   Gal. 3. 26
The light of the world,
   Matt. 5. 14
Complete in Him, Col. 2. 10
W.T.R.

## Man's Destitution.

1. No righteousness,
   Rom. 3. 11
2. No understanding,
   Rom. 3. 11
3. No desire for God,
   Rom. 3. 11
4. No goodness,   Rom. 3. 12
5. No peace,   Rom. 3. 17
6. No fear,  -   Rom. 3. 18
7. No defence,   Rom. 3. 19
   H.K.D.

## Points for Runners.

1. Kind of Men Required—A strong man to run
   a race,  -   -   -   -   - Psa. 19. 5
2. The Course—I will run the way of Thy
   commandments,  -   -   - Psa. 119. 32
3. The Day to Enter—Now is the accepted time, 2 Cor. 6. 2
4. The Training—And every man that striveth
   for the mastery is temperate in all things, - 1 Cor. 9. 25
5. The Conditions—Except ye be converted . . .
   ye cannot enter,  -   -   -   -Matt. 18. 3
6. The Prize—Ye shall receive a crown of glory
   that fadeth not away,  -   -   - 1 Peter 5. 4
7. Have You Given Up Running—Ye did run
   well.  Who did hinder you?  -   - Gal. 5. 7
8. The Result.  Which?—Well done, or depart
   from Me,  -   - Matt. 25. 12; 25. 41   J.W.

# SUBJECTS FOR SPEAKERS AND STUDENTS.

## All Things.

1. The believer's persuasion, - - - - Rom. 8. 28
2. The believer's riches, - - - - - ,, 8. 32
3. The believer's victory, - - - - - ,, 8. 37

H. K. D.

## "Do," a Little Word with Great Issues.

What must I do to be saved? (Acts 16. 30). One of the
most momentous questions ever asked.

Some of the wisest counsel ever given (John 2. 5).

One of the noblest acts ever witnessed (2 Sam. 15. 15).

Two of the greatest promises ever given (Rev. 22. 14). G. H.

## Divine Secrets in Psalm 16.

1. Secret of a Life of Trust—I trust in Him, - verse 1
2. Secret of a Surrendered Life—I belong to Him, ,, 2 R.V.
3. Secret of a Separated Life—I side with Him, ,, 3, 4 R.V.
4. Secret of a Happy Life—I am satisfied with Him, ,, 5, 6
5. Secret of an Instructed Life—I listen to Him, ,, 7
6. Secret of a Steadfast Life—I am engaged
   with Him, - - - - - - ,, 8 F.F.

## A Salvation Plan.

I. GOD'S LOVE.
   1. Divine, - - - - God
   2. Great, - - - - world
   3. Practical, - - He gave

II. GOD'S GIFT.
   1. Royal, - - - - His
   2. Liberal, - - - only
   3. Costly, - begotten Son,
   4. Exclusive, - whosoever

III. GOD'S PURPOSE.
   1. Negative,
      should not perish,
   2. Positive,
      have Everlasting Life

IV. GOD'S WAY.
   1. Freeness, - whosoever
   2. Condition, - -believeth
   W. C. J.

## Our Father, God.

1. His grace, - - 2 Cor. 9. 8
2. His glory, - - ,, 9. 13
3. His gift, - - ,, 9. 15

H. K. D.

## Precious Things.

1. Precious trial, 1 Peter 1. 7
2. Precious blood, ,, 1. 19
3. Precious stone, ,, 2. 6
4. Precious faith, 2 Peter 1. 1
5. Precious promises,
   2 Peter 1. 4 F. K.

## David : A Pattern for Boys.

Humble occupation,
   1 Sam. 17. 15
Slender resources,
   1 Sam. 19. 40
Trusted, - - 1 Sam. 17. 32
Brave, - - - 1 Sam. 17. 45
In secret, victorious,
   1 Sam. 17. 35 S. J. S.

# SUBJECTS FOR SPEAKERS AND STUDENTS.

## Rejoicing.

Precept—Rejoice in the Lord alway, - Phil. 4. 4
Purpose—We will . . . rejoice, . . . - - Isa. 25. 9
Promise—Your heart shall rejoice, - John 16. 22 w.t.r.

## Three Triumphant Notes.

1. A BLESSED ASSURANCE—The Lord, He it
   is that doth go before thee; He will be
   with thee, - - - - - Deut. 31. 8
2. A JOYFUL EXPERIENCE—Thou art with me, Psa. 23. 4
3. A GLORIOUS PROSPECT—So shall we ever
   be with the Lord, - - 1 Thess. 4. 18 G.H.

## In Time of Famine.

1. Abraham went down to Egypt, - - Gen. 12. 10
2. Isaac went down to Gerar, - - Gen. 26. 1
3. Egyptians went to Joseph, - - - Gen. 41. 55
4. Naomi went to Moab, - - - Ruth 1. 1
5. David went to the Lord, - - - 2 Sam. 21. 1
6. Prodigal went to the father, - - Luke 15. 20
7. Famine shall not separate from love of Christ, Rom. 8. 35
   H.K.D.

## The Sinner's Race.

1. THE START—Born in sin, - - - Psa. 51. 3
2. THE RACE—All gone out of the way, - Rom. 3. 12
3. THE FINISH—After death the judgment, - Heb. 9. 27
4. THE WEIGHING ROOM—Weighed and found
   wanting, - - - - - Dan. 5. 27
5. THE SETTLING DAY—What shall it profit a
   man if he gain the whole world and lose
   his own soul? - - - - Mark 8. 36
   L.W.

## Seven Bible Settings.

1. Set at Nought—Councils, - - - Prov. 1. 25
2. Set Thine House—Command, - - Isa. 38. 1
3. Set My Feet—Conversion, - - - Psa. 40. 2
4. Set Apart for Him—Consecration, - Psa. 4. 3
5. Set Me as a Seal—Chosen, - - Cant. 8. 6
6. Set His Love Upon Me—Comeliness, - Psa. 91. 14
7. Set Him on High—Consummation, - Psa. 91. 14
   These last two settings doubtless refer to Christ personally.
I have SET—PURPOSE, - - - Psa. 16. 8
SET not thine Heart—PRECEPT, - - Psa. 62. 10
   J.M.

# SUBJECTS FOR SPEAKERS AND STUDENTS.

## Christ Our Example.

1. In Loving.—Love one another as I have
   loved you, - - - - John 13. 34
2. In Receiving.—Receive one another as
   Christ also received us, - - Rom. 15. 7
3. In Forgiving.—Forgive one another as
   Christ also forgave you, - - Col. 3. 13
   
   H.K.D.

## The Lord Carries His People.

1. On His shoulders, the place of strength, Exod. 28. 12
2. In His bosom, place of confidence, Isa. 40. 11
3. On His heart, place of affection, - Exod. 28. 29
4. On His hands, place of safety, - Isa. 49. 16
5. On His forehead, place of thought, - Exod. 28. 38
6. On His wings, place of power, - Exod. 19. 4
7. In His arms, place of support, - - Deut. 33. 27

F.F.

## Our Lord's Service (John 9. 4).

1. Compulsion—I must work.
2. Consecration—The works of Him.
3. Compression—While it is day.
4. Completion — The Night cometh.    H.K.D.

## The Blessing of Joseph (Gen. 49. 22)

TELLS OF—

1. Fact—"Joseph is a fruitful bough."
2. Source—"by a well."
3. Result—"whose branches run over the wall."

*Conference Note.*

## Fire from God

HAS SMITTEN OR SHALL SMITE

1. Sodomites, - Gen. 19. 24
2. Nadab and Abihu,
   Lev. 10. 2
3. Israelites, - Num. 11. 1
4. Princes in Israel,
   Num. 16. 35
5. Messengers of Ahaziah,
   2 Kings 1. 10
6. Messengers of Ahaziah,
   2 Kings 1. 12
7. Those who fight against
   Christ at the end of the
   Millennium,    Rev. 20. 9

## Without the—

1. Precious Blood
   of Christ  - 1 Pet. 1. 19
   There can be no
2. Peace with God, Col. 1. 20
   Neither
3. Pardon from God, Heb. 9. 22
   Nor
4. Praise to God, Heb. 13. 15
   But
5. Perdition - 2 Pet. 3. 7
   Must be the unending
6. Portion - 2 Thess. 1. 9
   Of all who have been
7. Polluted by sin, Rev. 22. 15

150

# SUBJECTS FOR SPEAKERS AND STUDENTS.

## His Right Hand

1. Hath Saved Me—Past, - - - - Psa. 108. 6
2. Doth Embrace Me—Present, - - - S. of S. 2. 6
3. Shall hold me—future, - - Psa. 139. 10. W.T.R.

## The Importance of Service.

Your work of *faith*, - - - - 1 Thess. 1. 3
And labour of *love*, - - - - ,,
And patience of *hope* in our Lord Jesus Christ, ,,
Ye turned to God from idols - - - 1 Thess. 1. 9, 10
To serve the living and true God, - - - ,,
And to wait for His Son from Heaven, - ,,
   *Faith, hope, love*—the greatest of these is LOVE. A.B.B.

## The Christian's Race.

1. THE START—Born of God, - - 1 John 3. 1
2. THE RACE—Looking unto Jesus, - Heb. 12. 3
3. THE FINISH—Unto Him that is able to keep
   you from falling, - - - - - Jude 24
4. THE WEIGHING ROOM—Found in Him - Phil. 3. 9
5. THE SETTLING DAY—From henceforth there
   is laid up for me a crown of righteousness, 2 Tim. 4. 8
                                 L.W.

## Marks of a True Child of God.

1. Believeth that Jesus is the Christ - - 1 John 5. 1
2. Doeth righteousness, - - - - ,, 2. 29
3. Keeps His commandments, - - - ,, 2. 3
4. Does not practise sin, - - - - ,, 3. 9
5. Hated by the world, - - - - - ,, 3. 13
6. Loves the brethren, - - - - - ,, 3. 14
7. Overcometh the world, - - - - ,, 5. 4
                                W.J.M.

## The Last Words of New Testament (Rev. 22. 20).

### HE COMES TO

1. Call us to a higher sphere of service—His
   servants shall serve Him, - - - Rev. 22. 3
2. Change us into His image—They shall see
   His face, - - - Rev. 22. 4, with 1 John 3. 2
3. Claim us as His own—His Name shall be on
   their foreheads, - - - - - Rev. 22. 4
4. Compensate us—(*a*) For keeping His word,
               Rev. 22. 7, with Rev. 3. 11
     (*b*) Doing His work, - Rev. 22. 12
                        H.K.D.

# SUBJECTS FOR SPEAKERS AND STUDENTS.

## Three Precious Truths.

Saved by Grace—The Principle, - - Eph. 2. 8
Seated with Christ—The Position, - - Eph. 2. 6
Shown in Glory—The Prospect, - - Eph. 2. 7

H..KD.

## How He Got Deliverance.

1. He was in Darkness, - - -Mark 10. 46
2. He was in Destitution, - - - ,, 10. 46
3. He was Drawn to Jesus, - - - ,, 10. 50
4. He got Deliverance, - - - - ,, 10. 52
5. He manifested Devotedness, - - ,, 10. 52

W.J.M.

## Take Salvation.

1. We are to take it freely, - - - Rev. 22. 17
2. We are invited to take it, - - Matt. 11. 28
3. We are entreated to take it, - -2 Cor. 5. 20
4. We are commanded to take it, - 1 John 3. 23
5. We are to compel the unsaved to take it, Luke 14. 23
6. Men are lost because would not accept, - John 5. 40

R.G.

## God and His People.

1. In Creation God is *above* us, - Deut. 33. 12
2. In Providence God is *around* us, - - Psa. 125. 2
3. In Incarnation God is *with* us, - - Matt. 1. 23
4. In Regeneration God is *in* us, - 2 Cor. 6. 16
5. In Preservation God is *beneath* us, - Deut. 33. 27
6. In Persecution God is *for* us, - - Rom. 8. 31
7. In the Assembly God is *among* us, - Matt. 18. 20

T.B.

## Never Man Like this Man.

1. NEVER MAN FASHIONED LIKE "THIS MAN." "All things were made by Him; and without Him was not any thing made that was made" (John 1. 3).
2. NEVER MAN KNEW LIKE "THIS MAN." "Because He knew all men" (John 2. 24). "Knowing their thoughts" (Matt. 9. 4).
3. NEVER MAN SPAKE LIKE "THIS MAN." "If any man thirst let him come unto me and drink" (John 7. 37, 46). "Come unto Me" (Matt. 11. 28).
4. NEVER MAN LOVED LIKE "THIS MAN." "Jesus loved Martha, and her sister, and Lazarus—Behold how He loved him" (John 11. 5, 36)—"He loved them to the uttermost" (John 13. 1).          HyP.

# SUBJECTS FOR SPEAKERS AND STUDENTS.

## Adam and Christ Contrasted.

Compare Psalm 8. 3, 9 with Philippians 2. 7, 8.

| | |
|---|---|
| Eden with its delights, | Wilderness and its privations. |
| Confidence in Satan, | Confidence in God. |
| Complete defeat, | Complete victory. |

F. F.

## What we are to Christ.

1. "Ye are My *disciples*," - - - - John 8. 31
2. "There shall also My *servant* be," - - John 12. 26
3. "I have called you *friends*," - - - John 15. 15
4. "Go to My *brethren*," - - - - John 20. 17

HyP.

## The Wrong Way——The Right Way.

| A WAY, - Prov. 14. 12 | THE WAY, - John 14. 6 |
|---|---|
| 1. Turned unto, Isa. 53. 6 | 1. Turned to the Lord, |
| 2. Trusted in, - Hosea 10.13 | Acts 11. 21 |
| 3. Taught others, Jer. 2. 33 | 2. Trusted in, - Eph. 1. 13 |
| 4. Turned upside down, | 3. Taught the way, Acts 4. 2 |
| Psa. 146. 9 | 4. Turned the world |
| | upside down, Acts 17. 9 |

A. M. P.

## Incomparable Glories.

"In an enigma " 1 Corinthians 13. 12 (Conybeare and Howson).

1. The *half* was not told me, - - - 1 Kings 9. 7
2. The *time* would *fail* me to tell, - - -Heb. 11. 32
3. The *world* itself could *not* contain, - - John 21.25
4. *More* in number than the *sand*, - - Psa. 139. 18
5. Love of Christ which *passeth* knowledge, - Eph. 3. 19
6. God's *Unspeakable Gift*, - - - - 2 Cor. 9. 15
7. The *unsearchable* riches of Christ, - - Eph. 3. 8

T. B.

## The Grace of God.

GOD'S grace that bringeth salvation hath appeared to all men, teaching us that, denying ungodliness and worldly lusts, we should live soberly,

RIGHTEOUSLY, and godly, in this present world; looking for that blessed hope,

AND the glorious appearing of the great God and our Saviour Jesus

CHRIST; who gave Himself for us. ... These things speak, and

EXHORT (Titus 2. 11-15.

T.M.

# SUBJECTS FOR SPEAKERS AND STUDENTS.

## A Message to Backsliders.

1. A loving invitation, Jer. 3. 12
2. A gracious promise, ,, 3. 12
3. A necessary confession, - - ,, 3. 13
4. Additional promises, ,, 3. 14

H.K.D.

## Missionary Qualifications

Two essentials. Acts 13. The

1. *Call* of God — "Separate me," - - - - v. 2
2. *Commendation* of elders— "*They* sent them away," v. 3 HYP.

## The New and Living Bread in John 6.

1. It is True—My Father giveth you the true Bread, **v. 32**
2. It is Living—Jesus said, I am the Living Bread, ,, 51
3. It is Life-giving—Jesus said, It gives life to the world, 33
4. It is Life-sustaining—He said, I am the Bread of Life, - - - - - - - ,, 48
5. It is Satisfying—The eater shall never hunger, ,, 35
6. It is Enduring—That which endures unto life eternal, 27
7. It is Divine—The Bread of God which gives life, ,, 33
8. It is Heavenly—The Bread from, or out of, Heaven, 41

H. J. VINE.

## The Power of the Word of our God.

1. Gives life eternal, John 5. 24
2. It wounds, Heb. 4. 12
3. Then heals, Psa. 107. 20
4. It tries us, Psa. 105. 19
5. It cleanses us, Psa. 119. 9
6. It keeps us from sin if obeyed, Psa. 119. 11
7. It lightens up our darkness, - Psa. 119. 105, 130
8. It energises us for service, Jer. 20. 9 M.S.

## How to Secure Abiding Results.

As at the beginning, so to-day, in Acts 2.

1. UNITED DISCIPLES—"Peter standing up with the eleven," - - - - verse 14
   No longer "who shall be greatest" (Luke 9. 46).
2. UPLIFTED CHRIST—"Jesus of Nazareth, ... crucified, ... raised up, ... to sit on the throne," - - - - verses 22, 23, 24, 30
   A Rejected—Risen—Reigning Christ.
3. UNPARALLELED BLESSING—"The same Day there were added unto them 3000 souls," verse 41
   The *same* mind (v. 1), the *same* Jesus (v. 36), the *same* Day (v. 41). Wherever you have points 1 and 2, 3 will follow.
4. UNWAVERING STEADFASTNESS — "They continued steadfastly in (1) doctrine, (2) fellowship, or service, (3) ordinances, (4) prayers.

*Result*—"Praising GOD (not Peter, who preached), and having favour with ALL the people" (v. 46). HYP.

# SUBJECTS FOR SPEAKERS AND STUDENTS.
## A Pattern Young Christian.

The Apostle Paul in Acts 9: "Lord, what wilt Thou have me to do?" What he did any young believer may be safe in following.

1. He PRAYED—"Behold, he prayeth,"  -  -  verse 11
2. Was BAPTISED — "*Brother* Saul ... was baptised,  -  -  -  -  -  -  „ 17, 18
3. PREACHED Christ—When "straightway," *what*—"that He is the Son of God,"  „  20
4. JOINED THE DISCIPLES—On the testimony of one man, Barnabas, to one thing, "that he was a disciple,"  -  -  -  -  „ 26, 27
5. CONTINUED STEADFAST — "With them, speaking boldly in the Name,"  -  -  „ 28, 29

HYP.

| The Glory of our Lord | True Minister of Christ. |
|---|---|
| AS REVEALED IN | Read Malachi 2. 5-7. |

| | |
|---|---|
| 1. The liberty of His glory, Rom. 8. 21 | 1. Fearing God—state of mind |
| 2. The Gospel of His glory, 2 Cor. 4. 4 | 2. Proclaiming the truth — message |
| 3. The body of His glory, Eph. 3. 21 | 3. Avoiding iniquity—purpose |
| | 4. Walking with God — habit |
| 4. The power of His glory, Col. 1. 11 | 5. Turning men to God—work |
| 5. The appearing of His glory,  -  Titus 2. 3 | 6. Teaching the law of God— duty |
| H.K.D. | 7. Acting as God's messenger —communion  N-B. |

## Marks of a Revival.

As seen in the first Gentile Revival in the City of Samaria.  Related in Acts 8.

1. BORN IN TROUBLE—"Death, persecution, scattering, burial, lamentation, HAVOC, jail," verse 1-3
2. BEGAN WITH AN INDIVIDUAL — "*Then* Philip went down PREACHING AN INDIVI-DUAL—Christ,"  -  -  -  -  -  „  5
3. BLENDED THE PEOPLE "with one accord— (1) heeding, (2) hearing, (3) seeing,"  -  „  6
4. BRINGS OUT DEMONS—"Unclean spirits, palsied, lame, were healed,"  -  -  „  7
5. BLESSES EVERYBODY—"There was great joy in that city,"  -  -  -  -  -  „  8

HYP.

155

# SUBJECTS FOR SPEAKERS AND STUDENTS.

## Three Great Themes.

1. The Work of the Lamb,    -    -    -    - John 1. 29
2. The Worth of the Lamb,    -    -    -    - Rev. 5. 11
3. The Wrath of the Lamb,    -    -    -    - Rev. 6. 16

HyP.

## Daily Things.

1. Bread,  -   -        Matt. 6. 11
2. Cross,  -   -   -  Luke 9. 23
3. Increase in church,
                           Acts 16. 5
4. Searching of Scriptures,
                           Acts 17. 11
5. Dying,  -   -      1 Cor. 15. 31
6. Exhorting,      - Heb. 10. 25
7. Watching, -    - Prov. 8. 34

F. F.

## Things Concerning Himself.

Psalm 135. 2-19.

1. The Presence of the Lord
2. The Possession of the Lord
3. The Pleasure of the Lord
4. The Power of the Lord
5. The Permanence of the Lord
6. The Portion of the Lord

H. K. D.

## About Believing.

1. A Pointed Question—Dost thou believe? etc., John 9. 35
2. A Plain Answer—I believe that Jesus Christ, etc., Acts 8. 37
3. A Prolific Result—Forgiveness (Acts 10. 43), Justification (Acts 13. 39), Salvation (Rom. 10. 9), Sonship (John 1. 12), Everlasting Life (John 5. 24), The Holy Spirit (John 7. 39), Full and Final Victory over Death (John 11. 26).

G. H.

## What the Bible Says About Jerusalem.

1. GOD'S CENTRE—"The Lord hath chosen Jerusalem" (Zech. 3. 2). Man's centre is Rome. God's centre is "the city of the great King."
2. GENTILE RULED—Until "the times of the Gentiles be fulfilled" (Luke 21. 24). "Until the veil be taken away" (Rom. 11. 25). Until they shall say, "Blessed is He that cometh" (Matt. 23. 39).
3. MOST TRAGIC SCENES will be enacted therein—"Tread them down like mire in the streets" (Isa. 10. 6).
4. THE WORLD'S METROPOLIS of the future—"Ten men shall take hold . . . of the skirt of him that is a Jew, saying, We will go with you" (Zech. 8. 23).
5. CREATION'S GLORY forever—"Holiness unto the Lord" everywhere (Zech. 14. 20, 21).

HyP.

# SUBJECTS FOR SPEAKERS AND STUDENTS.

## Three Visions.

1. A vision of God, - Isa. 6. 1
2. A vision of sin, - ,, 6. 5
3. A vision of Christ, ,, 6. 6
H. K. D.

## Christ Risen, Satisfied.

1. Weeping Mary, John 20. 16
2. Fearing disciples, ,, 20. 19
3. Doubting Thomas, ,, 20. 28
HyP.

## Five Great Events.

1. Christ Jesus came into the world,  John 3. 17; 1 Tim. 1. 15
2. Christ suffered for us, - - - - -Matt. 16. 21
3. Christ arose from the grave, - - Mark 16. 1-8
4. Christ ascended, - - - - -Acts 1. 9-11
5. Christ is coming again, - - John 14. 1-3, 18, 28
R. G.

## A Great Preacher's Subjects.
Psalm 40. 9, 10.

1. The Righteousness of God
2. The Faithfulness of God
3. The Salvation of God
4. The Lovingkindness of God
5. The Truth of God  H. K. D.

## No More's in Revelation.

1. No more sea, - Rev. 21. 1
2. No more sorrow, ,, 21. 4
3. No more crying, ,, 21. 4
4. No more pain, - ,, 21. 4
5. No more curse, - ,, 22. 3
6. No more night, - ,, 22. 5
7. No more death, - ,, 21. 4
R. G.

## True Discipleship.

1. Lead me in Thy righteousness, - - - Psa 5. 8
2. Lead me in Thy truth and teach me, - - ,, 25. 5
3. Lead me in a plain path, - - - - ,, 27. 11
4. Lead me for Thy Name's sake, - - - ,, 31. 3
5. Lead me to the Rock that is higher than I, - ,, 61. 2
6. Lead me in the way everlasting, - - - ,, 139. 24
7. Lead me into the land of uprightness, - - ,, 143. 10
F. S. B.

## Death—Resurrection—Glory.
In John 12 we have Christ as the

1. Suffering One—"Corn of wheat, ... die," - verse 24
2. Exalted One—"It bringeth forth much fruit," ,, 24
3. Humble One—"He that hateth his life," - ,, 25
4. Ruling One—"If any man serve Me," - ,, 26
5. Coming One—"Him will My Father honour," ,, 26
6. Obedient One—"For this cause came I unto this hour," - - - - - - ,, 27
7. Glorified One—"Then came there a voice from Heaven, ... I will glorify again," - ,, 28
HyP

# SUBJECTS FOR SPEAKERS AND STUDENTS.

## When We Awake.

WE WILL

1. See His glory, - - - - - - Luke 9. 32
2. Be Satisfied with His likeness, - - - Psa. 17.15
3. Sing His praise, - - Isa. 26. 19   H.K.D.

## Blind Bartimaeus.

1. His Condition—Blind and Begging, - Mark 10. 46
2. His Conviction—Heard of Jesus, and cried
   for mercy, - - - - - - - „ 10. 47
3. His Call—Jesus called him, - - - „ 10. 49
4. His Conversion—He came to Jesus, - „ 10. 50
5. Consecration—He followed Jesus, - - „ 10. 52

W.J.M.

## Bonds.

1. Of Life, - 1 Sam. 25. 29
2. Of Love, - Hosea 11. 4
3. Of Peace, - Eph. 4. 3
4. Of Union, - Col. 2. 19
5. In the Gospel, Phile. 13
6. In Christ, - Phil. 1. 13
7. In Service, 2 Cor. 4. 5

A.M.P.

## A Cluster of Grapes.

1. Saved, - - Deut. 33. 29
2. Secured, - „ 33. 27
3. Seated, - „ 33. 3
4. Satisfied, - „ 33. 23
5. Separated, - „ 33. 16

W.J.M.

## The Spirit's Might

IN THE

1. Regeneration of Believers,
   Eph. 2. 1
2. Confirmation of Believers,
   Eph. 1. 13
3. Illumination of Believers,
   Eph. 1. 17
4. Inspiration of Believers,
   Eph. 2. 18
5. Fortification of Believers,
   Eph. 3. 16
6. Sanctification of Believers,
   Eph. 2.22
7. Supplication of Believers,
   Eph. 6. 18   T-H.

## The Great Commission and the Response.

Mark 16. 15.

Command—Go. -

Who?—Ye. - -
Where?—Into all the
world, - -
What to do?—Preach
Preach what?—Gospel.
To whom?—Every
creature. - -

Mark 16. 19.

What was the disciples' decision?—
They went forth.

What did they do?—Preach.

Where?—Everywhere.
With whom?—The Lord.
Why?—To confirm the Word.

Result—Signs following.   W.H.K,

# SUBJECTS FOR SPEAKERS AND STUDENTS.

## The True Lord's Prayer
is found in John 17.   The Disciple's Prayer in Matthew 6.9.

### I. OUR LORD SPEAKS OF THREE GIFTS.

1. " That He should give *Eternal Life*," - - verse 2
2. " I have given them *Thy Word*," - - „ 14
3. " And the *Glory* I have given them," - - „ 22

### II. HE ALSO MAKES FOUR REQUESTS.

1. " Holy Father, *keep* through Thy Name," - „ 11
2. " *Sanctify* them through Thy Truth," - „ 17
3. *Unite* " that they all may be one," - - „ 21
4. *Glorify* " that they may behold My glory," - „ 24
HyP.

## Identification with Christ.

1. In Sonship, - Gal. 4. 4, 5
2. In Heirship, - Rom. 8. 17
3. In Sanctification,
   John 17. 19
4. In Crucifixion, Gal. 2. 20
5. In Persecution, John 15. 20
6. In Resurrection, Col. 3. 1
7. In Glorification, John 17.22
T.-H.

## " Perfect."

1. A peerless Saviour,
   Heb. 11. 10
2. Has done a perfect work,
   Heb. 10
3. Which gives a purged
   conscience to all
   who believe on His
   Name, - - Heb. 10
S-S.

## Two Specimen Results
from the first Gentile Revival.   Acts 8.

1. A SHAM SORCERER—" Believed *also* (or copied others), was baptised, and wondered," verse 13
   " Thy money perish with thee," - „ 20
2. A SAVED PREMIER—Converted through Isaiah 53, " read, heard, believed, and was baptised," - - - - - - „ 27-38
   " He went on his way rejoicing," - „ 39
HyP.

## Visions of Christ
in Psalm 22.

1. The Reproached One, v. 6
2. The Rejected One, „ 7
3. The Risen One, - „ 22
4. The Rejoicing One, „ 22
5. The Ruling One, - „ 28
6. The Righteous One, „ 31
W. J. M.

## The Lord Preserveth—

1. The faithful, Psa. 31. 23
2. The souls of His saints,
   Psa. 97. 10
3. The simple, - Psa. 116. 6
4. All them that love Him,
   Psa. 145. 20
5. The strangers, Psa. 146. 9
6. The way of His saints,
   Prov. 2. 8   F. F.

# SUBJECTS FOR SPEAKERS AND STUDENTS.

## The "Greatest" of Texts (John 3. 16).

| | |
|---|---|
| God - - - - | - The greatest Lover. |
| so loved - - - | - The greatest degree. |
| the world, - - - | - The greatest company. |
| that He gave - - | - The greatest act. |
| His only begotten Son, - | - The greatest Gift. |
| that whosoever - - | - The greatest opportunity. |
| believeth - - - | - The greatest simplicity. |
| in Him - - - | - The greatest attraction. |
| should not perish, - | - The greatest promise. |
| but - - - - | - The greatest difference. |
| have - - - - | - The greatest certainty. |
| Everlasting Life, - - | - The greatest possession. |

## The Will of God
### (Eph. 1. 1).

1. Mystery of His will, Eph. 1. 9
2. Counsel of His will, Eph. 1. 11
3. Understanding of His will, - - Eph. 5. 17
4. Doing His will, Eph. 6. 6

H.K.D.

## We Are to Pray For

1. Self, - - - Psa. 50. 1
2. Family, - - 2 Sam. 7. 27
3. Friends, - - James 5. 16
4. Workers, - 2 Thess. 3. 1
5. Church, - - Eph. 6. 18
6. Enemies, - Luke 6. 28
7. All men, - - 1 Tim. 2. 1

S. E. B.

## "The Lord is Thy Keeper" (Psalm 121. 5).

1. THE PRAYER.—"Holy Father, *keep* through Thine own Name those whom Thou hast given Me" (John 17.11).
2. THE PROMISE.—"I will be with thee, and *keep* thee" (Gen. 28. 15). "I will hold thine hand, and will *keep* thee" (Isa. 42. 6).
3. THE PERSUASION.—"I know whom I have believed, and am persuaded He is able to *keep* that which I have committed unto Him" (2 Tim. 1. 12).
4. THE POWER.—"*Kept* by the power of God through faith unto salvation" (1 Peter 1. 5).
5. THE PRAISE.—"Now unto Him that is able to *keep* you from falling, and to present you faultless before the presence of His glory with exceeding joy, to the only wise God our Saviour, be glory and majesty, dominion and power, both now and ever. Amen." (Jude 24, 25). **T. SHULDMAN HENRY.**

# SUBJECTS FOR SPEAKERS AND STUDENTS.

## A Great Salvation.

1. The PERSON who first published it—The Son of God (Heb. 2. 3).
2. The PRICE Paid to Procure it—The Precious Blood of Christ (1 Peter 1. 19).
3. The PEOPLE Saved by it—The Chief of Sinners, etc. (1 Tim. 1. 15; Luke 18; Luke 7).
4. The PLACE it Saves us for—The Paradise of God (Luke 23. 43; Rev. 2. 7).
5. The PIT we are Saved from—The Bottomless Pit (Rev. 20. 1; Job 33. 24).                   J.M.

## "We Have"

1. Scripture as our *Authority* (2 Peter 1. 10).
2. Redemption as our *Blessing* (Eph. 1. 7).
3. Eternal Life as our *Possession* (1 John 5. 13).
4. Peace as our *Comfort* (Rom. 5. 1).
5. Access as our *Privilege* (Rom. 5. 2).
6. Union with Christ as our *Security* (Rom. 6. 5).
7. Christ's Advocacy as our *Care* (1 John 2. 1). C-C.

## Products of Preaching
### In Apostolic Days.

| | |
|---|---|
| 3000 believed, | Acts 2. 41 |
| 5000 men, | „ 4. 4 |
| Multitudes, | „ 5. 14 |
| Great company of priests, | „ 6. 7 |
| City of Samaria, | „ 8. 8 |
| All who heard, | „ 10. 44 |
| A great number, | „ 11. 21 |
| Much people, | „ 11. 24 |
| A household, | „ 16. 34 |
| Many—not a few, | „ 17. 12 |
| Many *myriads* (R.V.) | „ 21. 20 |

WHY NOT NOW? HYP.

## "Ready"—A Study for All.

1. Condition of the sinner—"*Ready* to perish" (Deut. 26. 5; Job 29. 13; Prov. 31. 6; Isa. 27. 13).
2. Compassion of the Lord—"*Ready* to pardon" (Neh. 9. 17; Psa. 86. 5; Isa. 38. 20).
3. Conduct of the saint—"*Ready* to do" (2 Sam. 15. 15).
4. Commission of the servant—"*Ready* to preach" (Rom. 1. 15).
5. Coming glory and salvation—"*Ready* to be revealed" (1 Peter 1. 5).
6. Complaint of the sorrowful—"*Ready* to halt" (Psa. 38. 17).
7. Consequence of backsliding—Grace "*ready* to die" (Rev. 3. 2).                   F.E.M.

# SUBJECTS FOR SPEAKERS AND STUDENTS.

## God, our Past, Present, and Future Helper.

1. Past Helper—"Thou hast been my help,"   Psa. 63. 7
2. Present Helper—"A very present help,"   Psa. 46. 1
3. Future Helper—"The Lord will help me," Isa. 50. 9

P.T.M.

## Threefold Calling.

1. Called by the Gospel—PAST,  ..   .. 2 Thess. 2. 14
2. Called unto Holiness—PRESENT,   .. 1 Thess. 4. 7
3. Called unto Glory—FUTURE,     .. 1 Thess. 2. 12

W.J.M.

## Precious Words—John 16. 22.

1. The Fact—"And ye now therefore have sorrow."
2. The Promise—"But I will see you again."
3. The Result—"And your heart shall rejoice."
4. The Seal—"And your joy no man taketh from you."

B-E.

## Comforting Words.

1. The believer shall not come into judgment, John 5. 24
2. The believer shall not walk in darkness,   John 8. 12
3. The believer shall never hunger, Phil. 4. 19; John 6. 28-35
4. The believer shall never thirst,   ..   John 7. 37-39
5. The believer shall never perish,   ..   .. John 3. 15
6. The believer shall never be plucked out of Jesus' hands, John 10. 27-29
7. The believer shall never die,     ..   John 11. 25-27

S-S.

## "The Blessed Man."

1. He experiences Pardon—"Blessed is he whose transgression is forgiven,"   ..   Psa. 32 1
2. He practises Walking—"Blessed is every one..that walketh in His ways,"   ..   Psa. 128. 1
3. He suffers Persecution—"Blessed are they which are persecuted for righteousness' sake," ..   ..   .. Matt. 5. 10
4. He endures Temptation—"Blessed is the man that endureth temptation,"   James 1. 12
5. He enjoys Giving—"It is more blessed to give than to receive,"   ..   .. Acts 20. 35
6. He delights in Obedience—"Blessed is the man that doeth this,"   ..   .. Isa. 56. 2

T-H.

# SUBJECTS FOR SPEAKERS AND STUDENTS.

## Seven Wonders in Psalm 111.

1. His Work—Recommended, .. .. Psalm 111. 3
2. His Righteousness—Remaineth, .. ,, 3
3. His Covenant—Remembered, .. .. ,, 5
4. His Commandments—Reliable, .. ,, 7
5. His People—Redeemed, .. .. ,, 9
6. His Name—Reverend, .. .. .. ,, 9
7. His Praise—Repeated, .. .. .. ,, 10

W.J.M.

## About Nothing.

1. Profiting Nothing—The Flesh,.. .. John 6. 63
2. Knowing Nothing—The Proud, .. 1 Tim. 6. 4
3. Paying Nothing—The Bankrupt, .. Luke 7. 42
4. Judging Nothing—The Church, .. 1 Cor. 4. 5
5. Able for Nothing—The Independent,.. John 15. 5
6. Careful for Nothing—The Prayerful, .. Phil. 4. 6
7. Good for Nothing—The Carnal, .. Matt. 5. 13

JS. FS.

## What the Saviour Does.

1. He justifies, Luke 18. 14
2. He emancipates, Titus 2. 14
3. He saves, Matt. 1. 21
4. He unburdens, Matt. 11. 28
5. He satisfies, John 4. 14

F.F.

## "Salvation" (John 6. 47).

1. A Personal Salvation— He.
2. A Present Salvation— Hath.
3. A Permanent Salvation —Everlasting.
4. A Perfect Salvation— Life. H.K.D.

## Some Sins.

1. Sins of Omission, James 4. 17
2. Sins of Commission, Deut. 9. 7
3. Secret Sins, Psalm 90. 8
4. Besetting Sins, Heb. 12. 1
5. Scarlet Sins, Isa. 1. 18
6. Great Sins, Rev. 18. 5
7. Sins of the Flesh, Gal. 5. 19 F.K.

## Seven Things of God.

1. The Will of God, 1 Cor. 1. 1
2. The Church of God, 1 Cor. 1. 2
3. The Faithfulness of God, 1 Cor. 1. 9
4. The Power of God, 1 Cor. 1. 8
5. The Wisdom of God, 1 Cor. 1. 21
6. The Testimony of God, 1 Cor. 2. 1
7. The Deep Things of God, 1 Cor. 1. 1 H.K.D.

# SUBJECTS FOR SPEAKERS AND STUDENTS.

## The Lowliness of our Lord.

1. In His Birth—"Lying in a manger," - - Luke 2. 11
2. In His Life—"Not where to lay His head," Luke 9. 58
3. In His Death—"Him, and the malefactors," Luke 23.33

HyP.

## "Redemption" in Ephesians 1.

| | | | |
|---|---|---|---|
| PERSONS, | .. .. | "Us," .. .. .. | v. 3 |
| POSITION, | .. .. | "In Christ," .. .. | v. 3 |
| PLACE, | .. .. | "The Heavenlies," .. | v. 3 |
| PURPOSE, | .. .. | "Eternal," .. .. | v. 4 |
| PLEASURE, | .. .. | "His will," .. .. | v. 5 |
| PRAISE, | .. .. | "Glory of His grace," .. | v. 6 |
| POWER, | .. .. | "Mighty power," .. | v. 19 |
| POINT, | .. .. | "Far above all," .. | v. 21 |

*For blackboard a large P can be used.*　　　　w-w.

## The Story of the Fall
### (Genesis 3).

The Cause of Sin (v. 1),
　Satan.
The Curse of Sin (vv. 14-19),
　Suffering.
The Cure of Sin (v. 15),
　Saviour.　　H. K. D.

## What Jesus gave John.

Pardon—"Washed us from
　our sins," Rev. 1. 5
Power—"Laid His right
　hand upon me,"
　　　　Rev. 1. 17
Peace—"Fear not,"
　Rev. 1. 17. w. j. M.

## Our Worship (John 4. 23, 24).

1. The *Authority* for it, .. .. The Father seeks it.
2. The *Object* of it, .. .. The Living God.
3. The *Power* for it, .. .. The Holy Spirit.
4. The *Manner* of it, .. .. .. In truth.
5. The *Place* of it, (Heb. 10. 19), .. In the holiest of all.
6. The *Character* of it (Heb. 13-15), .. Spiritual.
7. The *Acceptance* of it (1 Peter 2. 5), "In Christ Jesus."

T.D.W.M.

## The Abundance of God's Provision
### to meet all our Need.

Abundant Mercy for the Lost, .. .. 1 Peter 1. 3
Abundant Life for the Dead, .. .. John 10. 10
Abundant Pardon for the Guilty, .. .. Isa. 55. 7
Abundant Peace for the Troubled, .. Psa. 37. 11
Abundant Grace for the Needy, .. .. Rom. 5. 17
Abundant Joy for the Sad, .. .. 2 Cor. 8. 2
Abundant Power for the Weak, .. Eph. 3. 20 T·H·

# SUBJECTS FOR SPEAKERS AND STUDENTS.

## Chinese Translation of John 3. 16.

"The True God so passionately loved mankind, even so far as to take His only begotten Son, bestowing Him upon them in order to cause all who believe on Him not to reach destruction, but to certainly obtain eternal life."

*Teachers could quote and use as lesson.*  T.R.C.

## Negative and Positive Commands.

Eph.    Eph.

4. 14, "Be no more deceived," BUT "Grow up into Christ," 4. 15
4. 29, "No corrupt words," - BUT "That which is good," 4. 29
4. 28, "Steal no more," - - BUT "Give," - - - - - 4. 28
5. 4, "Nor foolish talking," - BUT "Giving of thanks," - 5. 4
5. 15, "Walk not as fools," - BUT "As wise, - - - - 5. 15
5. 17, "Be not unwise," - BUT "Understanding," - 5. 17
6. 6, "Not men pleasers," - BUT "Servants of Christ," 6. 6

Js. Fs.

## The Pattern Servant

Was revealed in Acts 20.  Served with

1. HUMILITY and tears, v. 19
2. REALITY.  Kept back nothing—free from blood, - - vv. 20, 26
3. PERSISTENCY. Night and day—all seasons—3 years, vv. 18, 31
4. EXPECTANCY.  They "wept sore, kissed, accompanied," vv. 37, 38

HyP.

## The Royal Proclamation.

Acts 13. 38.

1. Purchased, "*Through* this Man"
2. Present, - "*is* preached"
3. Personal, - - "unto *you*"
4. Precious, "*forgiveness* of sins,"
5. Plenteous, "*all* that believe"
6. Perfect, "justified from *all* things."

HyP.

## THREE PERFECT THINGS.

# GOD'S WORK AY ILL PERFECT

Deut. 32. 4; Psalm 18. 30; Rom. 12. 2.        A.J.P.

## Three Wonderful Sights.

PAST—We have seen Him,  ..  ..  John 20. 25
　　The Crucified One.
PRESENT—We now see Him,  ..  ..  Heb. 2. 9
　　The Crowned One.
FUTURE—We shall see Him,  ..  ..  1 John 3. 2
　　The Coming One.

W.J.M.

# SUBJECTS FOR SPEAKERS AND STUDENTS.

## The Last Tribunal.

1. The Court, .. The Great White Throne, Rev. 20. 11
2. The Judge, .. The Son of Man, .. John 5. 22
3. The Prisoners, The Dead, .. .. Rev. 20. 12
4. The Charge,.. Unbelief, .. .. Rev. 20. 13
5. The Witnesses, Three, .. .. Heb. 10. 29
6. The Verdict, Guilty, .. .. Rom. 3. 19
7. The Sentence, The Second Death, Rev. 21. 8 JS. FS.

## Things Opened.

1. The Eyes, - Isa. 42. 7
2. The Ears, - Isa. 50. 5
3. The Heart, - Acts 16. 14
4. The Mouth, Psa. 51. 15
5. The Scriptures,
   Luke 24. 32
6. The Understanding,
   Luke 24. 45
7. A Door for Service,
   1 Cor. 16. 9. F.F.

## Seven Covenants.

### in the Old Testament.

1. Covenant of Union,
   Jer. 50. 5
2. Covenant of Separation,
   Exod. 10. 3
3. Covenant of Search,
   2 Chron. 15. 12
4. Covenant of Obedience
   2 Kings 23. 3
5. Covenant of Walk,
   Neh. 10. 29
6. Covenant of Service,
   Joshua 24. 25
7. Covenant of Possession,
   2 Kings 11. 17
   S.C.U.H.

## A Fourfold Exhortation

### (Deuteronomy 5. 1).

Listen! Learn!
Love! Live G.H.

## An Abiding Saviour.

1. For us, - Heb. 9. 24
2. In us, - - John 15. 4
3. With us, - Luke 24. 29
   H.K.D.

## Comforting Thoughts.

HE KNOWS —He knoweth the way that I take,
Job 23. 10

HE LOVES — The Father Himself loveth you,
John 16. 27

HE CARES — Be careful for nothing, - Phil. 4. 6
E.R.M.

## The Blessed and Perfect Man.

### Christ as in Psalm 1.

His Purity, - - - v. 1
His Piety, - - - v. 2
His Prosperity, - - v. 3
W.J.M.

## Paul's Points.

### in his famous address. Acts 26.

1. What "I DID," - v. 10
   Punished, persecuted, mad.
2. What "I SAW," v. 13
   At midday—Lord—Jesus.
3. What "I AM," - v. 25
   Not mad (25)—persuaded (26)—happy even with bonds (29). HYP.

# SUBJECTS FOR SPEAKERS AND STUDENTS.

## Three Great Magnets
### in Mark 4. 19.

DISTRACTION, - - - "The *cares* of the world."
ABSTRACTION, - - "The *deceitfulness* of riches."
ATTRACTION, - "The *lusts* of other things." HYP.

### Bible Benedictions.
1. Sanctified,
     1 Thess. 5. 23-29
2. Stablished,
     2 Thess. 2. 16, 17
3. Subdued,
     Heb. 13. 20, 21
4. Strengthened,
     1 Peter 5. 10, 11
5. Sustained,   Jude 24, 25
6. Satisfied,   2 Cor. 13. 13
                    H.K.D.

### The Christian Life.
The Christian given to
Christ out of the world,
          John 17. 6
The Christian left in the
world,   John 17. 11, 15
The Christian not of the
world,   .. John 17. 14
The Christian hated by the
world,   .. John 17. 14
The Christian kept from the
evil of the world,
          John 17. 15
The Christian sent into the
world,   .. John 17. 18
The Christian preaching the
Word to the world,
     John 16. 20. N.B.

### Seven Danger Signals.
1. Beware of forgetting God,
          Deut. 6. 10-12
2. Beware of the unequal
     yoke,   .. 2 Cor. 6. 14
3. Beware of man's ap-
     proval,.. 2 Tim. 2. 15
4. Beware of secular mix-
     ture,   ..   Col. 2. 8
5. Beware of conceit,
          Rom. 12. 16
6. Beware of the "many
     things," Luke 10. 41, 42
7. Beware of the error of the
     wicked, 2 Peter 3. 17, 18
                    R.F.

### John's Theme.
#### (Revelation 1).
Cross of Christ,   ..   v. 5
Coming of Christ, ..   v. 7
Companionship of Christ,
     vv. 12-18.   W.J.M.

### The Spirit's Antidote
#### for an unquiet earthly mind.
Go on—with Him,
          John 15. 5
Go on—for Him,
          2 Cor. 5. 15
Go on—to Him,
     1 Thess. 4. 17.   S-S.

## A Fourfold Warning.
The angels cast down,   ..   ..   ..   2 Peter 2. 4
The Antediluvians perish,   ..   ..   2 Peter 3. 6
The Sodamites burned,   ..   ..   ..   Jude 7
The Jews cut off, ..   ..   ..   ..   Rom. 11. 20
                                        Js. Fs.

# SUBJECTS FOR SPEAKERS AND STUDENTS.

## The Word of God
(Psalm 119).

1. Receiving (v. 130),
    It gives light.
2. Resorted to (v. 9),
    It cleanses.
3. Retaining (v. 11),
    It preserves.
4. Relying on (v. 28),
    It strengthens.
5. Reading (v. 148),
    It instructs.
6. Reverence (v. 161),
    It is holy.
7. Rejoice at it (v. 162),
    It enricheth. w.j.m.

## The Death of Christ
(Acts 2. 23).
Seven facts associated with it.

1. We are sinners,
    Rom. 3. 23
2. There is judgment to
    come, - Heb. 9. 27
3. Sentence is pronounced,
    Rom. 6. 23
4. A Saviour has been pro-
    vided, - 1 Peter 2. 24
5. An eternal life of blessed-
    ness is offered, John 3.16
6. Eternal punishment
    awaits rejecters,
        John 3. 36
7. The Lord will come
    again, - Rev. 1. 7
                  F.F.

## Salvation.

GOD—Thought it.
JESUS—Bought it.
THE BIBLE—Taught it.
FAITH—Brought it.
THE HOLY SPIRIT—Wrought
    it.
THE DEVIL—Fought it.
    But I got it—GLORY!

## Christian Continuing.

1. Contend for the old faith,
        Jude 3
2. Continue in the faith,
        Col. 1. 23
3. Continue in prayer,
        Col. 4. 2
4. Continue in doctrine,
        1 Tim. 4. 16
5. Continue in things
    learned of God,
        2 Tim. 3. 14, 15
6. Continue in the love of
    Christ, - John 15. 9
7. Continue to entertain
    strangers, Heb. 7. 23
                  L.R.S.

## Wonderful Oneness
in Acts 4.

1. One aim—signs and
    wonders, - -    v. 30
2. One heart—the mul-
    titude, - - - - v. 32
3. One soul—them that
    believed, - - - v. 32
4. One purse—all things
    common, - - - v. 32
*Result*—"Great grace, great
    power."   HyP.

## My Life Story.

I am not what I was,
        Eph. 2. 2-12
I am not what I shall be,
        1 John 3. 2
I am not what I should be,
        Eph. 4. 1
I am not what I would be,
        Phil. 3. 12, 13
But by the grace of God,
I am what I am,
        1 Cor. 15. 10.   N-B.

# SUBJECTS FOR SPEAKERS AND STUDENTS.

## The Foolish Virgins.

A Bad Rebuff—The door was shut, - · Matt. 25. 10
A Mad Request—Lord, open to us, - · ,, 11
A Sad Reply—I know you not, - · ,, 12

W. J. M.

## Three Faithful Men.

1. Abram the Pilgrim, - - - · Neh. 9. 8
2. Daniel the President and Prophet,- - Dan. 6. 4
3. Paul the Preacher, - - - - 1 Tim. 1. 12
"Be thou faithful" (Rev. 2. 10). W. J. M.

## The Forsaken Slave.

The Young Man—
1. Forsaken, - 1 Sam. 30. 13
2. Famishing, ,, 12
3. Found, - ,, 11
4. Fed, - · ,, 11
5. Freed, · ,, 15

H.K.D.

## Four Therefore's.

1. Condemnation, Rom. 2. 1
2. Justification, - ,, 5. 1
3. Assurance of sal-
vation, - - ,, 8. 1
4. Consecration, · ,, 12. 1

W. J. M.

## The Model Maid.

She was little, - · · · · · 2 Kings 5. 2
She was a captive, - · · · · ,, 2
She was an Israelite, · · · · ,, 2
She confessed God, - · · · · ,, 3
She had sympathy, - · · · · ,, 3
She told of the prophet, - · · · ,, 3
She was the means of Salvation, - · ,, 15

JS. FS.

## Peace with God.

1. PEACE PROCURED. Having made peace through
the blood of His Cross, - - - Col. 1. 20
2. PEACE PROCLAIMED. Christ came and preached
peace to you which were afar off, and to
them which were nigh,- - - - Eph. 2. 17
3. PEACE POSSESSED. Therefore being justified
by faith, we have peace with God through
our Lord Jesus Christ, - - - - Rom. 5. 1
4. PEACE PERSONIFIED. He is our peace, - Eph. 2. 14

A.J.P.

## Christ is All.

In Christ,- · · Standing, · · Life
With Christ, · · Separated, · · Living
For Christ, · · Serving, - · · Labouring
Like Christ, · · Satisfied, - · · Likeness

2 Cor. 5. 17; Exod. 33. 16 and Acts 4. 13; 2 Cor. 4. 11;
1 John 3. 2. A.M.P.

# SUBJECTS FOR SPEAKERS AND STUDENTS.

## Our Divine Possessions.

Divine Forgiveness, Psa. 32. 1
Divine Assurance,  ,, 32. 5
Divine Protection,  ,, 32. 7
Divine Deliverance, ,, 32. 7
Divine Guidance,   ,, 32. 8
Divine Warning,    ,, 32. 9
Divine Joy,    ..  ,, 32. 11

W.J.M.

## Israel's First King.

His Display,    1 Sam. 9.  2
His Disobedience,  ,, 15. 11
His Dismay,        ,, 17. 11
His Displeasure,   ,, 18.  8
His Desolation,    ,, 18. 12
His Design,        ,, 19. 10
His Despair,       ,, 28. 4-6

JS. FS.

## The Lord's Negatives.

IT IS WELL TO REMEMBER THAT OUR LORD CAME

1. Not to destroy the Law,  ..   ..   Matt. 5. 17
2. Not to call the righteous,  ..   ..   Matt. 9. 13
3. Not to be ministered unto,  ..   ..   Matt. 20. 28
4. Not to destroy men's lives,  ..   ..   Luke 9. 56
5. Not to do His own will,  ..   ..   John 6. 39
6. Not to judge the world,  ..   ..   John 12. 47

H.K.D.

## Names of Our Lord.

The Word of Life, 1 John 1. 1
The Eternal Life,   ,, 1. 2
The Advocate,  ..  ,, 2. 1
The Righteous One, ,, 2. 1
The Propitiation,  ,, 2. 2
The Saviour of the
    World,    ..   ,, 4. 14
The Son of God,    ,, 5.  5

H.K.D.

## A Remarkable Cure.

CURE—Perfect and
    Patent,   ..  Acts 3. 7
CONDUCT—Walking,
    Leaping,
    Praising, Acts 3. 8
CONDITION—
    Helpless and
    Hopeless,  ..  Acts 3. 2

G.H.

## Wanted.

A LIST OF PERSONS WANTED EVERYWHERE TO-DAY.

Fathers like Abraham,    ..    ..    .. Gen. 18. 19
Mothers like Hannah,    ..    ..    .. 1 Sam. 1. 27, 28
Boys like the Lord Jesus, ..    ..    .. Luke 2. 51
Girls like the little Maid, ..    ..    .. 2 Kings 5. 1-4
Brothers like Nehemiah and Hanani,  .. Neh. 7. 2
Sisters like Mary and Martha,  ..    .. Luke 10. 38-42
Men in high places like Daniel, ..    .. Dan. 6. 5
Preachers like Paul,    ..    ..    .. 1 Cor. 2. 1-5
Servants of God like Barnabas, ..    .. Acts 11. 24
Everybody like the Bereans,  ..    .. Acts 17. 11

# SUBJECTS FOR SPEAKERS AND STUDENTS.

## The Lord as a "Stone."

Stumbling Stone to Israel (Isa. 8. 14; Rom. 9. 33; 1 Peter 2. 8).
Corner Stone to the Church (1 Peter 2. 6; Eph. 2. 20).
Smiting Stone to the Gentile Kingdom (Dan. 2. 45).   W.W.F.

## Three Things About Noah.

Sweet Invitation—"Come into the Ark,"   .. Gen. 7. 1
Wise Acceptation—"And Noah went in,"   ..   ,, 7
Grand Consolation—"Jehovah shut him in,"  ..   ,, 16
W.T.R.

## The Grace of our Lord
(2 Cor. 8. 9).

The Fact—He became poor.
The Purpose — That ye might be rich.
The Knowledge—Ye know.
H.K.D.

## We are

1. Called, .. 1 Cor. 1. 24
2. Saved, ..   ,, 18
3. Sanctified,   ,, 2
4. Enriched,   ,, 5
5. Despised,   ,, 28

## The Master and the Servants.

1. Where He found them—"out of the world" (John 17. 6).
2. What He gave them—Life (v. 2), the words (v. 8), the Glory (v. 22).
3. Where He sends them—"into the world" (v. 18).
4. What He does for them—"I pray for them" (v. 9).
5. Where He brings them—"Behold My glory" (v. 24). A. H.

## Pure Things (Phil. 4. 8).

1. Pure Wisdom, Jas. 3. 17
2. Pure Water, Heb. 10. 22
3. Pure Mind, 2 Pet. 3. 1
4. Pure Heart, 1 Pet. 1. 22
5. Pure Conscience, 1 Tim. 3. 9
6. Pure Religion, Jas. 1. 27
7. Pure Servant, 1 Tim. 5. 22

## What the Spirit Does.

1. Liberates, .. Rom. 8. 2
2. Indwells, ..   ,, 8. 9
3. Quickens, ..   ,, 8. 11
4. Leads, ..   ,, 8. 14
5. Witnesses, ..   ,, 8. 16
6. Helps, ..   ,, 8. 26
7. Intercedes,   ,, 8. 26, 27
W.J.M.

## Our Confidence:

1. As to temporal needs—"Ye are better than fowls" (Matt. 6. 26; Luke 12. 24).
2. As to personal safety—"Ye are of more value than many sparrows" (Matt. 10. 31).
3. As to joy—"Thy love is better than wine" (S. of S. 1. 2).
4. As to life—"Thy loving kindness is better than life" (Psa. 63. 3).
5. As to death—"The Lord's presence is very far better than earth" (Phil. 1. 23).   G.H.M.

# SUBJECTS FOR SPEAKERS AND STUDENTS.

## Bible Prayers.

1. Peter Cried, - Save Me, - - Matt. 14. 30
2. David Cried, - Search Me, - - Psalm 139 .23
3. Moses Cried, - Show Me, - - Exod. 33. 13
4. Samson Cried, - Strengthen Me, - Judges 16. 28
5. Isaiah Cried, - Send Me, - - Isaiah 6. 8
6. Solomon Cried, - Stay Me,- - - Song. 2. 5
7. Disciple Cried, - Suffer Me, -Luke 9. 59. JS. FS.

## What we Have to Take.

1. Take the *cup*—Implying Salvation, - Psa. 116. 13
2. Take *My yoke*—Implying Service, - Matt. 11. 29
3. Take *away* the stone—Implying Stum-
   bling-blocks, - - - - John 11. 39
4. Take *up* the Cross—Implying Suffering, Matt. 16. 24
5. Take *hold* of My strength—Implying
   Sufficiency, - - - - Isaiah 27. 5
6. Take *with* you words—Implying Prayer, Hosea 14. 2
7. Take *no* thought for your life—Implying
   Faith, - - - - - Matt. 6 25. J.S.

## God's "Fear Nots."

Isaiah 41. 10, 14.

Fear not
Abram, - Gen. 15. 1
Hagar, - Gen. 21. 17
Isaac, - - Gen. 26. 24
Jacob, - - Gen. 46. 3
Moses, - - Num. 21. 34
Joshua, - Josh. 8. 1
Gideon, - Judges 6. 23
Israel, - - Isa. 43. 1
Ezekiel, - Ezek. 3. 9
Daniel,- - Dan. 10. 12
Zerubbabel, Haggai 2. 5
Zacharias, - Luke 1. 13
Mary, - - Luke 1. 30
Simon, - Luke 5. 10
Jairus, - - Luke 8. 50
Paul, - - Acts 27. 24
John, - - Rev. 1. 17
Christian, - Matt. 10. 26

G.E.W

## By Royal Command.

Acts 17. 30, 31.

1. Who commands?- "God"
2. When? - - - "now"
3. Whom? - - "all men"
4. Where? - "everywhere"
5. What?- - "to repent"
6. Why? - day appointed—
   Judge appointed.

## Sufferings of Christ.

GREAT FACTS.

1. Foretold, - 1 Pet. 2. 12
2. Our example,
   1 Pet. 1. 11
3. His patience in
   1 Pet. 2. 23
4. His endurance,
   1 Pet. 3. 18
5. Our Aim, - 1 Pet. 4. 1
6. Partakers of 1 Pet. 4. 13
7. Our testimony of
   1 Pet. 5. 1. F.E.M.

# SUBJECTS FOR SPEAKERS AND STUDENTS

## Four Great "Pleasures" in the Bible.

1. **Sin's Pleasure,** - - - - - Heb. 11. 25
   Chokes the Word (Luke 8. 14); Evidence of death (1 Tim. 5. 6).
2. **God's Pleasure,** - - . . - Isa. 53. 10
   (1) To bruise His Son; (2) To prosper in His hand (Col. 1. 19).
3. **Christ's Pleasure,** - John 8. 29; Rom. 15. 3
4. **The Christian's Pleasure,** - 2 Cor. 5. 9, R.V.; Psa. 16. 11; 2 Tim. 2. 4  H.H.

## Psalm 4.

Divine help valued, - v. 1
Divine blessing desired, v. 6
Divine joy imparted, - v. 7
Divine safety enjoyed, v. 8
W. J. M.

## His Vineyard.
(Isa. 27. 2, 3)

It would not be difficult to find a long list of texts showing the ceaseless care the Master bestows. Here are a few:
He fences it, - Isa. 5. 2
He digs about it, Luke 13. 8
He dresses it, - Heb. 6. 7
He gathers out the stones, - Isa. 5. 2
He transplants it, Psa. 80. 8-10  G. M. T.

## A Divine Charter.

Everlasting Covenant made, - 2 Sam. 23.5
Assured of God's Everlasting love, Jer. 31. 3
Embraced in the Everlasting arms, Deut. 33. 27
Saved from the Everlasting burnings, Isa. 33. 14
Having instead an Everlasting righteousness, Dan. 9. 24
And crowned with everlasting joy, Isa. 51. 11
By the Everlasting God, Isa. 40. 28
JS. FS.

## Four Steps of the Christian Life (Mark 3. 13, 14).

1. He called, - - The Invitation, Matt. 11. 28
2. They came, - - The Acceptance, Luke 15. 20
3. That they should be with Him, - - The Life or Walk, John 15. 4, 5
4. That He might send them forth to preach, The Service, Matt. 28. 19, 20; John 15. 8

We see in this verse that there must be the living, or the abiding, with Him before any service can be rendered and blessed. H.G.

# SUBJECTS FOR SPEAKERS AND STUDENTS.

## David's Threefold Attitude.

Lying before the Lord as a Penitent,    - 2 Sam. 12. 16
Sitting before the Lord as a Worshipper,   - 2 Sam. 7. 18
Standing before the Lord as a Servant,    - 1 Chron. 28.2

N-B.

## Seven of God's Superlatives.

1. Unfeigned Faith,
       2 Tim. 1. 5
2. Abundant Life, John 10.10
3. Unspeakable Joy,
       1 Peter 1. 8
4. Manifold Grace 1 Pet.4.10

5. Incomprehensible
   Peace,   - Phil. 4. 7
6. Incomprehensible
   Love,   - Eph. 3. 19
7. Excellent Glory,
       2 Peter 1. 17

H.K.D.

## Great Truths in Isaiah 43.

1. Divine love set upon His own,   -   -   -   v.  4
2. Redeemed by His grace and love,   -   -   v.  1
3. His knowledge of His own,   -   -   v.  1
4. His assuring grace to all such,   -   -   v. 25
5. His covenant relationship with them,   -   -   v.  3
6. His abiding presence with them, -   -   -   v.  2
7. The Bright Hope set before them,   -   -   v.  5

G. H.

## The Lord's Coming.

### SOME OF THE GREAT FACTS CONNECTED THEREWITH.

1. Sure as to its occurrence, -   -   - Rev. 22. 20
2. Select as to individuals, -   -   - 1 Cor. 15. 23
3. Secret as to its method,   -   -   Acts 1. 11
4. Sudden in its operation,   -   -   1 Cor. 15. 52
5. Saving in its results,   -   - Phil. 1. 3; 20, 21

H.K.D.

## Little Things with Great Uses.

1. "He that offendeth in one *point*" (Jas. 2. 10). Illustrate by one link in chain, a black spot on white garment, etc.
2. "A Needle's *Eye*" (Matt. 19. 24). Explain meaning small door in city gate.
3. "A *Grain* of Mustard Seed" (Matt. 17. 20). Yet it becomes a great tree. Little sins, great results.
4. "The Very Last *Mite*" (Luke 12. 59). Equal to a farthing or a cent. Get saved now and keep out of Pit. *Objects* could be used for each.   HYP.

# SUBJECTS FOR SPEAKERS AND STUDENTS.

## Seven Reasons for Coming to the Lord's Supper.

1. It is to us, as His children, an act of obedience (Matt. 26. 26, 27; 1 Cor. 11. 24).
2. It is to us, as His children, an act of remembrance (Luke 22. 19; 1 Cor. 11. 24, 25).
3. A testimony to His death (1 Cor. 11. 26; 5. 7).
4. A confession that salvation is through His Blood (Matt. 26. 28; Rev. 1. 5).
5. An act of fellowship (1 Cor. 10. 16, 17).
6. An act of praise and thanksgiving (Luke 22. 19; 1 Cor. 10. 16; 11. 24).
7. An act silently but joyfully proclaiming His Second Coming (1 Cor. 11. 26).  W.H.

## New Things.

1. New creature, 2 Cor. 5. 17
2. New heart, Ezek. 36. 26
3. New tongue, Mark 16. 17
4. New song, - Psa. 40. 3
5. New food, - 1 Pet. 2. 2
6. New name, Rev. 2. 17
7. New covenant, Heb. 8. 8
8. New way, - Heb. 10. 20
9. New mercies, Lam. 3. 23
10. New fruit, Ezek. 47. 12
11. New home, Rev. 21. 1

F.F

## Ezekiel's Roll
(Ezek. 3. 1-17),

WAS TO HIM WHAT THE BIBLE SHOULD BE TO US.

1. Intellectually he had to "eat it"—get it into the head.
2. Experimentally he had to "digest it"—get it "in thine heart" (v. 10).
3. Practically he was "watchman"—work it out in the life. *Witness*.

## The Meaning of the Offerings.

1. The *burnt* offering (Lev. 1).—Man utterly unworthy in himself, without anything of his own to recommend him to God; and needing, therefore, to be identified with One who is altogether worthy, and an object of divine favour, that he might be accepted in God's Beloved.
2. The *meat* offering (Lev. 2).—Man fallen and depraved in nature, and needing as a substitute One who is holy, harmless, undefiled, and separate from sinners.
3. The *peace* offering (Lev. 3).—Man in heart alienated from God and needing reconciliation.
4. The *sin* offering (Lev. 4).—Man a sinner and needing an atoning sacrifice.  F.F.

# SUBJECTS FOR SPEAKERS AND STUDENTS.

## Seven Things About the Love of God.

1. The Original SOURCE, - - - - - God
2. The Infinite MEASURE, - - - - - so
3. The Costly SACRIFICE, - - - - only Son
4. The Unworthy OBJECT, - - - - the world
5. The Striking IMPARTIALITY, - - - whosoever
6. The Simple CONDITION, - - - - believeth
7. The Twofold PURPOSE, - (*a*) Salvation, not perish
(*b*) Life, Everlasting Life

R. LOGAN in "Suggestive Topics."

## "God our Rock."

1. Salvation, - - - - - 2 Sam. 22. 47
2. Stability, - - - Matt. 7. 24, 25; 16. 18
3. Security, - - - - Psa. 94. 22
4. Shelter, - - - - Psa. 62. 27
5. Satisfaction, - - - 1 Cor. 10. 4
6. Strength, - - - - Psa. 31. 2 (*margin*).
7. Shadow, - - - - Isa. 32. 2 R.L.B.

## "Unto Him."

Live, - - 2 Cor. 5. 15
Go forth, - Heb. 13. 13
Glory, - - Eph. 3. 21
The gathering, Gen. 69. 10
Our gathering, 2 Thess. 2. 1
Drawn, John 12. 32 R.L.B.

## The Meek and Lowly

SHALL BE

1. Satisfied, - - Psa. 22. 26
2. Exalted, - - Psa. 147. 6
3. Beautiful, - Psa. 149. 4
4. Guided, - - - Psa. 25. 9
5. Gladdened, - Isa. 29. 19

W. T. R.

## Three Stages in My History.

*Humble Past*—"So foolish was I, and ignorant,
I was as a beast," - - - - Psa. 73. 22
*Holden Present*—"I am continually with Thee,
Thou hast holden my right hand," - Psa. 73. 23
*Hopeful Future*—"Thou shalt...receive me
to glory," - - - - Psa. 73. 24 HYP.

## Past—Present—Perfect.

1. A PREVIOUS PURPOSE—"Chosen *before*
the foundation of the world," - Eph. 1. 4
2. A PRESENT INTENTION—"To the intent
that *now* unto principalities, etc.," - Eph. 3. 10
3. A FUTURE DISPLAY—"That in the Ages
to *come* He might show," Eph. 2. 7 T.B.

# SUBJECTS FOR SPEAKERS AND STUDENTS.

## Man's Giving and God's.

Man's giving: "That every one of them
    may take a little,"  -  -  -  John 6. 7-11
God's giving: "As much as they would,"  -  John 6. 7-11

G-T.

## When Israel Crossed Jordan.
#### They had to

1. Beware of Idolatry,  -  -  -  - Deut. 4. 15-24
2. Be not unequally yoked with unbelievers,  ,,   7. 1-4
3. Beware of being lifted up,  -  -  -  ,,   8. 11-18
4. Be separate,  -  -  -  -  -  ,,  18. 9-14
5. Be honest and upright,  -  -  -  ,,   19. 14
6. Be courageous,  -  -  -  -  ,,   20. 3, 4
7. Destroy Amalek,  -  -  -  ,,    25. 19
8. Give firstfruits to God,  -  -  -  ,,   26. 1-2
9. Love and obey the Lord,  -  -  ,, 30. 20 F.F.

## Concerning Abraham.

1. Abraham's faith,
    Gal. 3. 6
2. Abraham's children,
    Gal. 3. 7
3. Abraham's blessing,
    Gal. 3. 14
4. Abraham's seed,
    Gal. 3. 16-29
5. Abraham's inheritance,
    Gal. 3. 18. H.K.D.

## Christ as Lord.

1. A living Lord,
    Rev. 1. 18
2. A present Lord,
    Rev. 1. 13
3. A controlling Lord,
    Rev. 1. 16
4. A gracious Lord,
    Rev. 1. 13
5. An Active Lord,
    Rev. 2. 1   H.K.D.

## Christ Occupied for Us.

1. Heart sympathising,  -  -  -  - Heb. 4. 15
2. Arm strengthening,  -  -  -  - Psa. 89. 21
3. Hands encircling,  -  -  -  - S. of S. 2. 6
4. Eye guiding,  -  -  -  -  - Psa. 32. 8
5. Feet triumphing,  -  -  -  - Isa. 63. 3
6. Lips pleading,  -  -  -  - 1 John 2. 1
7. Ear hearkening,  -  -  Mal. 3. 16   R.L.B.

## The Wise Preacher.
#### "Because the preacher was wise" we note these marks in Eccles. 12.

1. PERSEVERANCE,   "*He* still taught,"  -  - verse 9
2. PREPARATION,  -  "He gave good heed,"  -   ,, 9
3. PLANNED,  -  "He set in order,"  -  -   ,, 9
4. PLEASED, -  - "Words of delight,"  -   ,, 10*m*
5. PRODUCED—as goads and nails,  -   v. 11    HYP.

# SUBJECTS FOR SPEAKERS AND STUDENTS.

## The Preacher's Instructions.
### (Acts 5. 20.)

| | |
|---|---|
| Command, | Go. |
| Attitude, | Stand. |
| Action, | Speak. |
| Where, | In the Temple. |
| To Whom? | The People. |
| Subject, | All the Words of this Life. |

S. J. S.

## The Feet.

1. A lamp for the feet, - - - - Psa. 119. 105
2. The path of the feet, - - - - Prov. 4. 26
     —Light and guidance for the Christian.
3. The feet receive strength, - - - Acts 3. 7
     —The walk of obedience.
4. Shoes on your feet, - - - - Luke 25. 22
     —For slippery places.
5. Sat at His feet, - - - - - Luke 10. 39
     —As a disciple to learn.
6. The feet kissed, - - - - - Luke 7. 38
     —The love of the saint.
7. The feet pierced, - - - - - Luke 24. 39
     —The love of Christ to the perishing.

H.R.F.

## Scriptural Causes for Thanksgivings.

1. For the UNSPEAKABLE GIFT, - - 2 Cor. 9. 15
     The Unspeakable Gift is the Lord
     Jesus (John 3. 16), the reception of
     whom leads to Unspeakable Joy
     (1 Peter 1. 8).

2. For present VICTORY OVER IN-DWELLING
     SIN, - - - - - Rom. 7. 25
     The present victory over in-dwel-
     ling sin is given as the eye is kept on
     the Risen Saviour day by day (Rom.
     6. 12).

3. For future VICTORY ASSURED IN RESUR-
     RECTION, - - - - - 1 Cor. 15. 57
     The future victory is assured when
     He comes back again. Then, and
     only then, shall we have full redemp-
     tion, Spirit, Soul, and Body.

W.A.T.

# SUBJECTS FOR SPEAKERS AND STUDENTS.

## "This Man."

"What manner of Man is this?"

1. Divine Man,    Mark 15.39
2. Faultless    ,,   Luke 23.14
3. Perfect    ,,   Luke 23.41
4. Eloquent    ,,   John 7. 46
5. Rejected    ,,   John 18. 40
6. Forsaken    ,,   Matt. 27.47
7. Sociable    ,,   Luke 15. 2
8. Powerful    ,,   Acts 13. 39
9. Hated    ,,   John 9. 24
10. Honoured ,,   John 9. 33
11. Supreme    ,,   Heb. 10. 12
12. Unchanging
     Man, - - Heb. 7. 24
13. Coming
     Man, - - Micah 5. 5
                W.H.

## The Blessed Man.

SEVEN STEPS AS RECORDED IN THE PSALMS.

1. Blessedly Saved,
            Psa. 32. 1, 2
2. Blessedly Separated,
            Psa. 1. 1, 2
3. Blessedly Satisfied,
            Psa. 34. 8, 9
   see also Psa. 84. 12 and
     40. 4.
4. Blessedly Sanctified,
            Psa. 65. 4
5. Blessedly Strengthened,
            Psa. 84. 5, 6, 7
6. Blessedly Subdued,
            Psa. 94. 12, 13
7. Blessedly Softened,
            Psa. 112. 1-9   G.S.

## The Lord Jesus Christ.

1. The Son of MARY,   -   -   -   -   Luke 1. 31
     As Son of Mary parental rule is acknowledged and obeyed (Luke 2. 51).

2. The Son of DAVID,   -   -   -   -   Matt. 22. 45
     As Son of David, Israel will again come into blessing (Luke 1. 32).

3. The Son of ABRAHAM, -   -   -   -   Matt. 1. 1
     As Son of Abraham all the nations of the earth will be blessed in Him (Gen. 12. 3; Gal. 3. 8).

4. The Son of MAN,   -   -   -   -   Luke 19. 10
     As Son of Man He will have dominion over the earth (Gen. 1. 26; Psa. 8).

5. The Son of GOD,   -   -   -   -   John 1. 34
     As Son of God He reconciles the things in the Heavens, and the whole universe is brought into subjection at His feet (Phil. 2. 10; Col. 1. 20).     V.A.T.

# SUBJECTS FOR SPEAKERS AND STUDENTS.

## The Joy of the Lord Jesus.

1. In Anticipation, - - - - Prov. 8. 31
2. In Obeying the Father, - - - Psa. 40. 8
3. In Resurrection, - - - - Psa. 16. 11
4. In Revealing Himself, - - - Luke 10. 21
5. In His Church - - - - Psa. 16. 3
6. In His People's Obedience, - - John 15. 11
7. Presenting them to His Father, Jude 24.   R.L.B.

## Name.

1. The Excellent Name,
   Psa. 8. 1
2. The Exalted Name,
   Phil. 2. 9
3. The Exquisite Name,
   S. of S. 1. 3   H.K.D.

## Christ's Invitations.

1. Look unto Me, Isa. 45.22
2. Come unto Me, Mat.11.28
3. Abide in Me, John 15. 4
4. Learn of Me, Matt. 11. 29
5. Follow Me,   Matt. 4. 19
                        F.F.

## The Coming One.
### John 14. 3.

I—The Person.
I will—The Power.
I will come—The Promise.
I will come again—The Prospect.
And receive you unto Myself—The People.
That where I am—The Place.
There ye may be also—The Purpose.   D.W.

## The Romance of Twelve Brothers.

How 11 bad were reconciled to 1 good brother.  In this picture of righteous
reconciliation we have

1. ROUGHNESS.—Spake *roughly* to them, -   Gen. 42. 7
2. REMEMBRANCE.—Put them altogether in
   ward three days, time to talk and
   think, - - - - - - Gen. 42. 17
3. REPENTANCE.—"We are verily guilty,"
   also his blood is required, - - Gen. 42. 21, 22
4. RECOGNITION of Guilt.—"God hath
   found out the iniquity of thy
   servants," - - - - - Gen. 44. 16
5. Reconciliation.—"I am Joseph;..come
   near unto me;..they came near;..he
   kissed all his brethren," - - Gen. 45. 4, 15
   SATISFACTION.—"It is enough,"   Gen. 45. 28  HYP.

# SUBJECTS FOR SPEAKERS AND STUDENTS.

## Blessings of the Believer.

1. Engraven on the Lord's hands, - - - Isa. 49. 16
2. Enrolled in His book, - - - Heb. 12. 23
3. Encouraged in His service, - - 2 Chron. 35. 2
4. Encamped round by His angel, - - Psa. 34. 7
5. Enlightened by the Father, - - Eph. 1. 18
6. Endued with the power by His Spirit, Luke 24. 49

## Practical Truths.

1. PRAISE, - "Rejoice evermore," - 1 Thess. 5. 16
2. PRAYER, - "Pray without ceasing,"- 1 Thess. 5. 17
3. PRACTICE, "In everything give thanks,
   for this is the *will of God*
   concerning you," - 1 Thess. 5. 18
   Hyp.

## Heavenly Provision.

1. DIVINE LOVE, - - - - Deut. 23. 5
2. ETERNAL SECURITY, - - - John 10. 28, 29
3. TRUE DISCIPLESHIP, - - - Luke 10. 39
4. SOUL ENRICHMENT, - - - John 17. 8 s. J. s.

## The Saint's Feast of Tabernacles.

In Isaiah 12, sung at the Feast of Tabernacles we have

| | | |
|---|---|---|
| 1. Behold, - - verse 2 | 4. Praise, - verse 4 |
| 2. Trust, - - ,, 2 | 5. Proclaim, - ,, 4*m* |
| 3. Draw, - - ,, 3 | 6. Sing, - - ,, 5 |

7. Cry out and shout, v. 6                    HYP.

## "John Mark."

1. His Generation, - - - Acts 12. 12
2. ,, Acceptation, - - - ,, 12. 25
3. ,, Ministration, - - - ,, 13. 5
4. ,, Isolation, - - - - ,, 13. 13
5. ,, Separation, - - - ,, 15. 37, 8, 9
6. ,, Salutation, - - - Col. 4. 10
7. ,, Valuation, - - - - I Tim. 4. 11 D. F.

## What Man Is and Needs.

1. Fallen, - - Eph. 2. 6, - Needs Raising
2. Condemned, - John 3. 18, - Needs Mercy
3. Corrupted, - John 3. 6, 7, - Needs Regenerating
4. Lost, - - Luke 19. 10, - Needs Saving
5. Dead, - - Eph. 2. 1, - Needs Quickening
   H. K. D.

# SUBJECTS FOR SPEAKERS AND STUDENTS.

## Condition of Heart
### Of the Emmaus Disciples, Luke 24.

1. Sad heart, -        -     v. 17—*Cure*, Himself, - verse 15
2. Slow heart,        -     v. 25—*Warmed*, Himself,    ,,   27
3. Satisfied heart, -     v. 33—*With*, Himself,        ,,   36
        Ends—"Worshipping Him," v. 52.        HYP.

## Things Broken.

1. Wall,        -        -   Destruction, -     - Neh. 1. 3
2. Spirit,      -        -   Reception,    -     - Psa. 51. 17
3. Law,         -        -   Contrition,   -     - Psa. 119. 136
4. Heart,       -        -   Affection,    -     - Psa. 147. 3
5. Box,         -        -   Adoration,    -     - Mark 14. 3
6. Partition,   -        -   Union, -      -     - Eph. 2. 14
7. Body,        -        -   Substitution, - 1 Cor. 11. 24   D.F.

## Four Figures
### In the vision of Ezekiel 1. 10.

1. MAN (front).  Sympathy intelligence,
        corresponding to    -     -     -     - Luke.
2. LION (right). Strength, power, corres-
        ponding to          -     -     -     - Matthew.
3. Ox (left). Perseverance, corresponding to Mark.
4. EAGLE (back).  Keen vision, corres-
        ponding to -        -     -     -     - John   HYP.

## Truths Spoken by Enemies of God.

1. Balaam—God is not a man, etc., -      - Num. 23. 19
2. Pharisees—This Man receiveth sinners,  Luke 15. 2
3. Jews—He saved others,      -     -     Matt. 27. 42
4. Pilate—King of Jews,       -     -     John 19. 19
5. Demons—Thou Holy One of God, Luke 4. 34   H.K.D.

## An Address in Itself.

1. It is a Gospel Address in itself,    -     - John 3. 16
2. Its theme is Love, -     -     -     - God so loved,
3. Love proved by the Gift,
                    He gave His only begotten Son,
4. It proclaims Salvation for all, -     -     - whosoever
5. In the easiest way, -     -     -     - believeth in Him
6. The Blessing it brings—*negative*,  - should not perish,
7. The Blessing it brings—*positive*, have Everlasting Life
                            WM. GILMORE, Bangor.

182

# SUBJECTS FOR SPEAKERS AND STUDENTS.

## Four Lessons From Noah.

| | | |
|---|---|---|
| The Ark, - | - Atonement, - | - Gen. 6. 14-22 |
| The Altar, - | - Acceptance, - | - Gen. 8. 20 |
| The Rainbow, - | Assurance, - | - Gen. 9. 13 |
| The Vineyard, - | Activity, - | - Gen. 9. 20 R.P. |

## Two Remarkable Men.

NAAMAN THE SYRIAN.

"I thought," - 2 Kgs. 5. 11
"I know," - 2 Kgs. 5. 15

THE APOSTLE PAUL.

"I thought," - Acts 26. 9
"I know," - 2 Tim. 1.12

D-W—e.

## Four Kinds of Ground.

LUKE 8. 1-18.

1. Trodden Ground,
   vv. 5, 12
2. Thin Ground, - vv. 6, 13
3. Thorny Ground, vv. 7, 14
4. True Ground, - vv. 8, 15

L.G.F.

## The Believer's Life.

| | |
|---|---|
| Received from Christ, - - - | - John 10. 28 |
| Hid in Christ, - - - - | - Col. 3. 4 |
| To be lived for Christ, - - - | - Phil. 1. 21 |
| To be spent with Christ for ever, - | - 1 Thess. 4. 18 |

## The Race (Heb. 12. 1).

1. Those who Run, - - - All "in faith."
2. Where to Run, - - - "Cross to Crown."
3. How to Run, - - - - "Let us lay aside."
4. Inducements to Run, - - "Joy set before."
5. Reward of Running, - - - "Crown." W.J.G.

## So Great Salvation.

WHY? Hebrews 2. 3.

1. Shows so *Great Mercy* and saves from so
   *Great Sin*, - - 1 Peter 1. 3; Titus 3. 5
2. So *Great to God*—Because it cost Him
   His Son to establish it, John 3. 16, 17; Rom. 8. 3;
   1 John 4. 14
3. So *Great to the Lord Jesus Christ*—
   Because it cost Him His life to
   secure it, - - John 10. 15; 1 John 3. 16
4. So *Great to the Holy Spirit*—Because it
   is His one commission to reveal it, - John 16. 7-11
5. So *Great to the Believer*—Because it saves
   him from such great condemnation,
   Rom. 8. 1; John 5. 24. A.W.R.

183

# SUBJECTS FOR SPEAKERS AND STUDENTS.

## What the Bible Says About "Peace."

| | |
|---|---|
| Lost, - - - Gen. 3. 10 | Proclaimed, - Eph. 2. 17 |
| Needed, - - Rom. 3. 17 | Bequeathed, - John 14. 27 |
| Prophesied, - Luke 1. 79 | Proved, - John 20. 19, 20 |
| Offered, - - ,, 2. 14 | Possessed, - Luke 2. 29, 30; |
| Precluded, - - ,, 12. 49- | 7. 50 |
| 51 | Pursued, - 1 Peter 3. 11; |
| Pretended, - - ,, 11. 21 | Rom. 12. 18 |
| Removed, - - ,, 19. 38 | Permanent, 1 Thess. 5. 23; |
| Postponed, - ,, 19. 42 | 2 Thess. 3. 16; Heb. |
| Made, - - - Col. 1. 20 | 13. 20, 21 W.F.C. |

## God's Epitaphs.

1. DIED UNTO SIN (Rom. 6. 10).
   The Person who thus died was God's
   Son, - - - - - - Matt. 16. 16
   He will never repeat this wondrous
   sacrifice, - - - - - Heb. 10. 10
2. DIED IN FAITH (Heb. 11. 15).
   Those who die in faith must first live
   by faith, - - - - - Gal. 3. 26
   They also have walked by faith, - 2 Cor. 5. 7
3. DIED WITHOUT MERCY (Heb. 10. 28).
   God is rich in mercy, - - - Eph. 2. 4
   All rejecters of Christ die without
   mercy, - - - - - John 8. 24
   A.G.

## What the Word of God Can Do.

1. It can pierce the heart and produce
   conviction of sin, - - - - Heb. 4. 12
2. It can regenerate and transform the
   life and character, - - - - 1 Peter 1. 23
3. It can produce a living faith in God, - Rom. 10. 17
4. It can cleanse and purify the heart and
   life, - - - - - - Psa. 119. 9-11
5. It can protect from heresy and error, - Acts 20. 29-32
6. It can bring joy and rejoicing to the heart, Jer. 15. 16
7. It can speak peace to the troubled soul, Psa. 85. 8
8. It can make us wiser than our teachers, - Psa. 119. 99
   T-H.

# SUBJECTS FOR SPEAKERS AND STUDENTS.

## Four Beholds.

Redemption, - - Luke 24. 39
Reception, - - Rev. 3. 20
Rapture, - - Rev. 22. 12
Review, - - Heb. 2. 13

J.E.B.

## Philip in Samaria.

Great Multitudes, Acts 8. 1-8
Great Miracles.
Great Blessing.
Great Power and Joy.

F.M'L.

## Hope for the Hopeless
### In the Remnant Days of Haggai.

1. "I am with you, saith Jehovah," - Haggai 1. 13
2. "My Spirit remainest among you," - ,, 2. 5
3. "The glory of the latter house shall
    be better than the former," - - ,, 2. 9
There is a good time coming, - - ,, 2. 23

HyP.

## A Sermon by the Greatest of Preachers.
### Luke 4. 16-19.

Note the omission of "day of vengeance"
(Isa. 61. 1, 2).

1. THE SIXFOLD DIVISION OF THE TEXT, - vv. 18, 19
2. THE SERMON (ver. 21), claiming all as
    fulfilled in Himself (19 centuries have
    proved it).
3. THE EFFECT! Admiration, Jealousy,
    Rejection, - - - - - vv. 22, 29
4. THE EXPLANATION (vv. 25, 27). They
    lacked the obedience of faith. Their
    eyes they had closed, - - - Matt. 13. 15

J.W.A.

## What the Bible Does for Spiritual Life.

The Bible is spoken of as God's seed (Luke 8. 11;
James 1. 21).

1. We are *born* of the Word, - - - 1 Peter 1. 23
2. We *grow* by the Word, - - - 1 Peter 2. 2
3. We are *cleansed* by the Word, - - John 15. 3
4. We are *sanctified* by the Word, - - John 17. 17
5. We are *protected* by the Word, - - Eph. 6. 17
6. We are *edified* by the Word, - - Acts 20. 32
7. We are *illuminated* by the Word, - - Psa. 119. 105
8. We are *converted* by the Word, - - Psa. 19. 11
9. We are *satisfied* with the Word, - - Psa. 119. 103

DR. GRIFFITH THOMAS.

# SUBJECTS FOR SPEAKERS AND STUDENTS.

## Seven Forms of Judgment in 1 Corinthians.

| | | | |
|---|---|---|---|
| 1. Motive judgment, | 4. 5 | 5. World judgment, | 6. 2 |
| 2. Self-judgment, - | 11. 31 | 6. Angelic judgment, | 6. 3 |
| 3. Divine judgment, | 12. 32 | 7. Civil judgment, | 6. 6 |
| 4. Assembly judgment, | 6. 5 | "Judge ye." | T.B. |

## Job a Type of the Lord Jesus Christ.

Job 1. 3, - - His Former Glory, - Prov. 8
Job 16. 15, - - His Humility, - - - Phil. 2. 8
Job 42. 10-12, - His Latter Glory, Phil. 2. 9; Rev. 1.8

D.W.

## Last Days of Old and New Testament.

Malachi's day corresponds with Laodicea. Six things marked their condition—

1. DOUBTED LOVE. "Wherein hast Thou loved us"— Mal. 1. 2.
2. DEFILED HONOUR. "Ye offer polluted bread upon Mine altar."—Mal. 1. 6.
3. DESPISED TABLE. "The table of the Lord is contemptible"—Mal. 1. 7.
4. DEGRADED MORAL STANDARD. "Every one that doeth evil is good"—Mal. 2. 17.
5. DEPLETED STOREHOUSE. "Ye have robbed Me"— Mal. 3. 8.
6. DISCONTENTED SERVICE. "It is vain to serve God"— Mal. 3. 14.

*Contrast* "Then they that feared the Lord spake often one to another"—Mal. 3. 16.            W.H.

## Four Examples of Lowliness.

In Philippians 2 we have four examples of "lowliness"—

1. THE LORD HIMSELF. Unselfishness brought Him from above. I can learn a great deal from my brethren, but I only see perfection in the Man Christ Jesus.
2. PAUL (verse 17). "Offered upon the sacrifice." Margin reads, "poured out." He likens the faith of the Philippians to the "bullock," and his martyrdom to the "cup of wine" poured on the offering. Forty years buffeted.
3. TIMOTHEUS (verse 19). "Like-minded." All seek their own, but Timotheus "cared for you."
4. EPAPHRODITUS (verse 25). The man who could carry a parcel for Paul from Philippi to Rome at the risk of his life (verse 30). When sick he thought not of his sickness, but of their anxiety about his sickness (verse 26). W.W.F.

# SUBJECTS FOR SPEAKERS AND STUDENTS.

## Four Rests.

Rest for the Sinner, - - - - - - Matt. 11. 28
Rest for the Pilgrim, - - - - Exod. 33. 14
Rest for the Disciple and Servant, - - Matt. 11. 29
Rest for the Obedient One, - - - Jer. 6. 16

F.C.M.

## "What is Man?" (Psa. 8. 4).

1. As Created—God's Masterpiece, - - Gen. 1. 27
2. As a Sinner—The Devil's Puppet, - Eph. 2. 2
3. As Saved—A Trophy of Grace, - - Eph. 2. 8
4. As a Saint—Christ's Reproduction, - Gal. 2. 20
5. As a Temple—God's Dwelling, - - 1 Cor. 3. 16
6. As a Servant—A Channel of Blessing, - John 7. 38
7. As Glorified—Like Christ, - - - 1 John 3. 2

T-H.

## Witnessbearing
### (Acts 1. 8).

1. What is it to be a witness? - - Evidence
2. Where is the place? - - - Begin at Home
3. What is the power? - - - Holy Spirit

A.E.J.

## Secrets of Unanswered Prayers.

1. SIN, - - - - Isa. 59. 1, 2; Prov. 15.29
2. Regarding iniquity in the heart, - - Psa. 66. 18
3. Not doing that which is pleasing in His
   sight, - - - - - - 1 John 3. 22
4. Idol in the heart, - - - - Ezek. 14. 3
5. Omitting to return thanks, - - Phil. 4. 6, 7
6. Selfishness, - - - - - Prov. 21. 13
7. Unforgiving spirit, - - - - Mark 11. 25
8. Wrong motive for asking, - - - James 4. 3

T.P.

## God Has Spoken.

1. In Creation, - - - - Rom. 1. 20
2. By implanted knowledge, - - Rom. 2. 14
3. By conscience, - - - - Rom. 2. 15
4. By the prophets, - - - Heb. 1. 1
5. By His Son, - - - - Heb. 1. 2
6. By His Word, - - - - 2 Tim. 3. 16, 17

The first three in absence of the last three. The last,
now complete, settles everything. D.W—e.

# SUBJECTS FOR SPEAKERS AND STUDENTS.

## Three Attitudes of the Soul.

1. Aspiration, - "My soul thirsteth," - - Psa. 63. 1
2. Realisation, - "My soul satisfied," - - Psa. 63. 5
3. Dedication, - "My soul followeth," - Psa. 63. 8 J.M.H.

## Jacob's Two Pillars.

1. Bethel—Joy, - Gen. 35. 14
2. Bethlehem—Sorrow, 35. 20
W. W. F.

## A Threefold Death.

1. Dead *in* sin, - - Eph. 2. 1
2. Dead *for* sin, - 1 Cor. 15. 3
3. Dead *to* sin, Rom. 6. 2 G.H.

## "The Begotten of God" in John's Epistle.

### 1. NEGATIVELY.

1. Sinneth not, - 1 John 5. 18
2. Cannot sin, - 1 John 3. 9
3. Evil one toucheth not,
1 John 5. 18

### 2. POSITIVELY.

1. Overcometh the world,
1 John 5. 14
2. Knoweth God, - 1 John 4. 7
3. Loveth his brother,
1 John 5. 1 H. K. D.

## Pentecostal Power Produced.

1. Conviction of sin, - - - - Acts 2. 37
2. Conversion to God, - - - - ,, 2. 38
3. Confession of faith in Christ, - - - ,, 2. 41
4. Continuance in the ways of God, - - ,, 2. 42
5. Consecration to God, - - - - ,, 2. 45
6. Continual joy in God, - - - Acts 2. 46, 47 G.H.

## Points of Agreement.

1. In prayer, - Matt. 18. 19
2. In offence, - Matt. 5. 25
3. In communion, Amos 3. 3
4. Of Scripture, Acts 15. 15
5. Of the Trinity, 1 John 5. 7
6. In deceit, - - Acts 5. 9
7. Satanic, - - Rev. 17. 17
T. B.

## Gifts of Jesus.

1. His life, - - John 10. 11
2. Eternal life, - ,, 10. 28
3. An example, - ,, 13. 15
4. A new commandment, - ,, 13. 34
5. Peace, - - - ,, 14. 27
6. God's Word, - ,, 17. 14
7. Glory, - - - ,, 17. 22
W. J. M.

## Within and Without.

1. Within and without the garden, - - Gen. 3. 24
2. Within and without the ark, - - - Gen. 7. 16
3. Within and without the sprinkled door, - Exod. 12. 22
4. Within and without the scarlet cord, - Josh. 2. 19
5. Within and without the camp, - - - Num. 12. 14
6. Within and without the Church, - - 1 Cor. 5. 12
7. Within and without the city of gold, - Rev. 22. 15 Js. Fs.

# SUBJECTS FOR SPEAKERS AND STUDENTS.

**Six Divine Appointments** | **Six Things in Daniel 6.**
FOUND IN THE WORD OF GOD. | WHAT DANIEL WAS AND DID

| | |
|---|---|
| 1. Sinner's wages, - Heb. 9. 27 | 1. Preferred, - - Dan. 6. 3 |
| 2.   ,,    doom, -Acts 17. 31 | 2. Persecuted, -  ,, 6. 4 |
| 3.   ,,    refuge, - Josh. 20 9 | 3. Prayed, - - -  ,, 6. 10, 11 |
| 4. A full salvation, -1 Thes. 5. 9 | 4. Praised, - -  ,, 6. 10 |
| 5. God-given service, Num. 4. 19 | 5. Preserved, - -  ,, 6. 22 |
| 6. Glorious kingdom, Lu. 22. 29 | 6. Prospered, - -  ,, 6. 28 |
| G.H. | W.J.M. |

## The Callings of the New Testament.

1. The Gospel calling, - Proclamation, - - Matt. 22. 14
2. The Christian calling, Profession, - - - 1 Cor. 1 26
3. The Father's calling, - Regeneration, - - 1 Cor. 1. 9
4. The Heavenly calling, Separation, - - - Heb. 3. 1
5. The Holy calling, - - Occupation, - - - 2 Tim. 1. 9
6. The High calling, - - Consecration, - - Phil. 3. 14
7. The Glory calling, - Exaltation, - 1 Pet. 5. 10 JS. FS.

## A Meditation about the Master.

### I. CHRIST, OUR PRIEST (Heb. 4. 14; 5).

1. The Maker of Reconciliation, - - - - Heb. 2. 7
2. The Obtainer of Eternal Redemption, - Heb. 9. 11, 12
3. The Succourer of the Tempted, - - - Heb. 2. 18
4. The Sympathiser with our struggles, - - Heb. 4. 14, 15
5. The Ever-living Intercessor for believers, Heb. 7. 24, 25

### II. CHRIST, OUR KING (John 19. 14).

1. The life of the kingdom, - - - - - John 3. 5-7
2. The laws of the kingdom, - - - - - Matt. 5, 6, 7
3. The love of the kingdom, - - - - - Gal. 5. 14
4. The liberty of the kingdom, - - - Gal. 5. 1; John 8. 36
5. The loyalty of the kingdom, - - Rev. 2. 10; 1 Cor. 4. 2

### III. CHRIST, OUR LEADER (Isa. 55. 4).

1. His unselfish will, - Matt. 26. 39, Submission to God
2. His undefiled walk, - Heb. 7. 26, - Separation from world
3. His unfaltering witness, Mark 1. 22, Straightness of appeal
4. His unceasing warfare, Gal. 5. 16, 17, Spiritual antagonism
5. His unapproachable work, Heb. 1. 3, Sin's slavery broken

### IV. CHRIST, OUR EXAMPLE (1 Peter 2. 21).

1. Continual prayerfulness, - - - Mark 1. 35; 6. 46; 9. 29
2. Compassionate tenderness, - - John 11. 3-5; Mark 3. 5
3. Calm restfulness, - - - - Mark 4. 35-41; Luke 4. 42, 43
4. Consistent righteousness, - - - - - - John 8. 46
5. Consecrated devotedness, - - - - - Luke 9. 51 A.M'F.

## A Garden Study.

" A garden enclosed " (S. of S. 4. 12).   Taking the simile of a garden, it needs to be—

1. Chosen.
2. Hedged in.
3. Planted.
4. Variegated in style, &c.
5. Needs care
6. And sunshine.
7. For use and en-joyment of others.

J. W. J.

## "Abundantly Satisfied."

Some of the provisions of His house (Psa. 36. 8)—

1. His abundant mercy for every sinner,   -     - Psa. 36. 5
2. His far-reaching faithfulness for the saint,   -   „   36. 5
3. His righteousness like a mountain high,   -   „   36. 6
4. His judgment as an ocean deep,   -     -     -   „   36. 6
5. His watchful care a theme of praise,   -   -   „   36. 7
6. His loving-kindness ever true,   -     -     -   „   36. 7
7. His sheltering wing a refuge near, -     -     -   „   36. 7

H. R. F.

## The Heart in Hebrews.
### SEVEN MARKS.

1. Erring heart, Heb. 3. 10
2. Hardened   „     „   3.8-15
3. Evil   „     „   3. 12
4. Discerned „     „   4. 12
5. Sprinkled „     „   10. 22
6. True   „     „   10. 22
7. Established „   „ 13.9 T.B.

## Seven Great Rocks
### OF SCRIPTURE.

1. Salvation,   - Psa. 89. 26
2. Stability,-   - Matt. 16. 18
3. Security,-   - Psa. 94. 22
4. Shelter,   -   - Psa. 61. 3
5. Satisfaction,- 1 Cor. 10. 4
6. Strength,-   - Psa. 31. 2
7. Shadow,   -   - Isa. 32. 2 x.

## Christian Appellations.

"WHOSE NAMES ARE IN THE BOOK OF LIFE" (Phil. 4. 3).

1. Sinner,   The Fallen Name,   -     -     - 1 Tim. 1. 15
2. Son,   The Hereditary Name,   -     - Rom. 8. 14
3. Saint,   The Separated Name,   -     - Acts 9. 13
4. Servant,   The Business Name,   •     - Acts 2. 18
5. Stranger,   The Unknown Name,   -     - 1 Peter 2. 11
6. Believer,   The Dependent Name,   -     - Acts 5. 14
7. Disciple,   The Scholar's Name,   -     - Acts 9. 36
8. Friend,   The Confidential Name,   -     - John 15. 15
9. Christian, The Relative Name,   •     - 1 Peter 4. 16
10. Brethren,   The Family Name, -     -     - Acts 6. 3
11. Children,   The Regenerate Name,   -     - Rom. 8. 16
12. Pilgrim,   The Traveller's Name,   -     - 1 Peter 2. 11
13. Apostle,   The Official Name, -     -     Acts 1. 2 JS.FS

# SUBJECTS FOR SPEAKERS AND STUDENTS.

## Arise.

1. The sinner for salvation,
   Luke 15. 18
2. The saint for separation,
   Eph. 5. 14
3. The servant for service,
   1 Chron. 22. 16
4. The pilgrim for the journey,
   Micah 2. 10
5. The bride for home,
   Song of Sol. 2. 10
   W.J.M.

## The Word.

1. His eternity—In the
   beginning,      - John 1.1
2. His equality — Was
   with God,      - ,,   1.6
3. His divinity —Was
   God,      -   - ,,   1.1
4. His humanity—Was
   made flesh, - - ,,   1.14
5. His testimony—Told
   the Father out,(mar.) 1.18
   H.K.D.

## Three Questions on Salvation.

THE INQUISITIVE QUESTION.

1. Are there *few* that be saved?   -   -   - Luke 13. 23
   *Ans.*—What matters it, whether few or many, if you
   are not one of them?

THE INCREDULOUS QUESTION.

2. Who then can be saved?   -   -   -   - Matt. 19.25
   *Ans.*—God is able to save all men whether rich or poor.
   Wealth is no aid to salvation.   Poverty is no barrier.

THE IMPERATIVE QUESTION.

3. What must *I* do to be saved?   -   - Acts 16. 30
   *Ans.*—God delights to reply to such a person, "Believe
   on the Lord Jesus Christ, and thou shalt be saved."
   Give up quibbling about salvation, and receive it. T.B.

## The Relation of the Believer to Christ.

is set forth in seven different forms of figure. Drawn from:

1. The purely animal kingdom, the sheep
   and the shepherd,   -   -   -   -   - John 10
2. The vegetable kingdom, vine and branches, John 15
3. The mineral kingdom, the building and
   the living stone,   -   -   -   -   - Eph. 2
4. The human form, the body and its members, Eph. 4
5. The family relation, the family and its
   members, or the state or commonwealth
   and its children,   -   -   -   -   - Eph. 2. 3
6. The marriage relation, the bride and the
   bridegroom,   -   -   -   -   -   - Eph. 5
7. The climax is reached in 1 Corinthians 6.
   17, "He that is joined unto the Lord is
   one spirit;" and in Romans 8. 35, "Who   Rom. 8
   shall separate us from the love of Christ?"   A.T.P.

191

# SUBJECTS FOR SPEAKERS AND STUDENTS.

### Signs of New Birth.

1. Hearing, - 1 Thess. 2. 13
2. Seeing, - 2 Cor. 4. 6
3. Eating, - - 1 Peter 2. 2
4. Drinking, - 1 Cor. 12. 13
5. Speaking, - Acts 9. 11
6. Walking, - Rom. 8. 4
7. Working, - 1 Thess. 1. 3

### Human Extremity.

1. No Wine, - John 2. 3
2. No Man to Help, John 5. 7
3. No Bread, - John 6.7
4. No Water, - John 7. 37
5. No Justifier, - John 8. 4
6. No Light, - John 9. 2
7. No Life, - John 11. 14

## Sins Covered or Uncovered.

"He that *covereth* his sins shall not prosper : but whoso confesseth and forsaketh them shall have mercy,"
Prov. 28. 13

"Blessed is he whose transgression is forgiven, whose sin is *covered*,"
Psa. 32. 1

Cover up your sins, and God will uncover them in *Judgment*.

Uncover your sins, and God will cover them *in Grace*.
A.J.P.

## The Alpha and Omega.

The Person who fulfilled all the expectation, the types, and the prophecies in Himself—"Behold Him," John 1. 29

The One who was in His walk and life here the object of divine complacency—"Behold Him," John 1. 36

The One who alone has power to open the Book of Judgment (Rev. 5. 1-6), even as He had closed it on making proclamation of grace, cf., Luke 4. 17-21; Isa. 61. 1, 2

The One who in the midst of the throne will be the theme of the eternal song of the redeemed from among men, .. .. .. .. .. Rev. 5. 8, 9

The One who shall Himself feed His martyred remnant of Israel, and shall lead them into fountains of living water, .. .. .. .. .. Rev. 7. 9-17

The One who shall be the centre to which all eyes shall look in the day of His espousals at the time of the great marriage supper of the Lamb, .. .. Rev. 19. 7-9

The One whose throne shall be in the midst of His own redeemed, when the perfection of divine government shall be seen in Heaven and on earth, and lawlessness shall hide its head for ever, .. Rev. 22. 3-5. T.D.W.M.

# SUBJECTS FOR SPEAKERS AND STUDENTS.

## Jesus in the Midst.

1. On the Cross, - John 19. 18, The central object of shame
2. In the Church, Matt. 18. 12, „ „ of worship
3. In the Glory, - Rev. 5. 6, - „ „ of praise

H.K.D.

## The Heart in Peter.

1. God in the heart, 1 Pet. 3.15
2. Humility „ „ 3. 4
3. Love „ „ 1.22
4. Hope „ 2 Pet.1.19

T.B.

## Preparation for Study.

1. Regenerate mind, 1 Cor. 2.14
2. Willing „ John 7.17
3. Obedient „ Jas.1.21,22
4. Teachable „ Matt.11.25

W.D.

## Three Things "at the Beginning."

Gen. 3. 2, POSITION in relation to God, -
- 1. Away from Him, Is. 53. 6
- 2. Separated by sin, Is. 59. 2

Gen. 3.12,13, CONDITION before God, - -
- 1. Guilty, - - Gen.3.12
- 2. Dead, - - „ 2.17

Gen. 3.21, REMISSION by blood,
- 1. Shadow, - - Gen.3.21
- 2. Substance, Heb.9.22 D.W.

## The Traveller's Guide to Glory (Hosea 12. 6).

1. "Turn to God," or conversion, - - 1 Thess. 1. 9
2. "Keep mercy and judgment," or consecration, Rom.12.1,2
3. "Wait on thy God continually," or communion,

Isa. 40. 31 G. H.

## Three Precious Portions for the Year.

1. To Israel at the end of the forty years' wilderness march: "The Lord thy God *hath been* with thee," Deut. 2. 7
2. To Joshua entering upon the conflict of Canaan: "The Lord thy God *is* with thee," - - Joshua 1. 9
3. By dying David to his son Solomon in view of his rearing the Temple: "The Lord God, even my God, *will be* with thee," - - - 1 Chron. 28. 20 HYP.

## The Trinity:
FATHER, SON, AND HOLY SPIRIT.

1. In creation, - Gen. 1. 26
2. In atonement, - Heb. 9. 14
3. In baptism, - Matt. 28.19
4. In access, - Eph. 2. 18
5. In election, - 1 Pet. 1. 2
6. In direction, - 2 Thes. 3. 5
7. In benediction, 2 Cor. 13.14

T.B.

## Manifestations of God
IN THE BELIEVER.

1. Dwelling, - - 1 Cor. 3. 16
2. Walking, - - 2 Cor. 6. 16
3. Speaking, - - 1 Pet. 4. 11
4. Working, - - Phil. 2. 13
5. Praying, - - Rom. 8. 26
6. Fighting, - - Gal. 5. 17
7. Ruling, - - Acts 20. 28

JS.FS.

## The Gift of God.

1. THE MOTIVE OF THE GIFT, God so loved, that He gave
2. THE PRECIOUSNESS OF THE GIFT, His only begotten Son
3. THE INTENTION OF THE GIFT, (a) Deliverance, not perish; (b) Beneficence, have Everlasting Life.
4. THE CONDITION OF THE GIFT, - - Believeth
   (a) Faith is necessary both for God and man; (b) Whosoever, no limitation or restriction.   J. R. THOMPSON.

## God's Great Love.

I. THE DIVINE LOVE.
   1. Its Marvellousness, God so loved the world,
   (a) Not the perfect material world
   (b) Not the world of unfallen angels
   (c) Not a world of creatures very good
   (d) But the world which lieth in wickedness
   2. Its Universality
   (a) Salvation is for all
   (b) Was meant for all
II. THE DIVINE GIFT.
   He gave His only begotten Son. God could give nothing dearer or greater. Christ is God's unspeakable gift. He gave His Son—                [tion
   1. To a humbling incarna-
   2. To a laborious servitude
   3. To an ignominious death
III. THE DIVINE DESIGN.
   1. What God wants to do—
   (a) To save all men from perishing            [Life
   (b) To give all Everlasting
   2. The conditions upon which He will do it—Faith in His Son
   M. DANIELS.

## The Story of Redemption.

1. Its Origin,  - God so loved
2. Its Object,  - - the world,
3. Its Expression, - that He gave His only begotten Son,
4. Its Cause,  - Should not perish
5. Its Purpose, Eternal Life,
6. Its Extent,  - whosoever
7. Its Condition,  - believeth
   JAMES SMITH.

## God's Pardoning Love.

I. THE GREAT GOSPEL MYSTERY.
   God so loved the world, that He gave
   1. Jesus is God's own Son
   2. In order to save, God gave His Son
   3. Herein God commends His love to the world
II. THE GREAT GOSPEL DUTY.
   Whosoever *believeth* in Him should not perish
III. THE GREAT GOSPEL BENEFIT.
   1. Saved from the miseries of Hell
   2. Entitled to the joys of Heaven
   MATTHEW HENRY.

# SUBJECTS FOR SPEAKERS AND STUDENTS.

## The Christian Occupied with Christ.

1. Heart yielded, - - - - - Prov. 23. 26
2. Arm leaning, - - - - S. of S. 8. 5
3. Hands working, - - - - Matt. 21. 23
4. Eye Looking, - - - - - Heb. 12. 2
5. Feet following, - - - - Luke 9. 59
6. Voice speaking, - - - - S. of S. 2. 14
7. Ear listening, - - - Luke 10. 39   R.L.B.

## Bondage to

1. Devil, - - 2 Tim. 2. 26 | 3. Sin, - - - John 8. 34
2. Death, - - Heb. 2. 4 | 4. Law, Gal. 3. 23   J.P.L.

## The Sinner and the Saviour.

THE FILTHY MAN.—"There is no difference, for all have sinned and come short of the glory of God" (Rom. 3. 22, 23). "They are all gone aside, they are altogether become *filthy*. There is none that doeth good, no, not one" (Psa. 14. 3).

THE FAITHFUL MAN.—"Lo, I come to do Thy will, O my God; yea, Thy law is within my heart" (Psa. 40). "His delight is in the law of the Lord; and in His law doth He meditate day and night" (Psa. 1. 2). "I have glorified Thee upon the earth, I have finished the work Thou gavest me to do" (John 17. 4).

THE FORSAKEN MAN.—"He hath made Him to be sin for us who knew no sin, that we might be made the right-eousness of God in Him" (2 Cor. 5. 21). "My God, my God, why hast Thou *forsaken* me? Why art Thou so far from helping Me?" (Psa. 22. 1). "He was wounded for *our* transgressions; He was bruised for *our* iniquities; the chastisement of *our* peace was upon Him, and with His stripes we are healed" (Isa. 53. 5).

THE FORGIVEN MAN.—"Blessed is he whose transgression is forgiven, whose sin is covered" (Psa. 32. 1). "Your sins are forgiven you for His Name's sake" (1 John 2. 12). "Be it known unto you therefore, that through this Man (Jesus) is preached unto you the forgiveness of sins, and by Him all that believe are justified from all things" (Acts 13. 37).

The faithful Man was *forsaken*, that the filthy man might be cleansed and *forgiven*.          *Our Record.*

# SUBJECTS FOR SPEAKERS AND STUDENTS.
## Four Blessed Facts.

1. God working *for* us,    -    - 1 Sam. 15. 6; John 17.4
2. God working *in* us,    -    - Phil. 2. 13; Heb. 13. 21
3. God working *by* us,    -    - 2 Cor. 5. 20
4. God working *with* us,    -    - Mark 16. 20    J.H.B.

## Three Precious Links.

1. Where I am, there ye may be *also*,   -   - John 14. 3
   The same *place*.
2. He that believeth on Me, the works that I
   do shall he do *also*,   -   -   -   - John 14.12
   The same *occupation*.
3. Because I live, ye shall live *also*,   -   - John 14. 19
   The same *life*.    J.B.

## The Blessed Servant (Matt. 24. 45-47).

1. He was faithful,    -    Character Godward, 1 Cor. 4. 2
2. He was wise,    -    Character manward, Matt. 7. 24
3. He had a Lord,    -    Under authority,   - 1 Peter 3. 6
4. He had an office,    Ruler,   -   -   - 1 Tim. 3. 1-5
5. He had a sphere,    The household,   - Eph. 2. 19
6. He had a work,    -    A feeder,   -   - 1 Peter 5. 2
7. He had a reward,    He reigned,   -   - 2 Tim. 2. 12
   JS.FS.

## David's Psalm of Praise.

| WHAT GOD IS. | | WHAT HE DOES. | |
|---|---|---|---|
| 1. Great, | - Psa. 145. 3 | 1. Upholdeth, | - Psa. 145. 14 |
| 2. Glorious, | - Psa. 145. 5 | 2. Giveth, | - Psa. 145. 15 |
| 3. Gracious, | - Psa. 145. 8 | 3. Satisfieth, | - Psa. 145. 16 |
| 4. Good,   - | - Psa. 145. 9 | 4. Fulfilleth, | - Psa. 145. 19 |
| 5. Righteous, | - Psa. 145. 17 | 5. Heareth, | - Psa. 145. 19 |
| 6. Holy,   - | - Psa. 145. 17 | 6. Saveth, - | - Psa. 145. 19 |
| 7. Nigh unto,&c., | Psa. 145. 18 | 7. Preserveth, | Psa. 145. 20 |

   W.B.S.

## A Trinity of Truth (2 Sam. 22. 31).

1. A Perfect Path. "His way is perfect." Amid the con-
   fusion and contradiction in the world there is "one
   sure way." "I am the way," &c. (John 14. 6).
2. A Tested Truth. "The Word of the Lord is tried."
   His promises are not untried bridges on which no
   foot has trod, but arches that have borne thousands
   on their way to heaven.
3. A Present Protection. "He is a shield," *e.g.*, Abraham,
   Job, &c.    W.R.

# SUBJECTS FOR SPEAKERS AND STUDENTS.

## Seven Aspects of God's Grace.

1. Preaching the Grace of God,     ..     Acts 20. 24
2. Seeing the Grace of God,     ..     Acts 11. 23
3. Receiving the Grace of God,     ..     2 Cor. 6. 8
4. Labouring by the Grace of God,     ..     1 Cor. 15. 10
5. Continuing by the Grace of God,     ..     Acts 13. 43
6. Giving by the Grace of God,     ..     2 Cor. 8. 1
7. Failing of the Grace of God,     ..     Heb. 12. 15

Js. Fs.

## A Divine Command
### As given in Joshua 1. 8.

This Book..shall not depart out of thy mouth—*Speak of it.*
But thou shalt meditate therein—*Study it.*
Observe to do according to all that is written—*Submit to it.*

W.J.M.

## The Soul.

1. A sinking soul, Matt. 14.30
2. A seeking soul, John 6. 24
3. A satisfied soul, Psa. 62. 5
   will be
4. A singing soul, Psa. 62. 5
5. A soaring soul, Isa. 40. 31
6. Soaring up to be for ever with the Lord, 1 Thess. 4. 7
   then
7. Satisfied perfectly, Psa. 17. 15.   F.B.

## Justification.

1. God, the Author, Rom. 3. 26
2. Grace, the source, ,, 3. 24
3. Blood, the ground, ,, 5. 9
4. Resurrection, the acknowledgment, ,, 4. 25
5. Faith, the channel, Rom. 5. 1
6. Works, the fruit, James 2. 24.   W.W.F

## The Saviour and the Sinner.
### Matthew 14. 29-31.

1. The Saviour's Invitation—"Come,"     ..     v. 29
2. The Sinner's Acceptation—Peter came out of the ship to Jesus,     ..     ..     ..     v. 29
3. The Sinner's Prayer—"Lord, save me,"     ..     v. 30
4. The Sinner's Immediate Salvation,     ..     ..     v. 31
5. The Sinner's Faith—Little Faith,     ..     ..     v. 31

F.B.

## The Salvation of God.

1. For God so loved - - - - GOD'S LOVE
2. the world, - - - - - - GOD'S WORLD
3. that He gave - - - - - GOD'S GIFT
4. His only begotten Son, - - - GOD'S SON
5. that whosoever believeth in Him - GOD'S FAITH
6. should not perish, - - - GOD'S PREVENTION
7. but have Everlasting Life, - • GOD'S LIFE T.B.

# SUBJECTS FOR SPEAKERS AND STUDENTS.

## An Old-Time Revival.
### Nehemiah 4. 2.

1. HINDRANCES TO REVIVAL.
   Opposition from the world, - - - vv. 1-8
   Much rubbish to be removed, - - - ver. 10
2. ESSENTIALS TO REVIVAL.
   We made our *Prayer* unto God, - - ver. 9
   The people had a mind to *Work*, - - ver. 6
   We set a *Watch*, - - - - - - ver. 9

S.H.

## Four Hours in John.
The Hour of
1. Saviour's Suffering, - - - - - John 17. 1
2. Sinner's Salvation, - - - - - John 5. 25
3. Saint's Service, - - - - - - John 4. 23
4. Son's Supremacy, - - - - John 5. 28, 29

G.W.B.

## Four Precious "Shalls."
1. "We shall all be changed," - - - 1 Cor. 15. 51
2. "We shall be like Him," - - - 1 John 3. 2
3. "Ye shall receive a crown," - - - 1 Peter 5. 4
4. "And your heart shall rejoice," - - John 16. 22

"Afar off"—calling for "mercy." W.T.R.

## Deep Things of God.
1. Joy, - - Unspeakable, - - 1 Peter 1. 8
1. Gift, - - ,, - - - 2 Cor. 9. 15
2. Riches, - - Unsearchable, - - Eph. 3. 8
2. Judgment, - ,, - - - Rom. 11. 38
3. Ways, - - Past finding out, - Rom. 11. 33
3. Peace, - - ,, - - - Phil. 4. 7
4. Love, - - Passing knowledge, - Eph. 3. 19

R.L.B.

# Index to Titles and Subjects

199

# INDEX TO TITLES AND SUBJECTS

# Index to Titles and Subjects

# INDEX TO TITLES AND SUBJECTS

# Index to Texts

213

# Index to Acrostics